S0-BOC-830

# 32-Bit Microprocessors

# 32-Bit Microprocessors

## Editor: H. J. Mitchell

**McGraw-Hill Book Company**

New York   St. Louis   San Francisco   Montreal   Toronto

**Library of Congress Cataloging-in-Publication Data**

32-bit microprocessors.

Includes index.
1. Microprocessors.  I. Mitchell, H. J.
QA76.5.A135 1986          005.26          86-19135
ISBN 0-07-042585-X

Copyright © 1986 by H.J. Mitchell. All rights reserved. Except as permitted under the United States
Copyright Act of 1976, no part of this publication may be reproduced or distributed in any form or by any
means, or stored in a data base or retrieval system, without the prior written permission of the publisher,
McGraw-Hill.

1234567890   DOCDOC   8932109876


ISBN 0-07-042585-X

This book was first published in Great Britain in 1986 by Collins Professional and
Technical Books, London.

Printed and bound in the United States of America by R.R. Donnelley & Sons Company.

# Contents

# Preface

With 32-bit microprocessors starting to appear in increasing numbers, the purpose of this book is to describe, in detail, a representative sample of these new devices.

In any book such as this, one is governed by the willingness of organisations to provide, in some cases, both pre-release information and the effort to prepare their chapters. As it would never have been possible to complete the book if we had tried to cover all devices, it was necessary to impose a limitation on both the number of contributions and the timescales allocated to contributors. While there are some omissions, the book provides a balanced view on what is here today, what is coming and a possible view of the future.

The book is intended to provide detailed information on the architecture and operation of the 32-bit microprocessors covered. The information is at a level suitable for the system designer, the engineer and the research student. Today a microprocessor cannot be considered in isolation. Microprocessors are only an element of a system. They must be considered with their related hardware and software components and the tools necessary to develop a system.

The first chapter is a discussion of RISC, which is now moving from the academic world to industry. With both microprocessors and systems appearing using this approach, it was felt appropriate to include a general review paper on this important subject area.

Subsequent chapters deal with specific devices. With the exception of the chapter on the Inmos Transputer, all contributions are produced by the device manufacturers.

H. M.

# CHAPTER 1
# Introduction

H. J. MITCHELL
*CAP Scientific Ltd*

For those of us who have worked with microprocessors since their inception, the progression to 32 bits has been a steady evolution. These new devices have been carefully researched and planned, unlike the early 1970s when devices appeared with such rapidity that users risked losing a large investment by a poor choice of device.

In the 1970s it was the fiercely competitive instrumentation market that led to the widescale use of the microprocessor. Today the 32-bit microprocessor is helping to create and expand the relatively new markets in areas from engineering workstations through to esoteric areas such as real time signal processing, where processor arrays will become commonplace. Even computer manufacturers are developing and selling their own 32-bit micro-processors for low end products, even if the Micro VAX II can be called a low end product!

Most of the established microprocessor manufacturers are moving their 16-bit architectures to 32 bits, while also adding increased functionality. The main rationale behind this approach appears to be the claim that they are protecting users' investment in software. For some applications this is obviously important. However, for many new applications this argument is totally irrelevant; we have the IBM PC using the Intel 8088 and the 80286. The next logical step would appear to be a move to the 80386; however, recent press reports are suggesting otherwise. In the same way Zilog appear to be planning to use the AT&T 31000 rather than their Z80000 for their next generation of Unix systems. It could be argued that some semiconductor manufacturers are trying to protect their own investment in development system software rather than the users'. The main area in which software portability is important is in the minicomputer market. While DEC realised this many years ago and produced the PDP11 and now the VAX machines, others, notably Hewlett-Packard, are still trying to catch up. Hewlett-Packard is now trying with its Spectrum range to unify its fragmented product range with a common architecture covering workstation through to mainframes.

While the concept of a unified product range is commonsense, what makes the Hewlett-Packard work interesting is their intention to adopt a reduced instruction set computer (RISC) as their basic architecture for future products. Hewlett-Packard will be the first major computer or semiconductor manufacturer to adopt this approach for all new products. However, IBM and others are being more cautious by only initially introducing workstations using RISC architecture. At the opposite end of the scale, the Inmos Transputer, with its RISC architecture, has the potential to change the face of computing as we know it today. With RISC devices coming from Fairchild, Acorn and others, we will all no doubt soon know which of the claims and counter claims are true in the RISC/CISC debate.

Probably the most common name appearing in this book is that of Unix. Over the past few years Unix has appeared as an operating system on most small to large scale computer systems. Whether one likes it or hates it, Unix will be around for many years to come. Recognising this, most of the semiconductor manufacturers have designed some features into their device to support Unix. As one might expect, the AT&T device is designed for efficient support for the programming language C. This device has also had included in it some primitives to improve Unix performance. Of the few 32-bit microprocessors on the market, the Unix operating system has appeared on systems incorporating Motorola, National Semiconductor and AT&T devices.

While Unix is now one of the standard operating systems for general purpose applications, there is no such standard for embedded applications. While Intel's RMX executive is probably one of the most widely used, we should slowly see a move to the use of Ada. However, unless the quality and performance of these early compilers improves, many users will be reluctant to move from languages and operating systems they know. It is also probable that the complexities of this language and its support tools may deter many organisations from embarking on developments using Ada.

For most complex systems the use of multiprocessors is becoming commonplace. Realising this, most manufacturers have designed some support into their products for multiprocessor applications. In particular, both Inmos and Zilog have designed extensive features into their products for such applications. The most novel of these features must be that found in the Inmos Transputer, with its (currently) four high speed serial links. Whether one is using a true multiprocessor configuration or co-processors, the basic 'hooks' need to be designed into a device at the start to ensure that these facilities are available to the user. Currently the most common type of coprocessor is for arithmetic or floating point applications. While these devices are still somewhat slower than the arithmetic processors in minicomputers, some improvement must be expected.

With users demanding higher performance from each product release and memory sizes forever on the increase, memory system design and control is now a complex area. While memory management support is an essential requirement for all 32-bit microprocessors, the system designer now has to consider whether to use external cache memory in his system. With small cache memory appearing in most of the new devices, it is probable that for high performance or large memory systems the use of external cache will be essential. To allow systems to operate at anywhere near their maximum speed, the designer only has the choice of using expensive high speed static memory or implementing a cache memory to front end slower memory, based on dynamic memory.

It can be assumed that most 32-bit microprocessors will be used in large and technically complex projects. These projects will need careful planning, resourcing and support to achieve their aims. Any medium to large scale project will need extensive and integrated support tools. These facilities will have to include management tools, office automation, system and software design aids and general support tools such as a code management system. While these support tools are becoming commonplace, the area where most work is needed is in the area of the software design and control process. With software reliability now appearing as contractual targets in military projects, the whole design process needs careful control.

With at least four devices currently available, and several more due in the near future, the era of the 32-bit microprocessor can be said to have arrived. Where the industry moves next will be in the hands of the users, their markets and the semiconductor manufacturers. Whether these moves are towards increased functionality, wider word lengths, RISC or parallelism, only time will tell.

CHAPTER 2
# A Perspective on RISC

H. M. BRINKLEY SPRUNT, E. DOUGLAS JENSEN,
CHARLES Y. HITCHCOCK III, AND ROBERT P. COLWELL
*Computer Science Dept, Dept of Electrical and
Computer Eng., Carnegie-Mellon University,
Pittsburgh, Pa., USA*

## 2.1 Introduction

An effective computer designer must make a large number of design decisions when creating a new computer architecture. These decisions are based upon both the designer's experience and system requirements. Recently, the Reduced Instruction Set Computer (RISC) design style has received much attention and many of its proponents feel strongly that the RISC philosophy offers the best methodology for designing computers. Claims have been made that RISC designs yield faster machines which are both easier and less expensive to design than Complex Instruction Set Computers (CISCs). However, we feel that though the RISC philosophy has merit, the implications of the RISC design style are not well understood. The RISC design philosophy poses a serious challenge to many of the implicit assumptions that have guided computer designs for years. Yet articles on RISC research often fail to explore properly many important issues and can be misleading. For example, comparisons have been made between RISC and CISC machines which are difficult to interpret because performance reports are monolithic in nature and do not properly assign performance gains to the appropriate mechanisms involved. Also, comparisons have been made between machines which have very different implementations and design goals (i.e. RISC I and the VAX) without accounting for these differences, making the results misleading. The goal of this chapter is to offer a more useful perspective of RISC/CISC research, a perspective that is supported by recent experimental results from Carnegie-Mellon University (CMU).

While not all of the distortions and misunderstandings can be redressed here, some of them lie at the heart of computer design and will be the focus of this chapter. For example, much of the RISC literature is devoted to discussions of the size and complexity of computer instruction sets. This is extremely misleading. Instruction set design is very important, but it should not be driven solely by adherence to religious convictions about design style, RISC or CISC. The focus of discussion should be on the more general question of the assignment of system functionality to implementation level within an architecture. This point of view encompasses the instruction set (in general, CISCs tend to install functionality at lower system levels than RISCs do) but also takes into account other design features such as register sets, coprocessors, and caches.

While the implications of RISC research extend beyond the instruction set, even within the instruction set domain there are limitations that have not been brought out. Casual perusal of typical RISC papers will give few clues, if any, as to where the RISC approach might break down. The claims for simple machines which provide high performances are attractive but as it has been said, 'Every complex problem has a simple solution . . . and it is wrong'. RISC ideas are not 'wrong', but a simple minded view of them would be. RISC philosophy has many implications which are not obvious. RISC research has helped to focus attention on some very important issues in computer architecture whose resolution has all too often been decided by default. Yet RISC proponents often fail to discuss the application, architecture, and implementation contexts in which their assertions seem to be justified. Even so, careful evaluation of the RISC design style, its claims, and the challenges it poses for CISC machines can yield a deeper understanding of hardware/software tradeoffs, computer performance, the influence of VLSI for processor design, and many other topics.

In this chapter we will briefly review the developments in computer design as well as the RISC research projects which have led to the RISC design style. We then review some of the significant challenges RISC presents for mainstream computer design and discuss several commercial RISC machines. Once the background information and a few examples of RISC machines have been presented we then discuss what we feel are major points of confusion and misunderstanding that are associated with RISC. This discussion leads into a summary of the research projects conducted at CMU which provide a better perspective on many of the issues involved in the RISC/CISC controversy.

## 2.2 RISC origins

To recognise the motivation for a reduced instruction set computer, it is important first to understand the historical trends of instruction set design. Since the earliest digital electronic computers, instruction sets have tended to grow larger and more complex. The 1948 MARK-1 had but seven instructions of trivial complexity such as adds and simple jumps, yet a contemporary machine like the VAX has over three hundred instructions. Further, its instructions can be rather complicated, like atomically inserting an element into a doubly linked list or evaluating a floating point polynomial of arbitrary degree. Any high performance implementation of the VAX, as a result, has to rely on complex implementation techniques such as pipelining, prefetching, and caches[31].

This type of progression, from small and simple to large and complex instruction sets, is most striking in single-chip processors, since their development has proceeded within only the past decade. The contrast between Motorola's 6800 and their 68020, for example, shows the addition of eleven addressing modes, more than twice as many instructions, and the addition of new functionality such as support for an instruction cache and coprocessors. Again, not only has the number of addressing modes and instructions increased, but so has their complexity.

This general trend towards CISC machines was fuelled by many things, including the following:

● New models within a computer family are often required to be upward compatible with existing models, resulting in the supersetting and proliferation of features. This allows new performance features to be incorporated into new machines without alienating large software bases.

● Many computer designers have desired to reduce the 'semantic gap' between programs and computer instruction sets. By adding instructions that are closer semantically to those needed by the programmer, these designers hoped to reduce software costs by providing a more easily programmable machine[5]. Note that such instructions have tended to be more complex due to their higher semantic level. (However, it is often the case that instructions with high semantic content do not exactly match those required for a specific language[33].)

● In striving for faster machines, designers have constantly migrated functions from software to microcode, or from microcode to hardware. But often, this has been done with an insensitivity to the pernicious adverse effects that an added architectural feature can have on the implementation of the design. For example, by adding an instruction that requires an extra level of decoding logic, a machine's entire instruction set can be slowed. (This has been called the '$n + 1$' phenomenon[18].)

● Tools and methodologies have aided designers in handling the inherent complexity of large architectures. Current CAD tools and microcoding support software are examples of this.

Microcode is a particularly interesting example of a technique that has encouraged complex designs, since it has done so in two ways. First, it provides a structured means of effectively creating and altering algorithms that control the execution of numerous and complex instructions in a computer. Second, the proliferation of CISC features is fuelled by the quantum nature of microcode memories. It is relatively easy to add yet another addressing mode or obscure instruction to a machine which has not depleted its microcode space.

Instruction traces from CISC machines consistently show that most of the available instructions are infrequently used in a given computing environment. This situation implies many things, as seen later in this chapter. It was such an observation of the System/360 characteristics that led IBM's John Cocke, in the early seventies, to contemplate a departure from traditional computer styles. The result was a research project, creatively named for the research group's building number, 801, which was based on a few coherent and synergistic design principles. Very little has been published about that project, but what has been released speaks for a principled and coherent research effort[27].

Three major ideas drove the 801 system design:

● Provide a hardware engine that can execute its instructions in one machine cycle and choose these instructions to be a good target for a compiler. This implies that the frequently executed primitive instructions should pay no performance penalties associated with the additional hardware needed to manage the execution of more complex instructions (which can involve extensive decoding and multi-cycle operation).

● Design the storage hierarchy so that the computing engine will generally not have to wait for storage access. The performance potential of a simple, fast computing engine would be lost if its execution were stalled frequently, waiting for instructions or data.

● Base the entire system design on the pervasive use of the 801 compiler. Programmers are now relying extensively on compilers for better program development and management reasons and only using assembly language when optimal performance is essential or for system operations which cannot be specified by the source language.

These ideas resulted in an instruction set architecture based upon three design principles. According to Radin[27], the instruction set was 'that set of run-time operations which:

● could not be moved to compile time,
● could not be more efficiently executed by object code produced by a compiler which understood the high level intent of the program,
● was to be implemented in random logic more effectively than the equivalent sequence of software instructions'.

The resulting 801 system relies on the tightly coupled nature of its hardware and software for its high performance. The hardware implementation, driven by a desire for leanness, featured hard-wired control and single-cycle instruction execution. All memory references were restricted to loads and stores and separate instruction and data caches were employed to allow simultaneous access to code and operands. The 801 CPU has 32 32-bit general purpose registers and all operations are register–register. The compiler uses many optimisation strategies including a powerful scheme of register allocation and global optimisation. The compiler also subsumes the responsibility for all reference checking and protection in the system.

Some of the basic ideas from the 801 research reached the United State's West Coast in the mid 1970s. At the University of California at Berkeley, these ideas grew into a series of RISC projects conducted in graduate courses that produced the RISC I, RISC II, and SOAR as well as the numerous CAD tools that facilitated these designs. These courses laid a foundation for related research efforts in performance evaluation, CAD and computer implementation.

Like the 801, the RISC I processor[24] is a hardwire controlled, load/store machine (i.e. data can only be operated upon when in a register and only load and store instructions access memory) which executes most of its instructions in a single cycle. Each of its 31 instructions fit in a single 32-bit word and use practically the same encoding format. A special feature of the RISC I is its large number of registers, well over a hundred, which are used to form a series of overlapping multiple register sets (MRS). This feature is used to make procedure calls on the RISC I less expensive in terms of processor–memory bus traffic.

It is reasonable to expect MRSs to yield performance benefits since procedure-based high level languages (HLLs) typically use registers for information specific to a procedure. Whenever a procedure call is performed, this information must be saved, usually on a memory stack, and restored on a procedure return. These operations are typically very time consuming due to their intrinsic data transfer requirements. RISC I uses its multiple register sets to reduce the frequency of this register saving and restoring. It also takes advantage of an overlap between register sets for parameter passing, reducing even further the memory reads and writes necessary when compared to parameter passing schemes which use memory as the passing medium (e.g. via a stack)[14].

RISC I's register file has 138 32-bit registers organised into eight overlapped 'windows' (see Fig. 2.1). In each window, six registers overlap with the previous window (for incoming parameters and outgoing results) and six registers overlap with the next window (for outgoing parameters and incoming results). During any procedure, only one of these windows is actually accessible. A procedure call changes the current window to the next window by incrementing a pointer and the six outgoing parameter registers become the incoming parameters of the called procedure. Similarly, a procedure return switches to the previous window and the outgoing result registers become the incoming result registers of the calling procedure. Assuming that six 32-bit registers are enough to contain the parameters, then a procedure call involves no actual movement of information (only the window pointer is adjusted). Note that the finite on-chip resources limit the actual savings due to register window overflows and underflows[24]. The register file also has 10 global registers which are always accessible.

The Berkeley papers describing the RISC I and RISC II processors claimed that their resource decisions produced large (2 to 4 times) performance improvements over CISC machines like the

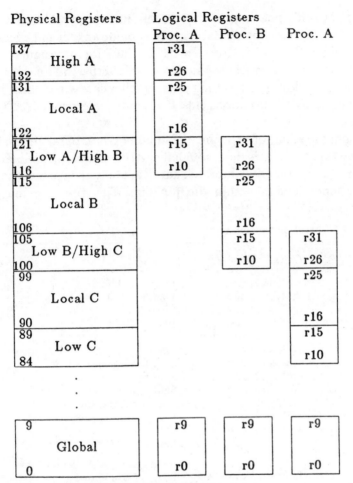

Fig. 2.1   RISC 1's overlapped register sets.

VAX and the 68000[24,26]. Many reservations can be expressed about these results and the methods used to obtain them. Foremost among these is that the performance effects of the reduced instruction set were not decoupled from those of the overlapped register windows, a feature which can be incorporated in any general purpose register machine. Since these performance factors were not evaluated independently, the claims for the performance due to the reduced nature of these machines are inconclusive. This point will be explained further in Section 2.6.

Not long after the first RISC I work at Berkeley, a processor named MIPS[17] (Microprocessor without Interlocked Pipe Stages) took shape at Stanford. The primary goal of MIPS is the high performance execution of compiled code. The basic principle used to achieve this goal was to expose the internal parellelism of the CPU to software control. Rather than provide an efficient encoding of a straightforward instruction set (as the RISC I designers did), MIPS presents the microengine to the user with a minimal amount of interpretation. The resulting processor is a hardwired, load/store machine whose instructions closely resemble microcode (see Table 2.1).

A unique result of exposing the microengine's parallelism at the instruction set level is that though the MIPS processor is pipelined, it contains no pipeline interlock hardware to manage resource and data dependencies within the pipeline. This function must be

**Table 2.1**   MIPS instruction set

| Operation | Operands | Comments |
|-----------|----------|----------|
| Add | src1, src2, dest | Integer addition |
| And | src1, src2, dest | Logical AND |
| Ic | src1, src2, dest | Insert byte |
| Or | src1, src2, dest | Logical OR |
| Rlc | src1, src2, src3, dest | Rotate combined |
| Rol | src1, src2, dest | Rotate |
| Sll | src1, src2, dest | Shift left logical |
| Sra | src1, src2, dest | Shift right arithmetic |
| Srl | src1, src2, dest | Shift right logical |
| Sub | src1, src2, dest | Integer subtraction |
| Subr | src1, src2, dest | Reverse integer subtraction |
| Xc | src1, src2, dest | Extract byte |
| Xor | src1, src2, dest | Logical XOR |
| Ld | A[src],dst | Load based |
| Ld | [src1 + src2],dst | Load based-indexed |
| Ld | [src1 $\gg$ src2],dst | Load based-shifted |
| Ld | A,dst | Load direct |
| Ld | I,dst | Load immediate |
| Mov | stc,dst | Load immediate |
| St | src1,A[src] | Store based |
| St | src1,[src2 + src3] | Store base-indexed |
| St | src1,[src2 $\gg$ src3] | Store based-shifted |
| St | src,A | Store direct |
| Bra | dst | Unconditional relative jump |
| Bra | Cond,src1,src2,dst | Conditional jump |
| Jmp | dst | Unconditional jump direct |
| Jmp | A[src] | Unconditional jump based |
| Jmp | (A[src]) | Unconditional jump indirect |
| Trap | Cond,src1,src2 | Trap instruction |
| SavePC | A | Save multi-stage PC after trap or interrupt |
| Set | Cond,src,dst | Set conditional |

performed by software (i.e. at compile time). Such a strategy is very different from techniques used in other heavily pipelined machines such as the IBM System/360 Model 91 in which pipeline interstage interlocking is performed at runtime by special hardware[1]. By moving this function from runtime to compile time the MIPS designers intended to provide a more efficient computing engine with a minimal cycle time.

Several other design decisions for the MIPS processor reflect the desire for minimal hardware complexity and high performance. Two memory interfaces are provided, one for instructions and one for data. This doubles the maximum bandwidth that only one memory interface would allow (an important factor for MIPS since its fast microengine would stall if sufficient memory bandwidth were not available). MIPS is also a word addressed machine which helps to reduce the hardware complexity from that required for a byte addressed architecture. Only one instruction size is provided in MIPS and all instructions execute in the same amount of time. This, along with the absence of condition codes, eases the problems associated with handling interrupts and page faults. Any MIPS instruction which can page fault is guaranteed not to modify any storage before the page fault is detected, thus removing the need to back up internal state for instruction restarting.

These three machines, the 801, RISC I, and MIPS, form the core of RISC research machines. The cited papers explain their principles in detail, but some of their features will be referred to throughout this article. While other RISC machines have been considered and explored, both within industry and academia, the discussions here concentrate on these three.

No comprehensive definition of a RISC has yet emerged, but one is needed. Proposed here are six synergistic elements that seem essential to the RISC philosophy. They are:

1. *Single-cycle operation.* This facilitates the rapid execution of simple functions which predominate a computer's instruction stream and it promotes a low interpretive overhead.

2. *Load/store design.* Follows from a desire for single-cycle operation.

3. *Hardwired control.* For the fastest possible single-cycle operation. Microcode leads to slower control paths and adds to interpretive overhead.

4. *Relatively few instructions and addressing modes.* This facilitates a fast, simple interpretation by the control engine.

5. *Simple instruction format.* The consistent use of a simple format eases the hardwired decoding of instructions, which again speeds control paths.

6. *More compile time effort.* RISC machines are predicated on running only compiled code. This offers an opportunity explicitly to move static runtime complexity into the compiler. A good example of this is the software pipeline reorganiser used by MIPS[18].

The list of RISC features enumerated above will be used in this chapter to weed out misleading claims as well as to provide a springboard for points of debate. Although some aspects of this list may be arguable, it will at least serve as a working definition throughout this chapter so that some of the issues and implications behind RISCs can be explored.

## 2.3   Challenges of RISC

As mentioned earlier, RISC ideas represent a serious challenge to some of the assumed design styles that have guided computer designs for many years. This section will examine each of the previously defined RISC features in this light. Each feature will be explored to bring out the ways in which it differs from past traditions and the ways in which it might contribute to future traditions.

Load/store architecture is not a new concept, but it certainly never was the *raison d'être* that it is for RISC designs. Load/store design provides a lower level of instruction atomicity than that provided by architectures which can have multiple memory accesses within a single instruction. While this lower level of atomicity requires more instructions, it can make for easier implementation. This is especially true for machines which have to support virtual memory and, hence, have to recover from memory access faults. Creating a machine that can recover from such a fault and restart coherently is trying enough on a RISC machine. It becomes even harder when multiple memory accesses may be required within a single instruction.

It is hard to argue against the desire for hardwired control. The faster cycle time and smaller control area which derive from having hardwired control are always attractive. This dovetails quite nicely with RISC philosophy which espouses a machine simple enough for hardwired control to be feasible. For larger machines, hardwired control can become a nightmare. The lesson for designers is 'RISC instructions must run at RISC speeds', meaning that the commonly used subset of instructions should run as if they were hardwired. Of course, the only way to do so is to hardwire them, leaving but two alternatives. One is to design a RISC. The other begs the question: 'Can hardwired and microcoded control systems be effectively mixed?' While there may be commercial examples of such machines, we are not aware of them.

Having relatively few instructions and addressing modes in an architecture can have two positive effects upon its implementation. First, it facilitates a speedy design. While designing any commercial processor design is by nature a complex task, with all the required documentation and testing, a smaller, simpler processor will still be easier to design than a larger, more complex one. The second positive effect deals with resources such as chip area, available power and board space. A simple processor will require fewer resources to implement than a complex processor. This could potentially leave resources for non-architectural features such as caching, address translation, or on-chip (on-board) I/O. This provides a flexibility not found in more constrained and complicated processor designs.

Not all points of our RISC definition can be applied only to small, simple processors. For example, RISC is not the only style of architecture that can benefit from simplified instruction formats. CISC implementers have long felt the pain of having to support complex, variable length, vertically encoded instructions. Architectures like the VAX have a performance limiting Achilles tendon in their tangled addressing modes and multiple operand instructions. Decoding such instruction streams is by nature either slow or resource expensive, or both. It will not be at all surprising if future complex, massive architectures appear with much cleaner instruction formats than what now commonly exist. Some recent large architectures, like the Ridge 32/100 series, show this trend.

The emphasis on compiler technology that RISC designs have shown is also bound to have a positive effect on all mainstream computer designs. While writing assembly code for the 360 is still all too prevalent, efficiently running compiled code is a proper goal for any new architecture. Further, the notion of moving functionality from runtime to compile time has finally been given its proper regard in the RISC world. This principle should be given the same high level of attention in all computer designs.

The utility of single-cycle operation is a RISC feature that, while intuitively appealing to many, has not been demonstrated. Unfortunately, computer design is not a science; no theorem can be proved that would demonstrate the superiority of single-cycle designs. While it is easy to believe that single-cycle machines have advantages over traditional microcoded engines, there has been little exploration of hybrid schemes that might effectively mix single- and multi-cycle operations.

## 2.4    Commercial RISCs

So far, our discussion of RISC machines has been limited to research projects. In this section we will discuss a few commercial machines which we feel have some RISC qualities. More specifically, we will discuss machines whose specification has been closely tied to their hardware implementations for performance reasons. This is a key attribute of the RISC design philosophy and it is worth discussing machines which have made significant design decisions that cross the traditional hardware/software boundaries. We will close this section with a brief discussion of several commercial machines which, for various reasons, have been labelled as RISCs but stray far from the definition we presented in the last section.

### 2.4.1   THE INMOS TRANSPUTER

The transputer[29] represents a novel approach to designing VLSI microprocessor systems. Typical microprocessors are designed for uniprocessor applications and are standardised at the instruction set level. Inmos' principal goal is to provide a family of high performance programmable VLSI components (transputers) containing high bandwidth communication links for the creation of concurrent multi-processor systems. The level of standardisation for transputers is *occam*, a programming language in which concurrent processes communicate via message passing along specified channels. The occam models of processes and communication are directly supported by transputer implementations.

The motivation for standardising the transputer family at the level of occam is to allow transputer hardware to evolve with advancing VLSI technology and to be optimised for special purpose processing while maintaining compatability with the occam software base. As such, each transputer will be designed to make the most efficient use of the available technology in order to maximise performance. This is where the transputer begins to be associated with the RISC design philosophy. The transputer designers are free to make decisions which cross the conventional architecture/implementation, hardware/software, and compile time/runtime boundaries to achieve high performance as long as the occam models of processes and communication are supported. The first results of such freedom can be seen in the initial implementations of transputers.

Two major characteristics of the first member of the transputer family, the IMST424, are a simple microcoded CPU and 2 kbyte of on-chip memory. The reasons for choosing a large on-chip memory and a simple micro-engine can be traced to current silicon implementation constraints. The on-chip memory provides fast access to a large amount of data without having to pay the expensive communication delays associated with off-chip memory. Memory is also very well suited for VLSI implementation because of its regular structure (also, Inmos' main products have always been semiconductor memories). However, the 2 kbyte of on-chip memory uses a significant portion of the silicon area, limiting the hardware resources available for the micro-engine. This has direct implications for the instruction set because the large amount of microcode space needed for a complex instruction set is not available. As such the T424 instruction set has a very simple, byte-encoded format and most instructions execute in a single cycle.

The T424 has only six registers (see Fig. 2.2). This small number is no great detriment to the processor's performance because of the on-chip memory which provides access to data at speeds close to that of registers. The small number of registers also reduces the amount of state that needs to be saved and restored across procedure boundaries and on process swaps. The six registers are:

- The A, B and C registers which form an evaluation stack. These registers are referred to implicitly by instructions which removes the need for instruction bits to specify registers, simplifying the instruction format.
- The workspace pointer which points to the area in memory where the local variables reside.
- The next instruction pointer.
- The operand register which is used to form instruction operands.

The T424 instruction set has only one instruction format. All instructions are one byte long and are divided into two parts: a 4-bit function field and a 4-bit data field (see Fig. 2.3). The instructions are divided into three groups:

- *Direct functions.* These 13 opcodes make up some of the most

Registers           Locals           Program

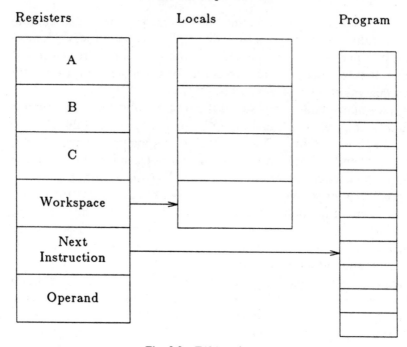

**Fig. 2.2** T424 registers.

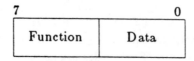

**Fig. 2.3** T424 instruction format.

common operations performed by a program, such as the loading and storing of local variables from the workspace, loading and adding constants, and program jumps and procedure calls.

- *Prefix functions.* Since only four bits of data can be expressed in an instruction, a provision is needed for forming longer operands. This is the function of the two prefixing instructions: *prefix* and *negative prefix*. The *prefix* instruction loads its four bits of data into the low order four bits of the operand register and then shifts the contents of the operand register up four bits. The *negative prefix* operates in a similar manner except that the contents of the operand register are complemented before shifting. Thus, operands of any length (not longer than the operand register) can be constructed.

- *Indirect functions.* The *operate* opcode causes its operand to be interpreted as an operation to be performed upon the values

in the evaluation stack. An example of such an operation would
be to add the contents of the A and B registers, store the result
in A, and copy the contents of C into B. This instruction allows
16 operations on the evaluation stack to be specified in one
byte. It is also possible to specify any number of operations
through the use of the prefixing instructions.

The T424 also has support for occam's model of concurrency.
The processor has a scheduler which time shares the processor
among active processes. These processes are maintained in two
linked lists of different priority. Hardware registers are used to
point to the first and the last processes on a list. New processes
are added at the end of the list. When a process is unable to
proceed, its instruction pointer is saved in its workspace and the
next process on the list is taken.

Occam's model of communication is also implemented in the
T424. Messages are passed along channels which can be internal
to the processor or connected between two processors. Internal
channels are implemented on the T424 using single words in
memory, and external channels are constructed using the T424's
point-to-point communication links. The same code sequences can
be used for either internal or external channels which allows
processes to be written without knowledge of the actual hardware
placement of the processes. Thus, an occam program can run on
any combination of transputers; only the information regarding
the configuration details of the system needs to be changed.

Inmos has reported impressive performance figures for the T424.
Colin Whitby-Strevens has stated that for the T424 'typical instruction sequences of commonly used instructions can deliver a 15
MIPS execution rate'[29]. MIPS rates should always be viewed with
some suspicion, especially when used as a metric for comparing
different machines. One needs to know the type of instructions
being executed (operations, data types, and addressing modes)
and where those instructions and the data they manipulate are
found (e.g. in a cache, prefetch queue, or main memory) to understand exactly what type of performance is being indicated. This
is especially true for the T424's 15 MIPS execution rate. This is
the maximum rate for single-cycle instructions which are found
in the on-chip memory. The performance degradation of off-chip
memory (a likely case since only 2 kbyte of memory are on-chip)
and slower instructions (e.g. context swaps and multiply instructions) are not incorporated into this instruction mix. One also

should remember that the 'typical' T424 instruction performs only a very simple operation whereas an instruction on a more complex machine can accomplish in one instruction what may require a whole sequence of instructions on the T424.

The T424's on-chip memory provides fast access to both instructions and data. However, the contents of the memory must be managed explicitly by the programmer. The management of this memory is not transparent to the programmer as a cache usually is. As such, the designer who needs more than 2 kbyte of memory must carefully allocate the on-chip memory to the most time critical processes in order to obtain high performance.

It should be noted that though the transputer and occam could be effective tools for constructing highly concurrent systems, they do not provide a general solution for decomposing a problem into its concurrent parts or scheduling the interaction of those parts. The system designer must still make the decisions concerning which processes are most effective when operating concurrently, how concurrent processes should be distributed over transputers, and when those processes should communicate with one another. These are the same problems that have plagued parallel computer projects for years. Norman Weizer, senior consultant for Arthur D. Little Inc., was quoted in *Electronics Week* saying that 'Except for raw signal processing, the massively parallel market has a history of failure'[21]. This is not to say that the transputer family will be unsuccessful, but instead it is meant to point out that occam and the transputer are not offering a total system solution. Many non-trivial design decisions still need to be made in order to realise effectively a concurrent system using transputers.

### 2.4.2 THE ACORN RISC MACHINE ARM

Acorn Computers of Cambridge, England, has announced the development of the Acorn RISC Machine (ARM), a 32-bit VLSI processor[2]. ARM was designed in a period of 18 months and first silicon met all design objectives. ARM is reported to exceed the performance of commercially available microprocessors such as the Motorola 68000 and the National Semiconductor 32016.

ARM is the response to Acorn's desire to build low cost personal computers and workstations using 16- or 32-bit technology. Existing 16- and 32-bit microprocessors were evaluated and Acorn came to the conclusion these processors could not be incorporated into low cost personal computers without significantly compromising system performance. Acorn cited the long uninterruptable operations typical in the existing microprocessors, which can slow interrupt response time, as the limiting factor for system performance. Acorn felt that existing microprocessors could not support the high I/O bandwidth they required without expensive DMA hardware.

Since available microprocessors were deemed inappropriate for low cost, high performance machines, Acorn began considering designing their own microprocessor. Some of the design criteria they had in mind were:

1. The processor interrupt latency should be low for the reasons cited above.

2. The performance of the new machine should be at least comparable to that of commercially available machines.

3. Virtual memory systems should be supportable using the new microprocessor, implying that all instructions need to be restartable.

4. The design task needed to be simple, considering the resources available to Acorn.

A RISC approach was taken primarily to meet the fourth design criterion. However, a simple machine can greatly improve interrupt latency and simplify the hardware necessary to allow instructions to be restarted (criteria one and three).

Some of the important characteristics of ARM are:

● ARM has a 32-bit data bus and a 26-bit address bus. Memory is byte addressed. All instructions are 32 bits and are word aligned. ARM has 16 general purpose registers, two of which are used for the program counter and the subroutine return link register. All operations are performed on 32-bit words. Load and store instructions are used to convert between bytes and words.

● In ARM all arithmetic and logical operations are performed on registers. These instructions specify one source register, a second register or an 8-bit constant, and a third destination register. The second source operand can be shifted/rotated before being used as an operand.

● Load and store operations can use either general base plus index or base plus a 12-bit constant for addressing memory. Any register can be used as a base and the index register can be shifted before being added to the base. The base register may be updated before or after the transfer, or not at all, as desired. Multiple register save and restore instructions are also available for consecutive memory addresses.

- Branch instructions use a word-aligned, 24-bit offset which allows branching anywhere within addressable memory. The branch instruction can specify that the program counter be saved in the link register for implementing procedure calls and returns.

- Supervisor and interrupt modes have access to nine registers unavailable to the user mode programs. These registers are used to minimise the interrupt latency and context switching times as well as provide support for simulating a DMA channel.

- Instruction restarting after an abort is not completely handled by the hardware. The criterion used for ARM was that it should be possible to restore the processor state. As such, the only guarantee is that all the information necessary to restore the processor state after an abort is preserved. The software must take over and restore the proper state before an instruction is retried.

- The ARM processor directly supports page mode cycles for DRAMs. This can yield a higher memory bandwidth than is available without using the page modes cycles.

### 2.4.3　THE RISC BANDWAGON

RISC has become a popular term in the technical community and has, to an extent, developed into a bandwagon. Several computer companies are jumping onto the bandwagon with new computer systems which they are claiming to be RISCs but which have characteristics very different from those we outlined earlier.

As an example of computer companies hopping onto this bandwagon, consider the two companies that have both claimed to create the first commercial RISC computers: Ridge Computers and Pyramid Technology. Both of their machines have restricted instruction formats, a feature they share with RISC machines. But Pyramid's is not a load/store machine, and both the Ridge and Pyramid machines have variable length instructions, involve multi-cycle interpretation, and employ microcoded control engines. Further, while their instruction counts might be reduced compared to a VAX, the Pyramid has almost 90 instructions and the Ridge has over one hundred. The use of microcoding in these machines is unsurprising for price/performance reasons. The Pyramid machine also has a system of multiple register sets which is derived from the Berkeley RISC I but, as will be argued later, this feature is independent of the RISC design philosophy. From both a technological and marketing standpoint, these may be successful machines, but they are not RISCs.

## 2.5 Points of confusion about RISC/CISC

There are two prevalent misconceptions about RISC and CISC. The first is due to the RISC and CISC acronyms, which seem to imply that the domain for discussion should be restricted to selecting candidates for a machine's instruction set. Although specification of instructions, their format and their number, is the primary focus of most of the RISC literature, the best generalisation of RISC philosophy goes well beyond this narrow activity. More properly, it connotes a willingness freely and consciously to make design trade-offs across architecture/implementation, hardware/ software, and compile-time/runtime boundaries in order to maximise performance (as measured in some specific context).

The RISC/CISC acronyms also seem to imply that any given machine can be classified as being either one or the other, and that the primary task confronting an architect is to choose the most appropriate design style for a particular application. But the RISC/CISC classification is not a dichotomy. RISCs and CISCs are at different corners of a continuous, multi-dimensional design space. What is needed is not some algorithm by which one can make a choice of building a RISC or a CISC; rather, the goal should be the formulation of a set of techniques, drawn from CISC experiences and RISC tenets, which can be used by a designer to assign functionality appropriately to implementation level within a computer system[9,15,6].

Unfortunately, as has been pointed out[7], the terms *reduced* and *complex* have been contraposed in discussions of the philosophy. In fact, two orthogonal instruction set dimensions are at issue here: size (reduced *vs.* massive) and complexity (simple *vs.* complex). The first dimension concerns the number of instructions (addressing modes, number of possible values in instruction fields in general) that characterise an architecture. The other concerns the functional complexity of the instructions as might be represented by the number of 'primitive' operations that would be needed to synthesise them. This dimension is much harder to quantify since various mixtures of simple and complex instructions can exist within the same computer architecture.

It is true that 'reduced' and 'simple' take on a mutually reinforcing relationship in the context of RISC design, as 'massive' and 'complex' normally do in the CISC domain. This does not have to be the case. Simplicity means different things to chip designers, computer architects, and all other people involved in the design process. The VAX has often been singled out as being a complex architecture. Yet, from the designer's point of view, the VAX was to be a simple yet massive instruction set. The definition of simplicity used in this context was:

Those attributes (other than price) that make minicomputer systems attractive.
These include approachability, understandability, and ease of use[28].

It is questionable whether or not this goal was achieved, especially given that massive items tend to be complex. It will be argued later that, in some ways, the issue of simplicity may not be of prime importance.

In support of having only simple operations, RISC proponents often warn of detrimental effects due to the use of complex instructions. Nevertheless, the popularity of installing support for specialised functions such as interprocess communication (IPC) seems to be undiminished. The designers of the ELXSI 6400 report[23], for instance:

A key architectural feature which allows the operating system to cope with the tremendous variability in its hardware environment is the microcode and hardware implemented message system. The use of messages allowed us to make choices in the CPU and operating system architecture which greatly enhance the effectiveness of additional processors.

But we concur with one of the RISC criticisms of the published accounts of these machines: it is not enough to show that a complex instruction executes faster than an equivalent sequence of primitive instructions. It must also be shown that the net effect is to improve system performance. We believe that this aspect of the problem must be part of the design effort.

There are many other computing environments, such as real time or signal processing systems, where it would be hard to argue against supporting complex functions directly in the computer architecture and implementation. More generally, Radin has written[27]:

> It is often true that implementing a complex function in random logic will result in its execution being significantly faster than if the function were programmed as a sequence of primitive instructions. Examples are floating point arithmetic and fixed point multiply. We have no objections to this strategy, provided the frequency of use justifies the cost and, more important, provided these complex instructions in no way slow down the primitive instructions.

We subscribe to this statement, but we assert that frequency of use is an insufficient criterion for justifying a given instruction. As Clark and Levy have pointed out[8]:

> Aggregate statistics alone cannot guide the design of an instruction set intended for different languages and applications. In particular, instructions that are infrequently used overall can be critical for some intended users.

The notion that complex functions slow down the simple actions of a computer seems to be the real problem that prevents us from having the best of all worlds. We believe that serious research efforts in the areas of functional partitioning, instruction interpretation, and distributed decoding will produce computer structures which reduce or eliminate this effect. Until research is directly aimed at this problem, a greater understanding of the scientific truths and principles involved, as opposed to the folklore currently being disseminated, is not possible.

One consequence of the us-or-them attitude evinced by most RISC publications is that the reported performance of a particular machine (e.g. RISC I) can become very hard to interpret if the contributions made by the various design decisions are not individually presented. A designer faced with a large array of choices needs more specific guidance than a monolithic all-or-nothing performance measurement.

An example of how the issue of scope can be confused is found in a recent article[3]. By creating a machine with only one instruction, its authors claim to have delimited the RISC design space, with their machine at one end of the space and the RISC I (with 31 instructions) at the other end. But an absolute number of instructions cannot be the sole criterion for categorising an architecture as to RISC or CISC. This model is far too simplistic to be useful: it ignores aspects of addressing modes and their associated complexity; it fails to deal with compiler/architecture coupling; and it provides no way to evaluate the implementation of other non-instruction set design decisions such as register files, caches, memory management, floating point operations, and coprocessors.

Another fallacy propagated by this article is that the total system is composed of hardware, software, and application code. This unfortunately leaves out the operating system, and the overhead and the needs of the operating system cannot be ignored in most systems. This area has received far too little attention from RISC research efforts (in contrast to the many CISC efforts that have focused on this area[4,5]).

One consideration for computer system design that did receive a lot of attention in some of the early arguments made in favour of the RISC design style was that simpler designs could be realised more quickly, giving them a performance advantage over complex machines. Besides the economic advantages of getting to market first, this was supposed to avoid the performance disadvantages of introducing a new machine based on relatively old implementation technology. In light of these arguments, DEC's MicroVAX-32[19] is especially interesting.

The VAX easily qualifies as a CISC. According to published reports, the MicroVAX-32, a VLSI implementation of the preponderance of the VAX instruction set, was designed, realised and tested in a period of several months. One might speculate that this very short gestation period was made possible in large part by DEC's considerable expertise in implementing the VAX architecture (existing products included the 11/780, 11/750, 11/730, and VLSI-VAX). This would not have been feasible if DEC had not first created a standard instruction set. But standardising at this level is precisely what RISC philosophy argues against. Such standards constrain the unconventional hardware/software trade-offs that RISCs capitalise on. From a commercial standpoint, it is significant that the MicroVAX-32 was born into a world where compatible assemblers, compilers and operating systems abound, which would certainly not be the case for a RISC design where every new generation must start anew.

Such problems with RISC systems designs may encourage commercial RISC designers to define a new level of standardisation in order to achieve some of the advantages of multiple implementations supporting one standard interface. A possible choice for such an interface would be to define an intermediate language as the target for all compilation. The intermediate language would then be translated into optimal machine code for each implementation. This translation process would simply be performing resource scheduling at a very low level (e.g. pipeline management and register allocation).

It should be noted that the MicroVAX-32 does not directly implement all of the VAX architecture. The suggestion has been made that this somehow supports the RISC inclination towards emulating complex functions in software[26]. This insinuation is unreasonable. The VAX does not come close to fitting this chapter's definition of a RISC, violating all six stated RISC criteria. To begin with, any VAX by definition has a variable length instruction format and is not a load/store machine. Further, the MicroVAX-32 has multi-cycle instruction execution, relies on a microcoded control engine, and interprets the whole array of VAX addressing modes. Lastly, the MicroVAX-32 executes 175 instructions onchip, not a 'reduced' number by any stretch of the imagination.

A better perspective on the MicroVAX-32 would show that there are indeed cost/performance ranges where a microcoded implementation of certain functions is inappropriate, and software emulation is better. The importance of carefully making this assignment of function to implementation level (software, microcode or hardware) has been amply demonstrated in many RISC papers. Yet this simple concern is also evidenced by many CISC machines. In the case of the MicroVAX-32, floating point instructions are migrated either to a coprocessor chip or to software emulation routines. The numerous floating point chips currently available attest to the contemporary wisdom of this partitioning. Also migrated to emulation are the console, decimal, and string instructions. Since many of these instructions are infrequent, not time critical, or are not generated by many compilers, it would be hard to fault this approach to designing an inexpensive VAX. The MicroVAX-32 also shows that it is possible for intelligent, competent computer designers who understand the notion of correct function-to-level mapping still to find microcoding a valuable technique. Published RISC work does not accommodate this possibility.

As VLSI technology improves, the level of integration will increase until one will be able to include main memory and memory management on the same chip as the CPU. Once these technology increases have been realised, the RISC philosophy offers no advice as to how to take advantage of even higher gate densities. The RISC philosophy seems to be basically at odds with approaches which will be based on millions of transistors on a chip. It is probably well suited for current technology (e.g. current GaAs chips are restricted to 10 to 20 thousand gates) but will become less attractive as fabrication capability improves.

The application environment is also of crucial importance in system design. The RISC I instruction set was designed specifically to run the C language efficiently, and it appears to do that quite well. The RISC I researchers have also investigated the SMALL-TALK-80 computing environment[30]. Rather than evaluate RISC I as a SMALLTALK engine, however, the RISC I researchers designed a new RISC and report encouraging performance results from simulations. But designing a processor to run a single language well is a qualitatively different endeavour from creating a single machine which must exhibit at least acceptable performance for a wide range of languages (e.g. the VAX). While RISC research thus far offers valuable insights on a per-language basis, more emphasis on cross-language anomalies, commonalities and tradeoffs is badly needed.

Especially misleading are RISC claims concerning the amount of design time saved by creating a simple machine instead of a complex one. Such claims sound reasonable. However, substantial differences exist between the design environments for an academic one-of-a-kind project (such as MIPS or RISC I) and for a machine with a lifetime measured in years requiring substantial software and support investments. As was pointed out in an *Electronics Week* article, R. David Lowry, market development manager for Denelcor, 'notes that commercial product development teams generally start off a project by weighing the profit and loss impacts of design decisions'. Lowry is quoted as saying 'A university doesn't have to worry about that, so there are often many built-in dead ends in projects. . . . This is not to say the value of their research is diminished. It does, however, make it very difficult for someone to reinvent the system to make it a commercial product'[21]. For a product to remain viable a great deal of documentation, user training, coordination with fabrication or production facilities, and future upgrade paths must all be provided. These factors skew such design time comparisons and comparisons of this nature should therefore be viewed with suspicion.

Throughout the RISC literature there is a largely unstated but pervasive bias towards those aspects of a computer system dealing with performance. Clearly, if all other attributes are equal, higher performance must be considered an improvement to a machine. However, we believe that it is possible to ascribe too much importance to the performance dimension of a computer system. Since performance is the most quantifiable measure of a machine, it is the most frequently discussed and measured – not because performance is always inherently so much more valuable than other system parameters, but because benchmarking is the easiest way of comparing system alternatives. It is a mistake to pursue performance blindly without explicitly acknowledging what is being traded for it.

Even so, the performance claims for RISC designs, perhaps the most interesting of all the RISC assertions, are not unambiguous. Performance as measured by narrowly compute-bound low level benchmarks which have been used by RISC researchers (e.g. recursively solving the Towers of Hanoi puzzle) is not the only metric in a computer system, and in some it is not even one of the most interesting. For many current computers, the only performance figure of merit is 'transactions per second', which has no direct or simple correlation to the time it takes to calculate Ackermann's function. While millions of instructions per second might be a meaningful metric in some computing environments, reliability, availability and response time are of much more concern in others, such as spaceborne and avionics computing. The extensive error-checking incorporated into these machines at every level may slow the basic clock time and substantially degrade peak performance. But reduced performance is tolerable; downtime may not be. In the extreme, naive application of the RISC rules for designing an instruction set would result in a missile guidance computer optimised for running its most common task: diagnostics. In terms of instruction frequencies, of course, flight control applications constitute a trivial special case and would not be given much attention. While this example is humorously implausible, it is worth emphasising that in the efforts to quantify performance, and to apply those measurements to system design, one must pay attention not just to instruction execution frequencies, but to cycles consumed per instruction execution. Levy and Clark make this point regarding the VAX instruction set[22], but it has yet to appear in any RISC-related papers.

For applications where performance (such as throughput, response time or transactions per second) is a first-order concern, one is faced with the task of quantifying it. The Berkeley RISC I

project's efforts in attempting to establish their machine's throughput is laudable, but before sweeping conclusions are drawn one
must carefully examine the benchmark programs that were used.
To quote from a recent article:

> The performance predictions for (RISC I and RISC II) were
> based on small programs. This small size was dictated by the
> reliability of the simulator and compiler, the available simulation
> time, and the inability of the first simulators to handle UNIX
> system calls[26].

Some of these 'small' programs actually execute millions of instructions, yet they are very narrow programs in terms of the scope of
function. For example, the Towers of Hanoi program, when executing on the 68000, spends over 90% of its memory accesses in
executing procedure calls and returns. The RISC I and II researchers have recently reported results from a large benchmark[26], but
the importance of large, non-homogenous benchmarks in performance measurement is still lost on many commercial and academic
computer evaluators who have succumbed to the misconcep-
tion that 'micro-benchmarks' represent a useful measurement in
isolation.

Measuring real computer systems requires that a processing load
be devised such that the results of the measurements can be
interpreted in some useful way. The art of benchmaking has
evolved to provide programs which, taken as a whole, are thought
to be representative of the processing load seen by the machine
in actual use.

Benchmarking is still an art, however. Little agreement exists
on how even to characterise typical processing loads, much less
to create benchmarks which accurately represent those loads. Even
for benchmarks that can be shown to correlate well with the steady
state average behaviour of a large scale processing load, small
benchmarks do not capture or duplicate such important systems-
level conditions as process swap overhead and I/O interrupts. For
systems with caches, small benchmarks may fit entirely within the
cache, exaggerating the performance benefits of such caches[32].

As Levy and Clark have pointed out[22], many other subtle effects
are present when high level benchmarks are used to compare
systems. For instance, they argue that benchmarks implemented
in different languages should not be used to draw architectural
conclusions. As an example of how the language semantics can
affect the results, they discuss the C string manipulation scheme

(pointers used to access characters) *vs.* Pascal (which indexes into an array of characters), and report that in languages such as Bliss and PL/1, the VAX *MatchC* string matching instruction would be used with a speed-up of nearly a factor of five.

Other problems with high level language benchmarks relate to the quality of compiled code (a very significant issue for the Intel 432, as will be discussed in Section 2.7). Clark and Levy show examples of variations in execution times of more than 2 : 1 just for different compilers of the same language on a single architecture.

Another issue in measuring system performance concerns the load represented by operating system code. Since there is wide variability in the use of OS functions, it can be very difficult to characterise that load, but it is often estimated that a substantial number (greater than 50%) of the processor cycles are typically dedicated to the operating system. Processing loads of that magnitude should not be ignored.

Despite the problems associated with using benchmarks, their use can be of great value in architectural design. In discussing the performance of Lisp systems, Gabriel and Masinter[13] argue for an architectural evaluation based on benchmark performance combined with analysis of mechanisms and structure.

> Computer architectures have become complex enough that it is often difficult to analyse program behaviour in the absence of a set of benchmarks to guide that analysis. It is often difficult to perform an accurate analysis without doing some experimental work to guide the analysis and keep it accurate; without analysis it is difficult to know how to benchmark correctly.

We take the position that, although there are many problems with system measurements using benchmarks, there are also good reasons to use them. If the benchmarks are constrained to be implemented in a single language, and for a single architecture that is incrementally changed in various ways, then it is possible to draw unambiguous conclusions about the effects of those architectural decisions.

RISC work generally chooses to trade away the traditional benefits of an architecture/implementation dichotomy for greater flexibility in implementation which can make architectural evaluation more difficult. However, providing a few examples of where CISC designers may have gone too far in optimising the architecture at the expense of implementation efficiency does not imply that the problems are inevitable. It has been suggested that architectural evaluation is 'folly' because one such study ignored the effects of pre-fetched bytes that weren't used (a problem largely obviated by the 'delayed branch' technique common to RISC I, MIPS, and the 801)[25]. This argument is specious and can be dealt with in several ways:

1. The study should have included those bytes.

2. Any machine, RISC or CISC, can use delayed branches (the 432 uses delayed branches in its microcode routines), so this point is irrelevant.

3. One study that errs does not invalidate the method from which it derives.

4. It is not necessarily the case that the faster machine has the better architecture or provides optimum utility or lowest life cycle cost, metrics that lie at the heart of architecture studies but are ignored in RISC publications.

5. Without architectural metrics we have no way to compare the processor families of various manufacturers, and cannot then abstract away the artifacts of implementation from the innovations. What is really needed are better metrics that combine both architecture and implementation to reflect best the expected life cycle cost.

Much of the current RISC work is relevant and useful to computer designers, but is best absorbed within a context derived elsewhere. The RISC bias is not towards analysis of the practical problems faced by manufacturers who must create, produce and support a line of processors along with a range of languages and operating systems. RISC work aims at illuminating the low level performance aspects of computer inplementations within a narrow range of usage. It can criticise CISC mistakes effectively, but offers only higher performance on simple operators in exchange. Arguments that purport to show that complex machines like the VAX are faster when only their simple instructions are used show only the inadequacy of current compilers, or that errors can creep into microcoded instructions, making them slower than their design specification calls for. Such arguments do not shed light on the performance tradeoffs associated with designing a microcoded engine.

RISC proponents have argued that micro-instructions should not be faster than simple instructions, since that implies that the simple instructions are not as fast as they could have been. We believe this argument has merit, but its implications are not what they seem. This premise has been used to conclude that the micro-coding technique is counterproductive, since a general purpose machine should be designed to optimise execution of the operations that make the greatest contribution to overall perform-ance (the simple operations), and microcode is not needed for those. Faced with such a choice, the RISC approach is worth considering.

But the hidden premise is that such a choice must be made at all. There is no reason that a CISC realisation could not decouple the simple RISC-like engine required for simple operations from the microcode necessary for more complex operations (e.g. the 432's *Send*). In fact, that is precisely the approach RISC pro-ponents advocate for floating point; why not consider it for other functions as well? The point is argued repeatedly in RISC publica-tions that 'microcode is not magic', meaning that whatever micro-code can do, software can do. Microcode is not magic, but neither is it isomorphic to software. In fact, there are at least two important ways in which a function implemented in microcode differs from its software analogue.

The first difference is in security. Von Neumann machines place instructions and data into the same memory. Architectural mechan-isms attempt to regulate access to the various types of information contained in memory, but this protection is necessarily at a fairly gross level. Even for a machine with fine-grained protection domains such as the 432, it is possible intentionally or accidentally to misuse memory. When a function is placed into microcode, the operation of that function cannot be altered or subverted by changes to its instructions or immediate data. The 432 relies on its on-chip microcode to implement correctly its addressing and protection mechanisms, which underlie all of the machine's com-putations. With a secure kernel implemented where no activity can ever change it, the possibility for a completely reliable operat-ing system is raised. Such a prospect is not feasible for machines where one set of bits in memory guards another set of bits.

Another difference between microcode and software may seem magical if the right point of view is taken. Given that a machine can be constructed such that its microcode does not slow the execution of its simple operators, whatever functionality that resides in the microcode could be viewed as a software routine that has been instantly loaded into the instruction cache, which instantly became large enough to hold the entire routine. The routine has then executed without even a threat of a cache miss, resulting in no memory accesses, and finishing with the cache exactly as it was before the routine began. Of course, microcode memory is much more efficient than a cache since read-only memory is much denser, so larger functions can be provided than if the program really had to execute from cache. The open research questions here are to determine the functions that would be appropriate for such coprocessor implementation, and to find the most efficient communication mechanisms between the processor and its coprocessors. Keep in mind that a coprocessor may or may not reside on the same chip as the central processor; where technology permits, this may be a better use of chip real estate than larger caches or massive register files.

## 2.6　The multiple register set study

Probably the most publicised RISC-style processor is Berkeley's RISC I. The most well known feature of this chip is its large number of on-chip registers organised as a series of overlapping register sets. However, this is ironic since the register file is a performance feature independent of any RISC (as defined earlier) aspect of the processor. Multiple register sets (MRS) could be included in any general purpose register machine.

It has been claimed that the small control area needed to implement the simple instruction set of a VLSI RISC leaves enough chip area for a large register file[24]. The relatively small amount of control logic used by a RISC does free resources (in any technology) for other uses, but a large register file is not the only way to use them, or even necessarily the best. For example, the 801 and MIPS chose other ways to use their available hardware; these RISCs have only a single, conventional size register set. Of the many possible uses for those resources 'freed' by a RISC's simple instruction set, caches, floating point hardware, and interprocess communication support are but a few. Moreover, as chip technology improves, the tradeoffs between instruction set complexity and architecture/implementation features become less constrained. Computer designers will always have to make decisions on how best to use their available resources, but in doing so they should realise which interrelationships are intrinsic and which ones are not.

The Berkeley papers describing the RISC I and RISC II processors claimed that their resource decisions produced large (2 to

4 times) performance improvements over CISC machines like the VAX and the 68000[24,26]. These studies, however, did not decouple the performance effects of the reduced instruction set from those of the overlapped multiple register sets. As such, we feel that the RISC-derived performance of these machines was not demonstrated in those studies because the different performance features were not independently evaluated.

Some of the performance comparisons between different machines, especially the earlier ones, were based upon simulated benchmark execution times. While absolute speed is always interesting, other, less implementation dependent, metrics can provide more useful design information to computer architects, such as the processor-memory traffic necessary to execute a series of benchmarks. It is also difficult to draw firm conclusions from comparisons of vastly different machines unless some effort has been made to factor out implementation dependent features not being compared (e.g. caches and floating point accelerators).

Based upon these reservations, experiments were conducted at CMU to test the hypothesis that the effects of multiple register sets (MRSs) are orthogonal to instruction set complexity[10]. Specifically, the goal was to see if the performance effects of MRSs were comparable for RISCs and CISCs. For these experiments, simulators were written for two CISCs (the VAX and the 68000) without MRSs, with non-overlapping MRSs, and with overlapping register sets. Simulators were also written for the RISC I, RISC I with non-overlapping register sets, and RISC I with only a single register set. In each of the simulators, care was taken not to change the initial architectures any more than absolutely necessary to add or remove MRSs. Instead of simulating execution time, the total amount of processor-memory traffic (bytes read and written) for each benchmark was recorded as the metric for comparison. To use this data fairly, only different register set versions of the same architecture were compared (avoiding some ambiguities which arise from comparing vastly different architectures like the RISC I and the VAX). The benchmarks used were the same ones originally used to evaluate RISC I. A summary of the experiments and their results can be found in a recent paper[20].

As expected, the results show a substantial difference in processor-memory traffic for an architecture with and without MRSs. The MRS versions of the VAX and 68000 both show marked decreases in processor-memory traffic for procedure-intensive benchmarks, as seen in Figs. 2.4 and 2.5. Similarly, the single

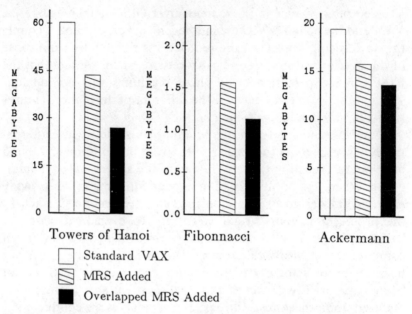

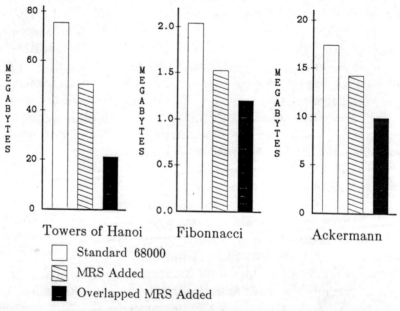

**Fig. 2.4** Total processor-memory traffic for benchmarks on the standard VAX and two modified VAXs, one with multiple register sets and one with overlapping multiple register sets.

**Fig. 2.5** Total processor-memory traffic for benchmarks on the standard 68000 and two modified 68000s, one with multiple register sets and one with overlapping multiple register sets.

register set version of RISC I requires many more memory reads and writes than RISC I with overlapped register sets (Fig. 2.6). This is due in part to the method of handling register set overflow and underflow, which was kept the same for all three variations. By using a more intelligent scheme, the single register set RISC I actually requires fewer bytes of memory traffic on Ackermann's function than its multiple register set counterparts (see Fig. 2.7). For benchmarks with very few procedure calls (e.g. The Sieve of Eratosthenes), the single register set version has the same amount of processor-memory traffic as does the MRS version of the same architecture. Again, a recent paper describes this result, and others[20].

Clearly, MRSs can affect the amount of processor-memory traffic necessary to execute a program. A significant amount of the performance of RISC I for procedure intensive environments has been shown to be attributable to its scheme of overlapped register sets, a feature independent of instruction set complexity. Thus, any performance claims for reduced instruction set computers that do not remove effects due to multiple register sets are inconclusive, at best.

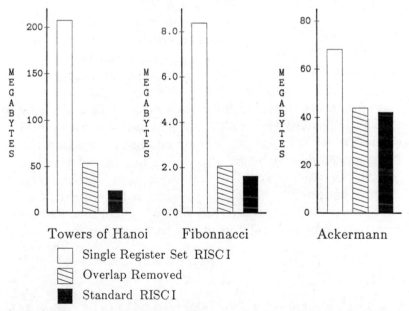

Fig. 2.6  Total processor-memory traffic for benchmarks on the standard RISC I and two modified RISC Is, one with no overlap between register sets and one with only one register set.

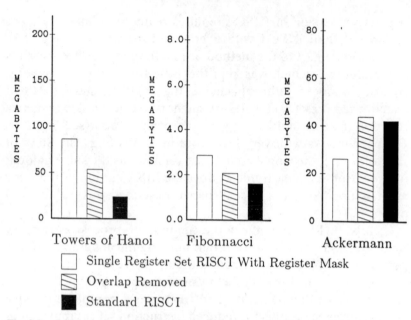

**Fig. 2.7** Total processor–memory traffic for benchmarks on the standard RISC I and two modified RISC Is, one with no overlap between register sets and one with a single register set which makes use of a register mask to indicate which registers should be saved and restored on procedure calls and returns.

These CMU experiments used benchmarks drawn from other RISC research efforts for the sake of continuity and consistency. Some of these benchmarks, such as Ackermann, Fibonacci and Hanoi, actually spend most of their time performing procedure calls. The percentage of the total processor–memory traffic due to 'C' procedure calls for these three benchmarks on the single register set 68000 ranged from 66 to 92%. It was no surprise that a machine such as the RISC I, with an overlapped register structure which allows procedure calls to be almost free in terms of processor–memory bus traffic, would do extremely well on these highly recursive benchmarks when compared to machines with only a single register set. However, it has not been established that these benchmarks are representative of any computing environment.

## 2.7  The Intel 432

As a classic example of a CISC, the Intel 432 has few peers. It is an object-orientated VLSI microprocessor chip set designed expressly to provide a productive Ada programming environment for large scale, multiple process, multiple processor systems. The nature of its architectural support for object orientation is such that every object is protected uniformly without regard to traditional distinctions such as 'supervisor/user mode' or 'system/user data structures'. The 432 has a very complex instruction set. Its instructions are also bit-encoded and range in length from 6 to 321 bits. The 432 also incorporates a significant degree of functional migration from software to on-chip microcode (the interprocess communication SEND primitive is a 432 machine instruction, for instance).

Published studies of the performance of the Intel 432 on low level benchmarks (e.g. Towers of Hanoi[16]) show that it is very slow, requiring approximately 10–20 times as long to complete them as did the VAX 11/780. Such a design would appear to be an ideal candidate for scrutiny in the RISC/CISC controversy.

Intuitively, one would be tempted to blame the machine's object-oriented runtime environment for imposing too much overhead. Every memory reference is checked to ensure that it lies within the boundaries of the referenced object, and the read/write rights of the executing context are verified for that object. RISC proponents would argue that the complexity of the 432's architecture, plus the additional decoding required for a bit-encoded instruction stream, contributes to its poor performance. To address these and other issues, a detailed study of the 432 was undertaken which evaluated the effectiveness of the architectural mechanisms (functional migrations) the 432 provided in support of its intended runtime environment. This is one of the central differences in the RISC and CISC design styles: RISC designs avoid hardware/microcode structures intended to support the runtime environment, attempting instead to place such support into the compiler or software. This runs contrary to the mainstream history of computer instruction set design, which reflects a steady migration of such functionality from higher levels (software) down to lower ones (microcode or hardware) in the expectation of improved performance.

Unlike much RISC work, this study did not assume that any and all aspects of system architecture or implementation are fair candidates for alteration or disposal as long as overall system throughput on the benchmarks appears to be higher. The study pursued the question of how large an inherent overhead object orientation appears to be, and how effectively functional migration can be used to combat that overhead. Consequently, the highest performance subject to certain runtime constraints which are intrinsic to the 432 class of object-oriented systems was sought.

The performance of the 432 was evaluated using a set of benchmarks to drive the 432 microsimulator. This simulator created cycle-by-cycle log files, which were then analysed. Proposed architectural changes to the 432 were then modelled using the number of cycles per instruction given in the log files as a guide. A detailed treatment of these experiments and their results can be found in a recent thesis[11].

Simulations of these benchmarks revealed several performance problems with the 432 and its compiler.

1. The 432's Ada compiler performs almost no optimisation. As a consequence, the machine is frequently forced to make unnecessary changes to its complex addressing environment, costly subexpressions are recomputed unnecessarily, and parameter passing is always done by 'call by value result', which in some cases requires substantially more memory traffic than would 'call by reference'. This seriously skews many results from benchmark comparisons. Such benchmarks do reflect the performance one can expect to achieve from the present version of the 432, but say very little about the efficacy of the architectural tradeoffs made in that machine.

2. The 432 is very memory-bandwidth limited. This is the result of several factors, especially the following. The 432 has no on-chip data caching, no instruction stream literals and no local data registers, which cause it to make far more memory references than it would have to otherwise. This also makes the code size much larger, since many more bits are required to reference data within an object than a local register. Due to pin limitations, the 432 must multiplex both data and address information over only 16 pins. Also, the standard Intel 432/600 development system, which supports shared memory multiprocessing, uses a slow asynchronous bus that was designed more for reliability than throughput. All of these implementation factors combine to make wait states consume 25–40% of the processor's time on the benchmarks.

3. On highly recursive benchmarks, the object-oriented overhead in the 432 does indeed appear in the form of a slow procedure call. But even here the performance problems should not be attributed to object orientation or to the machine's intrinsic complexity. The designers of the 432 made a decision to provide a new protected context for every procedure call; the user has no

option in this respect. If an unprotected call mechanism was used where appropriate, the Dhrystone benchmark[32] would run 20% faster.

4. The bit-aligned nature of the instructions means that the 432 must almost of necessity decode the various fields of an instruction sequentially. Since such decoding often overlaps with instruction execution, the 432 stalls waiting for the instruction decoder 3% of the time on these benchmarks. However, this percentage will only get worse when other problems above are eliminated.

Several of the cycle sinks mentioned above have significant impact upon the overall performance of the 432, yet are unrelated to architectural complexity, functional migration, or object orientation. Consequently, several architectural improvements were explored to determine the number of cycles actually wasted during execution. These improvements were:

- Better management of addressing environments (*enter-environments*).
- Better code optimisation by the compiler.
- Appropriate mechanism used for procedure calls (protected calls *vs.* branch-and-link).
- Use of the fastest parameter passing mechanism available.
- A non-bit-aligned instruction stream.
- Provision for literals in the instruction set.

Table 2.2 shows the combined cycles saved when the above assumptions are made.

The implications of Table 2.2 must be clearly understood. This table shows that 35–45% of the 432's total benchmark execution cycles are wasted. These cycles are not spent in pursuit of object

**Table 2.2** New baseline cycles and percent improvement over original baseline

| Benchmark | Cycles saved | Original base cycles saved | Synthetic base cycles |
|---|---|---|---|
| | | % | |
| Acker | 8 864 736 | 2.2 | 385 785 657 |
| Sieve | 1 130 839 | 14.9 | 6 472 647 |
| CFA5 | 15 228 248 | 43.6 | 19 688 197 |
| CFA5R | 24 207 058 | 39.6 | 36 930 835 |
| CFA10 | 21 795 608 | 44.7 | 27 007 880 |
| Dhrystone | 655 452 | 93.7 | 44 168 |

orientation; they are not the inevitable fallout of a complex instruction set; they do not reflect the alleged inefficiency of a microcoded processor. We assert that these cycles are consumed because of sub-optimal design decisions or outright errors, and that such errors could have been committed on any new system design, whether object-based or not.

The relative contributions of each of the improvements itemised above are shown as percentages in Table 2.3. Note that these percentages represent the cycle savings when each improvement is considered individually, whereas the percentages in Table 2.2 represent the combined effects of all the architectural improvements (this is the reason the percentages for Table 2.2 do not add up to those in Table 2.3).

**Table 2.3**  Relative contributions of improvements over original baseline, in percentages

| Benchmark | Enters | OptCode | Pr. calls | Params. | Align. | Consts. |
|---|---|---|---|---|---|---|
|  | % | % | % | % | % | % |
| Acker | 0 | 0 | 0 | 0 | 67 | 33 |
| Sieve | 0 | 0 | 0 | 0 | 60 | 40 |
| CFA5 | 44 | 27 | 12 | 6 | 5 | 6 |
| CFA5R | 25 | 19 | 8 | 39 | 5 | 4 |
| CFA10 | 35 | 17 | 8 | 26 | 8 | 6 |
| Dhrystone | 1.2 | 0 | 1.8 | 90.0 | 0.2 | 0.3 |

Since every category in Table 2.3 contributes substantially to the speed-up of one of the benchmarks, this data suggests that each of these improvements is significant and should have been incorporated into the 432 originally. The running times of Acker and Sieve are not vastly improved overall by the instruction alignment and literals, but cycles should never be wasted in such fundamental elements of an architecture unless a very strong case can be made on grounds other than performance; here it cannot.

These factors which account for wasted performance had to be established, analysed and removed from architectural consideration since they are irrelevant to architectural analysis of functional migration. The next step taken to determine the performance costs necessarily incurred to support the 432's runtime, object-oriented invironment was to establish the performance benefits possible if an incrementally better technology (smaller feature size, for instance) were available for a new instantiation of the 432. Such information would suggest the overall price for object orientation for contemporary implementation technology.

The following improvements were considered for the 432:

● Provision for local data registers.
● Expansion of internal and external buses from 16 to 32 bits.
● Expansion of the Top-of-Stack register from 16 to 32 bits.
● An extra bit for the μInstruction Bus.
● An address descriptor cache (AD-Cache).
● A memory clearing primitive operation.

Table 2.5 shows the overall cycle improvement in percentages if these improvements were incorporated. Table 2.4 shows how each improvement changes for each benchmark. Note again that the interactions between the improvements account for the differing percentage sums in these tables.

Table 2.6 shows the combined effect of all the changes to the architecture, compiler and implementation technology listed above.

**Table 2.4** Cycles saved with incrementally better implementation technology by percentage

| Benchmark | Data regs | 32-bit buses | 32-bit TOS | 17-bit μInstr. | AD cache | Mem. clr. |
|---|---|---|---|---|---|---|
| | % | % | % | % | % | % |
| Acker | 0 | 45 | 0 | 1 | 12 | 42 |
| Sieve | 82 | 18 | 0 | 0 | 0 | 0 |
| CFA5 | 34 | 32 | 17 | 0 | 15 | 2 |
| CFA5R | 19 | 47 | 15 | 1 | 17 | 1 |
| CFA10 | 40 | 35 | 3 | 0 | 20 | 2 |
| Dhrystone | 8 | 43 | 1 | 1 | 26 | 22 |

**Table 2.5** New benchmark cycles and percent improvement over original baseline

| Benchmark | Cycles saved | Original base cycles saved | Improved tech. cycles |
|---|---|---|---|
| | | % | |
| Acker | 130 452 160 | 33 | 264 021 113 |
| Sieve | 4 489 605 | 59 | 4 489 605 |
| CFA5 | 15 212 797 | 44 | 19 692 875 |
| CFA5R | 25 998 902 | 43 | 25 983 605 |
| CFA10 | 21 027 060 | 43 | 27 769 185 |
| Dhrystone | 23 866 | 35 | 45 150 |

**Table 2.6**   Total synthetic baseline cycles, percent improvement over original baseline, and real time in milliseconds

| Benchmark | Final total cycles | Original base cycles saved | Real time |
|-----------|-------------------|---------------------------|-----------|
|           |                   | %                         | MS        |
| Acker     | 257 319 033       | 35                        | 32 165    |
| Sieve     | 2 653 785         | 65                        | 332       |
| CFA5      | 11 025 390        | 68                        | 1 378     |
| CFA5R     | 21 050 576        | 66                        | 2 631     |
| CFA10     | 15 394 492        | 68                        | 1 924     |
| Dhrystone | 28 709            | 58                        | 3.59      |

The 432 designers have long asserted that for compute bound benchmarks (like Sieve) the 432 should exhibit no major performance liabilities once the object-oriented operations have been done. The 65% overall improvement shown for Sieve brings its performance up to a level where it is competitive with other machines like the Motorola 68000 and the Intel 8086 and as such provides the first direct evidence for that claim.

Acker represents the worst case situation for an object based machine, executing only operations at which it is slowest (procedure calls). As such it is estimated that for procedure call intensive code, the object-oriented overhead is roughly a factor of four.

These results establish a position from which the object-oriented overhead evinced by the 432 can be evaluated. Overall, the price for object orientation appears to range from a factor of 1 to 4 (Sieve to Acker) over conventional architectures.

This 432 experiment substantiates, at least for low level compute bound benchmarks, RISC's renewed emphasis on the importance of fast instruction decoding (regular, fixed instruction formats) and fast local storage (such as caches and registers). It has been demonstrated that the 432 paid significant performance penalties due to its lack of on-chip data caching and variable length, bit-aligned instructions. The Sieve benchmark was brought up to competitive execution speeds when just eight registers were added to the 432. The benchmark was also speeded up by 8% when the cycles spent stalled upon the instruction decoder were removed. It is most important to note here, though, that these mistakes are *not* the inevitable outcome of complex instruction set computer design. There is no reason that the same functionality of the 432's instruction set could not have been realised on a machine with a more regular instruction encoding and fast local storage. When making comments upon the performance of a computer system it is very important to attribute the reported performance (good or bad) to the proper cause. The 432 exhibits poor performance because of its chosen runtime environment and outright design errors, not because it is a complex instruction set computer.

RISC concerns over the importance of fast procedure *calls* and *returns* are vindicated in the 432, but not necessarily the RISC solutions. The 432 suffers from a comparatively slow *call* and *return*, which can make it run approximately four times slower than conventional processors. However, the protection that is provided by the object based paradigm may be such that this performance price is deemed acceptable. When comparing the execution times for object-oriented computers and more conventional machines, one must remember that differing amounts of work are being done on the respective machines. Object-oriented systems trade some performance for a potentially more productive programming environment and it is important to keep this in mind when making comparisons between such different computer systems.

Though the 432 exhibits poor performance, it cannot be considered compelling evidence that large scale migration of functions to microcode and hardware is ineffective. On the contrary, Cox *et al.*[12] have demonstrated that the 432's microcode implementation of interprocess communication, for instance, is much faster than an equivalent software version. On the low level benchmarks used in this study, the 432 could have achieved much higher performance with only minor changes to its implementation and a better compiler. With all of these points in mind, it would be wrong to conclude that the 432 constitutes evidence for the general RISC point of view.

## 2.8 Summary

In this chapter, many sides of RISCs and CISCs have been explored. By examining the claims, history, philosophy, challenges, commercialisation, confusion and re-evaluation of RISC, a broader perspective on computer design has been brought out. It is a perspective that does not dichotomise between RISC and CISC, creating unnatural divisions and monolithic answers. Rather, it seeks to understand the spectrum of the computer design space by examining the individual features that compose a machine. It is a perspective that is concerned with the mapping of function to a proper implementation level, regardless of what label is placed on the resulting design.

RISCs are undoubtedly going to be an important part of the computer scene for the near future. Yet it is not at all clear if such designs will eventually come to dominate computer architecture or not. Regardless of the outcome, some benefits of the RISC movement are already apparent. RISC designs have confronted the assumed design styles of traditional computers. In doing so, RISC philosophy questions many basic assumptions and makes some bold, insightful claims. This has brought about a healthy self-examination within many corners of computer design, a result that is always welcome.

## References

1. 'The IBM System/360 Model 91: Machine Philosophy and Instruction Handling', Anderson, D. W., Sparacio, F. A. and Tomasulo, R. M. *IBM J. Res. & Dev.*, **11**, 1, 8–24, Jan. 1967.
2. *The Acorn RISC Machine.* Acorn Computers Ltd., Fulborn Road, Cherry Hinton, Cambridge, England, CB1 4JN, 1985.
3. 'The MODHEL Microcomputer for RISCS Study', Azaria, Helnye and Tabak, Daniel. *Microprocessing and Microprogramming*, **12**, 3–4; 199–206, Oct.–Nov. 1983.
4. 'Sentry: A Novel Hardware Implementation of Classic Operating System Mechanisms', Barton, G. C. *Proc. 9th Ann. Symp. Comp. Arch.*, IEEE/ACM, Austin, Texas, 140–147, Apr. 1982.
5. 'The Operating System and Language Support Features of the BELLMAC-32 Microprocessor', Berenbaum, Allen D., Condry, Michael W. and Lu, Priscilla M. *Proc. Symp. Arch. Support for Prog. Lang. and Op. Syst.*, ACM, Palo Alto, California, 30–38, 1–3 Mar. 1982.
6. 'Understanding Execution Behavior of Software Systems', Browne, James C. *Computer* **17**, 7, 83–87, July 1984.
7. 'Comments on "The Case for the Reduced Instruction Set Computer"', by Patterson and Ditzel', Clark, Douglas W. and Strecker, William D. *Comp. Arch. News*, **6**, 6, 34–38, Oct. 1980.
8. 'Measurement and Analysis of Instruction Use in the Vax-11/780', Clark, Douglas W. and Levy, Henry M. *Proc. 9th Ann. Symp. Comp. Arch.*, IEEE and ACM, 9–17, Apr. 1982.
9. 'A Perspective on the Processor Complexity Controversy', Colwell, Robert P., Hitchcock III, Charles Y. and Jensen, E. Douglas. *Proc. Int. Conf. Comp. Des.: VLSI in Computers*, IEEE, Port Chester, New York, 613–616, 31 Oct.–3 Nov. 1983.
10. 'Peering Through the RISC/CISC Fog: An Outline of Research', Colwell, Robert P., Hitchcock III, Charles Y. and Jensen, E. Douglas. *Comp. Arch. News*, **11**, 1, 44–50, Mar. 1983.
11. *The Performance Effects of Functional Migration and Architectural Complexity in Object-Oriented Systems*, Colwell, Robert P. PhD thesis, Carnegie-Mellon University, May 1985.
12. 'Interprocess Communication and Processor Dispatching on the Intel 432',

Cox, George W., Corwin, William M., Lai, Konrad K. and Pollack, Fred J. *ACM Trans. Comp. Sys.*, **1**, 1, 45-66, Feb. 1983.

13. 'Performance of Lisp Systems', Gabriel, Richard P. and Masinter, Larry M. *ACM Symp. Lisp and Func. Prog.*, Aug. 1982.
14. 'Windows of Overlapping Register Frames', Halbert, Daniel C. and Kessler, Peter B. *CS292R Final Reports*, University of California, Berkeley, 9 June 1980.
15. *Tutorial: The Migration of Function into Silicon*, Hammerstrom, Dan, given at the *10th Ann. Int. Symp. Comp. Arch.*
16. 'A Performance Evaluation of the Intel iAPX 432', Hansen, Paul M., Linton, Mark A., Mayo, Robert N., Murphy, Marguerite and Patterson, David A. *Comp. Arch. News*, **10**, 4, 17-27, June 1982.
17. 'MIPS: A VLSI Processor Architecture', Hennessy, John, Jouppi, Norman, Baskett, Forest and Gill, John. *Proc. CMU Conf. VLSI Sys. and Comps.*, 337-346, Oct. 1981.
18. 'Hardware/Software Tradeoffs for Increased Performance', Hennessy, John, Jouppi, Norman, Baskett, Forest, Gross, Thomas and Gill, John. *Proc. Symp. Arch. Supp. for Prog. Lang. and Op. Sys.*, ACM, Palo Alto, California, 2-11, 1-3 Mar. 1982.
19. 'VLSI Processor Architecture', Hennessy, John. *IEEE Trans. Comp.*, C-33, 12, 1221-1246, Dec. 1984.
20. 'Analyzing Multiple Register Sets', Hitchcock III, Charles Y. and Brinkley Sprunt, H. M. *Proc. 12th Int. Symp. Comp. Arch.*, IEEE/ACM, Boston, MA, 55-63, 17-19 June 1985.
21. 'Money Starting To Flow As Parallel Processing Gets Hot', Iverson, Wesley R. *Electronics Week*, 36-38, Apr. 1985.
22. 'On the Use of Benchmarks for Measuring System Performance', Levy, Henry M. and Clark, Douglas W. *Comp. Arch. News*, **10**, 6, 5-8, Dec. 1982.
23. 'Messages and Multiprocessing in the ELXSI System 6400', Olson, Robert A., Kumar, B. and Shar, Leonard E. *Proc. Spring 1983 CompCon*, IEEE, Mar. 1983.
24. 'A VLSI RISC', Patterson, David A. and Sequin, Carlo H. *Computer*, **15**, 9, 8-21, Sept. 1982.
25. 'Reduced Instruction Set Computers', Patterson, David A. *CACM*, **28**, 1, 8-21, Jan. 1985.
26. 'RISC Watch', Patterson, David. *Comp. Arch. News*, **12**, 1, 11-19, Mar. 1984.
27. 'The 801 Minicomputer', Radin, George. *Proc. Symp. Arch. Support for Prog. Lang. and Op. Sys.*, ACM, Palo Alto, California, 39-47, 1-3 Mar. 1982.
28. 'VAX-11/780: A Virtual Address Extension to the DEC PDP-11 Family', Strecker, William D. In *Computer Engineering: A DEC View of Hardware Systems Design*, Digital Press, Bedford, MA, Ch. 17, 409-428, 1978. VAX-11/780: A Virtual Address Extension to the DEC PDP-11 Family; reprinted in SBN.
29. 'The Transputer', Whitby-Strevens, Colin. *Proc. 12th Int. Symp. Comp. Arch.*, IEEE/ACM, Boston, MA, 292-300, 17-19 June 1985.
30. 'Architecture of SOAR: Smalltalk on a RISC', Ungar, David, Blau, Ricki, Foley, Peter, Samples, Dain and Patterson, David. *11th Ann. Int. Symp. Comp. Arch. Proc.*, IEEE/ACM, Ann Arbor, Michigan, 188-197, 5-7 June 1984.
31. 'Design and Implementation of the VAX 8600 Pipeline', DeRosa, John, Glackemeyer, Richard and Knight, Thomas. *Computer*, **18**, 5, 38-48, May 1985.
32. 'Dhrystone: A Synthetic Systems Programming Benchmark', Weicker, Reinhold P. *Comm. of the ACM*, **27**, 10, 1013-1030, Oct. 1984.
33. 'Compilers and Computer Architecture', Wulf, William A. *Computer*, **14**, 7, 41-47, July 1981.

# CHAPTER 3
# AT&T's WE32100 32-Bit Microprocessor System

PRISCILLA M. LU
*AT&T, USA*

## 3.1 Introduction

WE™32100 is AT&T's second generation microprocessor. It is complemented by four peripheral chips, consisting of memory management support (MMU-WE32101, floating point arithmetic acceleration (MAU-WE32106), direct memory access controller (DMAC-WE32104), and dynamic random access memory controller (DRC-WE32103). Photographs of these five devices are shown in Figs. 3.1–3.5.

**Fig. 3.1**  WE32100 microprocessor.

**Fig. 3.2** WE32101 memory management chip.

The chip set forms the basic building blocks for a high performance 32-bit system. The architecture supports efficient implementation of the UNIX* operating system, provides high level language assists; the I/O architecture[1] is designed to simplify system design and maximise system level performance.

## 3.2 WE32100 microprocessor architecture

The WE32100 microprocessor is implemented in 1.5 μm CMOS technology. The first generation WE32000[2] was implemented in

* UNIX is a trademark of AT&T Bell Laboratories.

**Fig. 3.3**  WE32106 floating point arithmetic acceleration chip.

1981, in 1.75 μm CMOS technology. The WE32100, upward compatible with its predecessor, is enhanced with a 64-word I-cache, and a general purpose coprocessor interface. The I-cache has a hit rate of about 65–75% for most UNIX programs, and contributes about 20–25% improvement in performance of programs. The WE32100 operates at 18 MHZ, with an overall performance of 2–3 MIPS.

The microprocessor has a 32-bit bidirectional bus with status decoding, bus arbitration for external access, DMA control, interrupt handling, trace enable and pin out visibility to facilitate testing and debugging.

The WE32100 processor supports four data types: bytes, halfwords, words and bit fields (1 to 32 bits in length). Bytes, halfwords and words can be interpreted as either signed or unsigned in arithmetic or logical operations. Strings are supported by special block instructions (STRING COPY, STRING LENGTH). The string format conforms to the C language and is terminated by a 'null' or zero byte.

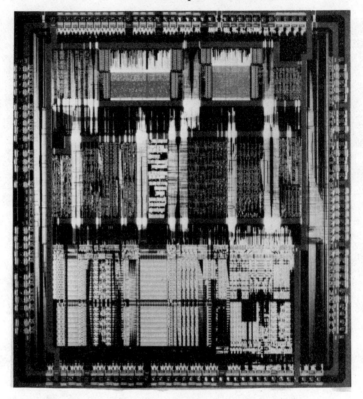

**Fig. 3.4** WE32104 direct memory access controller.

**Fig. 3.5** WE32103 dynamic random access memory controller.

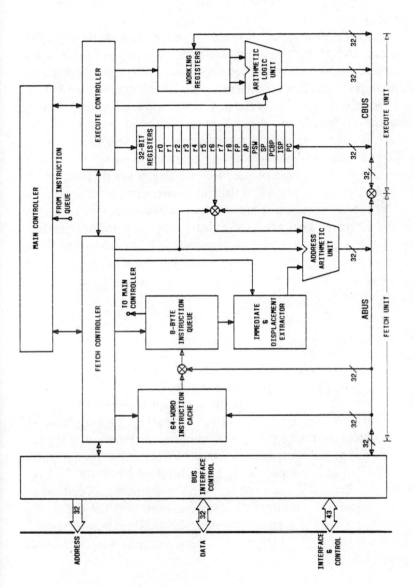

**Fig. 3.6** WE32100 microprocessor block diagram.

Instructions are byte addressable, and defined by a one or two-byte opcode followed by zero or more operand descriptors. All byte or halfword operands are sign or zero extended to 32 bits when they are fetched.

The operand descriptor indentifies the location of the operand. There are several addressing modes: literal, byte/halfword/word immediate, register, register deferred, short offset (for frame and argument pointers), byte/halfword/word displacement, byte/halfword/word displacement deferred, and expanded operand type. These are covered in more detail in the following sections.

There is a special program counter register and fifteen other registers in the processor that can be referenced in any of the addressing modes. Three of the fifteen registers are privileged, i.e. they can be written only when the processor is in kernel execution level. These three registers are used to support operations in the operating system. They are used as interrupt stack pointer, process control block pointer and processor status word. Another three registers are used by special instructions as a stack pointer, a frame pointer and an argument pointer. A block diagram is shown in Fig. 3.6.

## 3.3 Programming language support

In designing the WE32100 microprocessor a major goal was to provide support for the programming language C. The resulting architecture, however, supports the needs of high level programming languages in general, as well as C. Language support features include useful instructions for implementing arithmetic and logical operations, special instructions for manipulating strings and bit fields, and both simple and high level subroutine linkage operations. Several features of the WE32100 microprocessor simplify the interface to an operating system, including the machine's 'process oriented' design as needed for tasking and a special 'controlled transfer' mechanism which implements both user defined and system exception control.

### 3.3.1 ARITHMETIC AND LOGICAL INSTRUCTIONS

Instructions, addressing, and to some extent data types are fully orthogonal on the WE32100 microprocessor. The operation code defines the function to be performed, operand descriptor (or addressing mode) specifies the data type. The operand descriptor can be any one of the possible addressing modes. There are no register or data type restrictions on operands with any operation. Machine instructions associate a 'default' data type with the operands if their data type is not otherwise specified.

The WE32100 microprocessor offers a complete set of the 'usual' arithmetic and logical operations. Briefly the functions provided are:

logical:     clear (i.e. zero data) one's complement, inclusive or, and exclusive or

arithmetic:  negate, add, subtract, multiply, divide, modulus, increment and decrement (by one).

The unary operator's negate and complement are formulated as a move instruction; consequently, the result can either replace the existing datum or be placed in a new destination. All binary operators have both dyadic and triadic forms of instructions. All operations are internally performed as 32-bit functions; however, an overflow occurs if the computation result size exceeds that of the output operand's size.

Having all operations occur in all the same forms is convenient for compilers. For example, using dyadic and triadic forms for evaluating an expression is sometimes ignored in compiler optimisation because of operand restrictions. Coding the C expression

a = b + c*(d + e)

can be done easily with three instructions (assume all variables were integer words):

addw3    d,e,%r0    R0 = d + e
mulw2    c,%r0      R0 = c*(d + e)
addw3    b,%r0,a    a = b + c*(d + e)

where the variable names represent some operand descriptor to access the variable data. The same sequence could be used with different (binary) operators in the C expression with the corresponding opcode replacements; also, the variables need not be integer words.

One addressing mode of particular interest is the *short literal* mode that can represent a small integer (between −16 and 63) using only a single byte for data and descriptor. Using this mode provided an average space reduction of 5% and, as a consequence of this reduction, improved execution time by about 1.8%. The WE32100 microprocessor also has *immediate* modes for the different data types, where the data follows the mode descriptor. As with many machines, short literals and immediates need not be the same data type as the other instruction operands and these modes cannot be used as an operation destination.

An instruction associates a predefined data type with its operands, such as 'add word' and 'add byte.' However, this default data type is essentially a convenience that provides abbreviated addressing descriptions. The WE32100 microprocessor has an *expanded type* operand mode that explicitly specifies the data type of the operand along with its addressing form. The WE32100 microprocessor executes arithmetic and logical operations internally in words; the machine performs any data type conversion while fetching and storing operands.

As an example of expanded type operands consider adding a byte integer 'a' to a word integer 'b' and storing the result in a halfword integer 'c'. Typically, this computation requires several steps of instructions. The sequence of operations for most machines would look like:

```
movbw   a, temp   convert a to word
addw2   b, temp   compute the sum in a temporary
movwh   temp, c   convert result to a halfword.
```

Using the expanded type operands on the WE32100 microprocessor, this operation needs only one instruction:

```
addb3   a, {word}b.}halfword}c
```

Where the desired operand data type is specified in brackets. In this example 'add byte' was used as the instruction to specify the data type of the first operand; if the first operand also used an expanded type mode, then any of the add instructions would produce identical computations.

As seen in the above example, the expanded type mode is convenient when the operand data types happen to be inconsistent, since its use eliminates temporaries that can compete for registers. Expanded type also provides some operations that are not directly available with the instructions. For example, there is no unsigned multiplication operation, but this operation can be achieved with a multiplication instruction using unsigned expanded type'd operands. A final motivation for this is to permit future type extensions.

### 3.3.2   OTHER DATA TYPE OPERATIONS

Other data operations in the WE32100 microprocessor include functions to manipulate strings and bit fields. The string operations are designed specifically for a C string representation, where a *string* is a sequence of bytes ending in a null character (zero). There are two string primitives:

*string* *copy*: copy one string into another,
*string* *end*: locate the terminating (null) character in a string.

The addresses of the operands for these operations are specified in predefined registers. The *string end* operation can be used to compute the string length or in combination with *string copy* to produce a string append function. No length specification is given in either of these operations (string copy assumes target space is adequate and string end assumes the string is properly represented). These instructions are suitable for C but not necessarily for other languages. The WE32100 microprocessor also provides an instruction for moving a block of storage similar to the string copy, except the length is specified.

A *field* on the WE32100 microprocessor is a variable length sequence of bits occurring entirely within a word. Instructions are provided to extract a field from storage and to insert a field, with the operations specifying the number of bits and bit offset of the bit field as well as the target and source addresses. Fields can be manipulated in terms of bytes, halfwords or words. Using these operations, most of the necessary bit manipulation functions for high level languages can be easily implemented.

The WE32100 microprocessor chip supports floating point and decimal arithmetic coprocessor instructions. These instructions are supported by a coprocessor interface that allows the CPU to initiate instruction and operand fetch from memory. The coprocessor is activated by a coprocessor command from the CPU. The coprocessor proceeds to monitor the data bus for latching the operands for that operation. Data is fetched from memory by the CPU, and is latched by the coprocessor on the data bus.

The CPU is blocked during the coprocessor's execution of that instruction. Upon completion, the coprocessor would assert the 'done' signal. Status conditions are sent back to the CPU, and the result is put on the data bus by the coprocessor, and is written out to memory by the CPU.

### 3.3.3 PROCEDURE LINKAGE

The WE32100 microprocessor offers high level procedure linkage operations as well as a set of primitive instructions for subroutine jump and return. The high level operations are useful for many programming languages, including C.

The high level procedure linkage operations manipulate the stack frame, save registers, and transfer control between procedures. They are implemented to be efficient and include procedure call/return, and register save/restore. The push operation can be used to push arguments. The procedure linkage process manipulates the stack and execution. Four registers are modified:

pc: the program counter is changed to start executing in the subroutine and to return to the calling program.

sp: the stack pointer is adjusted properly to point to the top of the stack.

fp: the frame pointer points to the point in the stack just above the register save area (usually the start of local variable space for a procedure).

ap: the argument pointer points to a list of arguments used by the procedure. This list precedes the other linkage data on the stack.

In addition to these registers, other registers have a presumed semantics. Specifically, registers r0 through r2 are viewed as 'temporaries' whose values are not saved between procedure calls. Registers r3 through r8 can be saved across procedure calls.

A typical stack frame, such as used in C, contains the arguments, return information, saved registers and local variable. This stack frame is displayed in Fig. 3.7.

Stack frames using the WE32100 microprocessor's high level linkage operations can differ from the above in the number of registers saved.

There are four instructions used in procedure linkage. The calling procedure uses the Call instruction to save the ap and return address on the stack. The first instruction of each procedure is the Save instruction that saves the old fp and a specified sequence of registers from r8 to r3. Conceptually, only the registers to be used are saved. As noted earlier, registers r0–r2 are not saved and consequently can be used to store the result. When the procedure completes it executes a Restore instruction to restore any needed values in r3 through r8, and then a Return instruction that resets the stack frame to that of the calling procedure and resumes its execution. Arguments are typically placed on the stack with the Push or Push-Address instructions. The Return instruction automatically pops them off. Using these instructions proved to

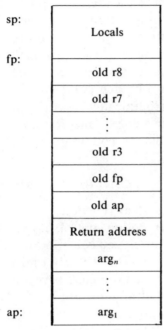

**Fig. 3.7** Sample stack frame.

give a 20% speed-up in execution time over direct coding of these four functions.

Coupled with the above procedure linkage scheme are two addressing modes called ap-offset and fp-offset. These modes provide a one-byte descriptor that can reference a datum whose address is an offset to the ap or fp registers in a range of 0 to 14. Since procedures typically have few arguments and often only a few local variables, most arguments and locals can be referenced with a one-byte descriptor. For an example of where these modes can be used, consider the variables in the C program:

```
foo(a,b,c)
int a,b,c;
{     int d,e,f;
      . . .
}
```

All the given variables (a–f) could be addressed with a one-byte descriptor. Our analysis showed that each of these addressing modes gave an average space reduction of 5% and an average execution speed improvement of 1.8% over not using these modes.

If it is inconvenient to use the above procedure linkage scheme, Jump to Subroutine and Return from Subroutine instructions are also provided. The Jump to Subroutine instructions act as in many machines by pushing the return address on the stack and changing control to the subroutine. This operation comes in both jump (that gives the address) and branch (which gives a pc offset) formats. The Return from Subroutine unwinds this operation but is interesting in that it comes in a conditional form, i.e. the execution of the return can depend on the condition codes, where all available codes can be tested.

### 3.3.4 ENVIRONMENTAL CONTROL: TASKS AND EXCEPTIONS

Providing 'operating system' functions in a programming language, such as tasking and exception control, have typically been difficult to implement. Many articles on compilers have cried for assistance in machine architecture. The WE32100 microprocessor provides some assistance to these problems, particularly with exceptions.

The process oriented architecture of the WE32100 microprocessor eases this requirement by establishing the process design with the machine architecture. A compiler can represent a task as a WE32100 microprocessor process with the appropriate memory mappings that can be constructed by either the language run time system or operating system. Also, this approach simplifies the mutual exclusion aspect of task rendezvous, since it is provided by the hardware. The other rendezvous issues, synchronisation and data exchange, are not directly assisted by the hardware and need some assistance by the system scheduler. Section 3.4 on operating system design discusses this process structure for the WE32100 microprocessor.

The WE32100 microprocessor has a table-driven *interrupt* mechanism that is used to manage system exceptions (and other system calls) and can be employed to implement user exceptions as well. When a system level exception occurs the WE32100 microprocessor effectively executes a *controlled transfer* call instruction using a predefined set of operand values. This transfer operation is best viewed as a form of jump-to-subroutine where tables select the appropriate subroutine address. If the operating system provides an interface for modifying the controlled transfer tables, a user-written exception handler can be called automatically by inserting its address into the appropriate table entry. The user defined exceptions can be managed with this operation, by adding exception handler addresses for each user exception and having the user execute a controlled transfer call instruction when the exception occurs. The controlled transfer can transfer to a normal user routine. To resume processing at the point of the exception (user or system) the code for the handler simply executes a controlled transfer return instruction.

3.3.4.1 *Common libraries and packages.* One approach to implementing common libraries and packages (abstract data types) is to use the controlled transfer mechanism discussed above. Conceptually, the call to a package entry can be viewed as a user exception.

One (or more) of the transfer tables could be allocated to package control. Each entry in this table would correspond to a function entry in some package. To invoke a package procedure a controlled transfer call instruction would be used and each package procedure would return via a controlled transfer return. A major advantage of this approach is that code for package procedures could be shared across processes and generating code for package calls would be simplified.

## 3.4 WE32100 microprocessor operating system support

The WE32100 microprocessor was designed to provide an efficient environment for a sophisticated operating system. An operating system is not built into the processor, nor is the processor optimised for any particular operating system. Instead, the processor provides two mechanisms that can be used to manipulate processes, control transfers to the operating system, and respond to interrupts and handling of exceptions.

### 3.4.1 PROCESSES

The WE32100 microprocessor supports a 'process oriented' operating system; a particular model of a process is implicit in the machine architecture. This model has several characteristics:

● There are four levels of privileged execution to allow flexibility in constructing multi-level operating systems. The hierarchy among the four levels is enforced only by the controlled transfer mechanism.
● There is only one execution stack per process. This stack is used by the procedure call mechanism as well as the controlled transfer mechanism, and it is used independent of execution level.

- A process is defined to the processor by a *processor control block* (PCB), which stores copies of the processor's resources used by the process (e.g. the on-chip registers).
- It is intended that at least the kernel of the operating system reside in the address space of every process.

With four execution levels, a system that required a separate stack for each execution level would have to maintain at least four growable segments for stacks. With a single stack, the operating system need maintain only one, and a single-stack overflow mechanism is sufficient to grow the stack. The stack fault mechanism, which handles overflow conditions as well as other violations, is described below in Section 3.4.6.2. In addition, at least four registers would be required to point to these four stacks, and the management of such special registers is expensive in a VLSI design. The execution stack can also be used to pass arguments from user code to system functions; the regular parameter passing mechanism can be used without elaborate copying operations.

If the kernel of the operating system is in the address space of every process, copying of data from user buffers to system buffers is not required, since the system can access user buffers, and *vice versa*. A common address space for user and operating system code is necessary if the single execution stack mechanism is to work: changing the address space would lose the stack and the procedure chain it contains. The exception mechanism of the WE32100 microprocessor expects the kernel to be in the address space of every process, so the processor does not change memory management to access an exception handler.

Two data structures are associated with processes on the WE32100 microprocessor, the PCB and the interrupt stack. The PCB (see Fig. 3.8) has space for the 14 registers used by a process. These are the 11 user registers plus three control registers, the *stack pointer* (SP), the *program counter* (PC) and the *processor status word* (PSW). Two words in the PCB are used to store the upper address limit and the lower address limit of the execution stack; these bounds are checked in the controlled transfer mechanism. The rest of the PCB is unbounded in length and is intended to be used by (but is not restricted to) memory management. The interrupt stack is not associated with any one process, and contains pointers to PCBs. One of the two on-chip registers not associated with any one process, the PCB pointer (PCBP), points to the PCB of the process running on the processor. The second of these

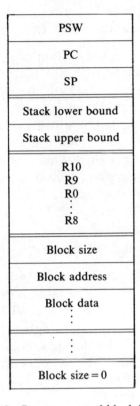

| PSW |
| :---: |
| PC |
| SP |
| Stack lower bound |
| Stack upper bound |
| R10<br>R9<br>R0<br>⋮<br>R8 |
| Block size |
| Block address |
| Block data<br>⋮ |
| ⋮ |
| Block size = 0 |

**Fig. 3.8** Processs control block layout.

registers, the *interrupt stack pointer* (ISP), points to the top of the interrupt stack. Both the PCBP and the ISP are privileged in that they can only be written when the processor is in the kernel execution level.

### 3.4.2 PROCESS SWITCH

The first of the two mechanisms used to support operating systems on the WE32100 microprocessor is the *process switch* mechanism, which is used in process switching, interrupt handling and exception handling. The process switch mechanism has four parts that are used by the microsequences in various combinations:

1. Store the control registers in the PCB pointed to by the PCBP (the 'old' PCB). Store the user registers in the 'old' PCB (optional).

2. Update the PCBP to point to the 'new' PCB. Load the control registers from the 'new' PCB. Move PCBP past the initial context of the 'new' PCB (optional).

3. Perform a series of block moves (optional).
4. Load user registers from 'new' PCB (optional).

The data in the block move section of the PCB is intended to be a memory map specification. Since all I/O on the WE32100 microprocessor is memory mapped, the starting address in the block move section would be the base of translation registers in a memory management unit. With this mechanism, the process switch would automatically establish the virtual address domain of the new process without any further intervention by the operating system. Of course, if the WE32100 microprocessor's mechanism is undesirable for some application, it can be disabled by setting the block move count to zero in all PCBs.

### 3.4.3 CALL PROCESS/RETURN TO PROCESS

Explicit instructions are provided in the WE32100 microprocessor for switching processes by the operating system. They are not used for scheduling processes, which in the WE32100 microprocessor are still the responsibility of operating system software. Instead, they provide a means of dispatching processes, and coordinating process switches determined by the operating system with those that arise unexpectedly from interrupts. The two instructions, Call Process and Return to Process, are analogous to the pair Jump to Subroutine and Return from Subroutine. In the subroutine transfer instructions, the starting address defines the subroutine. The jump pushes a return address on the execution stack and the return pops the return address off that stack. In the process transfer instructions, the address of the PCB defines the process. The call pushes the address of the current PCB on the interrupt stack and the return pops the address of a PCB off the interrupt stack. Like the subroutine transfer instructions, the process transfer instructions only transfer flow of control and do not explicitly pass arguments.

The Call Process instruction has the address of a PCB as its argument. It saves the context of the old process in the old PCB, with the saved PC pointing to the next instruction to be executed, and gets a new context from the new PCB. The Return to Process instruction just loads a new context from the new PCB.

### 3.4.4 INTERRUPTS

The interrupt mechanism of the WE32100 microprocessor is intended to be efficient, reliable and consistent with the process model of the processor. Since interrupts are asynchronous, they are not likely to be associated with the process running on the processor. Ideally, an interrupt should be handled by a new process, which is exactly what the WE32100 microprocessor does. This concept has a number of advantages. An interrupt process has an entirely new context and is unlikely to interfere with any other process. If the interrupting device is not a critical resource, the interrupt handler need not run in kernel mode, but can be dispatched directly in user mode. A special execution stack used by interrupts is not necessary, since each interrupt process gets a new execution stack that does not need any special treatment.

3.4.4.1 *Interrupt mechanism.* An interrupt in the WE32100 microprocessor is handled as an unexpected Call Process instruction. An interrupting device presents the processor with an 8-bit interrupt id. This id selects one of 256 PCB pointers in a table starting at a fixed virtual address. Each PCB pointer corresponds to an interrupt handler process. The microsequence is then exactly the same as in the Call Process instruction. The interrupt process will then run unless it is interrupted in turn by a higher priority interrupt. When the interrupt handler process is completed, a Return to Process instruction should be issued, which will restart the process that was suspended when the interrupt occurred.

The interrupt stack keeps track of the nesting of interrupts. Unless the interrupt stack is explicitly manipulated by the operating system, the PCBP at the bottom of the stack points to the PCBs of interrupt handler processes of increasing priority, with the PCBP pointing the PCB of the highest priority interrupt currently in a state of execution.

3.4.5 CONTROLLED TRANSFER

The controlled transfer mechanism in the WE32100 microprocessor provides a means for ccontrolled entry into a procedure or handler along with a new PSW. It can be used as the system call mechanism. The controlled transfer consists of a 'controlled call' and a 'controlled return'. The controlled call operates like the Jump to Subroutine instruction except that the PC/PSW pair is stacked and replaced. This instruction has two operands that operate as a double table index to determine the new PSW and the appropriate address to branch to. The PC/PSW pair is popped off the stack on a 'controlled return'.

At a predefined location in memory there is a 'first level' table of pointers, each of which can point to a 'second level' table of PC/PSW pairs. The first index operand selects the appropriate 'second level' table. The second index operand determines the appropriate address to branch to (see Fig. 3.9). The 'first level' allows for 32 entries and each 'second level' table can have up to 4095 entries. The 'second level' table can be located anywhere in memory. In particular, they may be shared by some (or all) of the users or be unique to a process.

3.4.5.1  *Use of controlled transfer.* In more conventional architectures, a single Supervisor Call instruction exists, which loads a new PC and PSW from a predetermined location. It is up to the operating system software to determine which procedure to invoke.

In the WE32100 microprocessor, this software procedure is assisted by the processor internal architecture. The controlled transfer mechanism is the only way a processor can change its

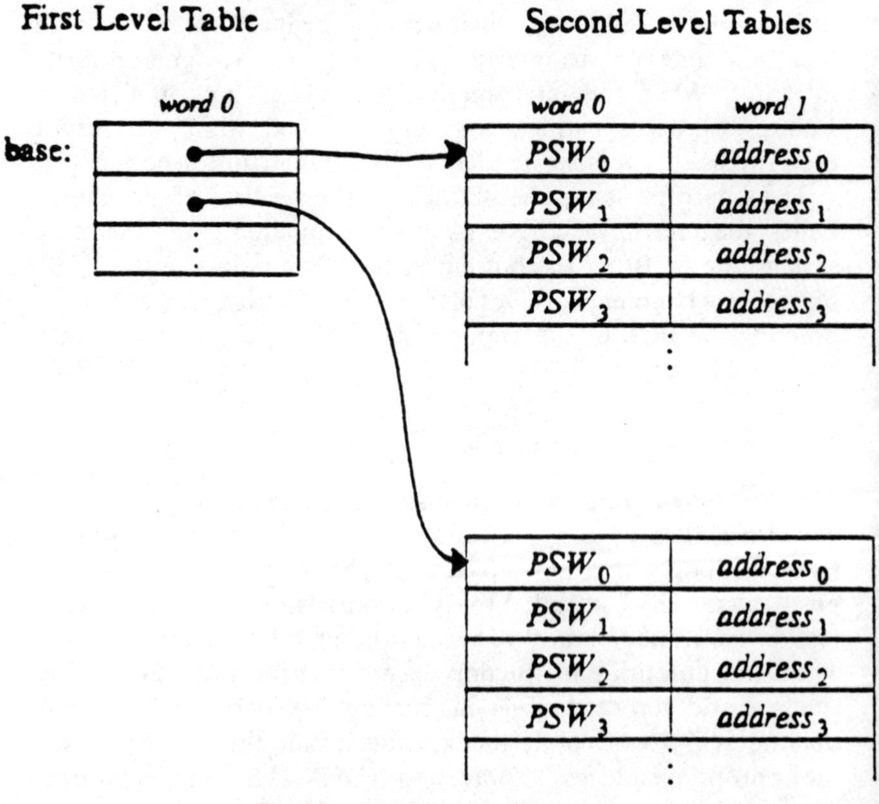

Fig. 3.9  Controlled transfer tables.

execution level. There is no notion of execution level in the micro-sequence implementing the call, because the new PSW will determine the execution level of the process. The controlled return instruction is the only place in the WE32100 microprocessor that explicitly identifies privilege: it will not allow a procedure to return to a more privileged one.

Since there is only one execution stack per process, it is especially important to maintain integrity of this stack. The controlled transfer mechanism is where the sanity of the stack is preserved. There are two entries in the PCB. These correspond to the upper and lower bounds of the execution stack. The controlled call instruction checks to make sure that the stack pointer lies between these boundaries before executing the transfer. The operating system on the processor has to maintain properly the stack bounds in the PCB.

### 3.4.6 EXCEPTIONS

Exceptions are events that indicate something is wrong with the current execution. They can be detected internally by the processor or generated externally. The WE32100 microprocessor can handle all exceptional conditions without halting and it uses the two basic mechanisms provided for the operating system, the controlled transfer mechanism and the process switch mechanism. Four levels of exceptions are invoked by the WE32100 microprocessor, depending on the severity of the error and the resources available at the time. These levels are: normal exception, stack exception, process exception and reset exception.

**3.4.6.1** *Normal exception.* Most exceptions are normal exceptions. These include such internal exceptions as illegal instruction, integer overflow and privileged register access as well as externally generated memory faults. The processor records an index of the exceptions in a 4-bit field of the PSW called the *internal state code* (ISC). The action the processor takes is exactly the same as the controlled transfer call. The first level index is always zero, and the second level index is the ISC. Therefore, when any normal exception occurs, the controlled transfer mechanism automatically transfers control to a routine that can handle the exception. The exception handler need not be privileged or even part of the operating system. If the user provides a handler for an exception, it is sufficient to change the table entry of that exception to point to that code.

3.4.6.2 *Stack exception.* The execution stack on the WE32100 microprocessor is a critical resource and hence must be maintained carefully. If the execution stack is bad, a normal exception sequence cannot be invoked, since the first thing a normal exception sequence does is push a PC/PSW pair onto the stack. Therefore, a special type of process switch is provided to handle stack exceptions. Stack exceptions are detected in the controlled transfer mechanism, either when the stack bounds check fails, or when a read from the stack or write to the stack fails. When a stack exception is detected, the processor fetches a pointer to a new PCB from a fixed virtual location. It then pushes the current PCBP onto the interrupt stack, saves the old control registers and loads a new set, obtaining a new stack. It does not execute the block moves, so the memory management is not forced to change. The new process can repair the stack, adjust the stack bounds, kill the process or whatever else it likes.

3.4.6.3 *Process exception.* A process exception occurs when a read from or a write to the PCB during a microsequence causes a memory fault. Since the PCB is bad, the process is effectively dead; there is no way registers can be saved or the process restarted. All that the processor can do is to start a new process. When a process exception occurs, the processor fetches a pointer to a new PCB from a fixed virtual location, pushes the current PCBP onto the interrupt stack and loads a new set of control registers. Because the process exception handler should do its job quickly, it is more efficient to include one in the domain of every process and avoid executing the block moves of the process switch.

3.4.6.4 *Reset exception.* A reset exception is invoked when all else fails or when the processor resets externally. It occurs during a microsequence, when a memory fault occurs when reading from or writing to the interrupt stack, when a memory fault occurs in reading an address vector, or it occurs when there is a memory fault in processing a process exception. When a reset exception occurs, the processor disables virtual addressing, fetches a pointer to a new PCB for a fixed physical location and loads a new set of control registers. If a memory fault occurs in processing a reset exception, another reset exception is generated and the processor tries again. The microprocessor is fully restartable on any fault.

### 3.4.7 UNIX USE OF THE HARDWARE PROCESS SWITCH AND THE MMU

The process switching features of the CPU and the virtual memory features of the MMU combine neatly to support operations typical in modern operating systems. Use of these features to implement a user-process to user-process switch is explained here.

The MMU provides the concept of 'sections' of virtual address space, where each section consists of one quarter of the 32-bit address space and is mapped through one segment descriptor table. The MMU can automatically flush its internal descriptor caches on a per-section basis, in response to a single write from the CPU. That is, in one operation, the operating system can change the mapping of one quarter of the virtual address space, and the MMU will guarantee that the appropriate portions of its internal caches are flushed.

A natural way to partition the virtual address space is to dedicate one or more sections to the operating system, and the remaining sections to the currently active user process. That is, all user processes will reside at the same virtual addresses (of course, only one user process can reside there at any one time). By rewriting the MMU registers that contain the addresses of the segment descriptor tables for those sections, the operating system can switch one user process out of the virtual address space, and another one into the virtual address space, in very few operations.

In fact, the complete operating system code for a user-process to user-process switch in such a system would be as follows:

{Currently running in user process A}

/*process switch to switcher process in operating system*/
MOVAW switcher,%r0
CALLPS

{Now running in switcher process in operating system}

/*rewrite MMU registers for two sections*/
MOVW newpointer1,mmureg1
MOVW newpointer2,mmureg2

/*process switch 'back' to new user process B*/
RETPS

{Now running in user process B}

This code has accomplished a complete user-process to user-process switch. The CALLPS (Call Process) instruction saved the register contents of the current process (user process A) and obtained the register contents of an operating system process designated as the 'switcher' process. The 'switcher' process, after determining which user process to switch to (not shown), wrote the addresses of user process B's segment descriptor tables into the MMU registers, thus making user process A 'disappear' from the virtual address space and making user process B 'appear' in it. Finally, the 'switch' process executed a RETPS (Return to Process) instruction, which obtained the register contents of user process B from where they were saved when process B last executed a CALLPS instruction to get to the 'switcher' process.

The advantages of providing support for the operating system are that the primitives are guaranteed to be correct, are guaranteed to be protected from alteration or corruption, and can access internal CPU facilities for disabling interrupts, initiating fault sequences, and so on.

### 3.5 Usage of common peripheral chips with the WE32100 microsystems

The WE32100 chip-set provides a pseudo-synchronous interface to the system designer. This interface protocol is compatible with common industry peripherals such as UARTs, interrupt controllers, etc. The WE32100 chip-set allows easy memory interface to dynamic RAMs, static RAMs and cache memory designs.

The basic memory transaction is a 3–7 clock cycle transaction (zero wait states) with an additional cycle used by the WE32101 MMU to provide a virtual memory environment when the designer uses the WE32101 MMU.

Some unique features of the hardware interface provided by the WE32100 chip-set are:

1. A dynamically selectable block fetch feature which improves CPU performance by eliminating trivial virtual address translations.

2. Delayed bus exceptions allowing a designer longer time to detect faults.

3. Two-wire bus arbitration.

#### 3.5.1 COPROCESSOR INTERFACE

The coprocessor interface supported by the WE32100 chip-set provides a high speed interface between the CPU and MAU, along with the flexibility for easy expansion to additional coprocessors. A total of 10 CPU opcodes have been reserved for coprocessor instructions, providing a flexible assortment of zero, one and two operand instructions with each operand being either one, two or three words in length. Communication between the CPU and a coprocessor takes the form of a minimum length bus transaction, with optional wait states. Data fetched from or written to memory is performed concurrently by the CPU and coprocessor in a single bus transaction, rather than routing data through the CPU as two separate bus transactions. This approach provides the highest possible speed for operand transfers.

A coprocessor operation is initiated with a 'coprocessor broadcast' transaction, in which an 8-bit coprocessor ID field allows the CPU to address up to 256 different types of coprocessors on the bus. The remaining 24 bits of the transaction word can be interpreted by the coprocessor in any fashion it desires, usually as opcode and operand information. All operands are then fetched, and taken in directly by the coprocessor. At this point, the coprocessor executes the requested operation, and indicates completion to the CPU with a DONE signal. The CPU then latches status from the coprocessor into its PSW, and provides the address for any memory writes which may be required for the result of the coprocessor operation. Any exceptions which may have been detected by the coprocessor during execution can be signalled to the CPU during the status transfer bus cycle.

### 3.6  WE32101 memory management unit architecture

The WE32101 is the second generation[3] memory management unit. The first generation was implemented in 2.5 $\mu$m CMOS technology and runs at 7.2 MHZ. The WE32101 is implemented in 1.5 $\mu$m CMOS technology and has a clockrate of 18 MHZ. It provides address translation for contiguous and paged segments simultaneously. The memory management architecture has the following attributes:

● Facilitates systematic memory organisation for operating systems by partitioning virtual address space into manageable units of sections, segments and pages.
● Access protection checking for contiguous and paged segments.
● Support of demand paging and segmentation algorithms by automatic update of 'referenced' and 'modified' bits.

- Automatic miss-processing for on-chip segment and page descriptor cache entries.
- Support of variable size segments from 8 bytes to 128 Kbytes.
- Support of shared segments through the use of indirect segment descriptors.
- Descriptor cache flushing facilities.
- Detailed fault detection and resolution.

To minimise memory translation time, the MMU has descriptor caches on the chip. There is a directly mapped, 32-entry segment descriptor cache and a two-way set associative, 64-entry page descriptor cache.

To translate an address, the MMU searches its descriptor caches for relevant descriptors. If the descriptors are present, the MMU checks for length violation and access permission violation.

For contiguous segments, translation is done by adding the segment base address, from the cached segment descriptor, to an offset, from the virtual address, to form the physical address.

For paged segments, the MMU concatenates a page base address, from the cached page descriptor, to the page offset, from the virtual address, to form the physical address.

If there is a miss in the cache, the MMU will perform 'miss-processing'. The MMU will access the descriptor tables in memory and fetch the descriptor into the on-chip caches.

### 3.6.1 ADDRESS SPACE PARTITIONING

The MMU supports up to $2^{32}$ bytes of virtual or physical memory. Virtual address translation can be selected dynamically by a virtual/physical signal from the CPU.

Virtual address space is divided into sections, and sections into segments. Segments can be paged or contiguous (non-paged).

The virtual address space of a process is divided into four sections. An important purpose of sections is to optimise the flushing of cache entries of shared virtual address space. The cached descriptors for a section can be flushed independently of the other sections during a process switch. Therefore, sections of the virtual address space (such as libraries of system calls or kernel routines) that are common among multiple processes can be maintained in the descriptor caches of the MMU between process switches.

Each section may consist of up to 8K segments. Section identifiers stored in the MMU chip designate the segment descriptor tables associated with the sections. Rewriting a section identifier in the MMU automatically flushes the corresponding entries in the descriptor caches for that section.

Segments can be contiguous or paged. Both types are supported simultaneously by the MMU. A paged segment is divided into 2 kbyte pages.

### 3.6.2 FEATURES

3.6.2.1 *Virtual address fields.* The subdivisions of virtual address space require the division of virtual addresses into three fields for contiguous segments and four fields for paged segments.

A virtual address that references a contiguous segment is divided into a *section ID* (SID) field (which section of virtual address space), a *segment select* (SSL) field (which segment within the section), and a *segment offset* (SOT) field (which byte within the segment). See Fig. 3.10.

For paged segments, the SOT field is subdivided into a *page select* (PSL) field (which page within the segment) and a *page offset* (POT) field (which byte within the page). See Fig. 3.11.

3.6.2.2 *Map tables and descriptors.* Segment descriptor tables (SDTs) and page descriptor tables (PDTs) specify mappings between virtual and physical address space in terms of segments and pages. The tables must always reside in physical memory whenever the MMU is using them. A contiguous segment is represented by only a single SDT entry, while a paged segment is represented by both an SDT entry and an entire PDT. In the latter case the SDT entry contains the physical base address of the PDT.

| 31‾‾‾‾30 | 29‾‾‾‾17 | 16‾‾‾‾0 |
|:---:|:---:|:---:|
| SID | SSL | SOT |

**Fig. 3.10**  Virtual address fields for a contiguous segment.

| 31‾30 | 29‾‾17 | 16‾11 | 10‾0 |
|:---:|:---:|:---:|:---:|
| SID | SSL | PSL | POT |

**Fig. 3.11**  Virtual address fields for a paged segment.

The MMU chip stores pointers to the tables in memory and also contains the length of each table. This information is used during miss-processing.

**3.6.2.3** *Segment descriptors and tables.* The mapping from virtual address space to physical address space for a section is defined by the SDT associated with that section. An SDT contains one 8-byte entry, a segment descriptor (SD), for each segment in the section. Each segment may consist of up to 128 kbytes. The segment select (SSL) field of the virtual address is used as an index into the SDT. (See Figs. 3.12 and 3.13.)

V~ (Valid). V = = 1 indicates a valid segment descriptor If V = = 0 an access causes a fault.

C~ (Contiguous). C = = 0 means the segment is paged and C = = 1 means that it is contiguous. If C = = 0 then the MMU uses the second word of the SD as the physical address of a PDT. If C = = 1 the MMU uses the second word of the SD as the physical base address of a contiguous segment.

P~ (Present). P = = 1 means the segment or PDT is present in memory. If the MMU attempts to use the SD during miss-processing and P = = 0, a fault occurs.

I~ (Indirect). I = = 1 indicates an indirect segment descriptor (one that points to another segment descriptor). During miss-processing, if I = = 1, the second word of the SD is used as the physical address of another SD and the second SD is fetched. If I = = 1 in the second SD also, another SD is fetched using the second word of the second SD. Up to six fetches may occur, but if the sixth SD has I = = 1, a fault occurs. Indirect segment descriptors may be used to implement shared segments that may

| 31⁻24 | 23⁻⁻⁻10 | 9⁻8 | 7 | 6 | 5 | 4 | 3 | 2 | 1 | 0 |
|-------|---------|-----|---|---|---|---|---|---|---|---|
| Acc | Max⁻ Off | Res | I | V | R | T | $ | C | M | P |

**Fig. 3.12** Format of first word of an SD.

| 31 ~~~~~~~~~~~~~~~~~~~~~~~~~~~~~~~~~~~~~~~3 | 2⁻⁻0 |
|-------------------------------------------|------|
| Address~ (high-order⁻27⁻or⁻29⁻bits) | Soft |

**Fig. 3.13** Format of second word of an SD.

be easily swapped out. The only segment descriptor that has to be modified by the operating system when the shared segment is swapped or moved is the last one (the one with I = = 0).

R~ (Referenced). If the MMU is configured to do so and a segment descriptor (in a segment descriptor table) is referenced via miss-processing and the reference is not faulted, then the R bit in the segment descriptor is set to 1.

M~ (Modified). If the MMU is configured to do so, it sets the M bit to one, if not one already, if the MMU successfully translates an address using this SD for a write access.

$~ (Cachable). Whenever the SD is used for a translation, the MMU sets its cachable pin to reflect the value of this bit. Cachable bits may be used by the system to prevent or allow the caching of instructions and data on a per-segment basis.

T~ (Object~ Trap). If there is a valid translation using the segment descriptor (maximum offset and access permissions are not violated), and the segment is contiguous (C = = 1), and the T bit is set, an object-trap fault occurs. The T bit is ignored on paged segments.

Res~ (Reserved). These bits are reserved for future MMU use.

Soft~ (Software~ Reserved). These bits are reserved for use by software and are guaranteed not to be changed by the MMU.

Max~ Off~ (Maximum~ Offset). This field is used to calculate the maximum offset from the beginning of the segment that a virtual address may specify. If a virtual address specifies a byte outside this limit, a fault is signalled to the CPU.

This value is equal to the number of double-words (8-byte) in the segment, minus one. Thus it is impossible to specify a segment containing 0 bytes via this mechanism.

Whenever a segment descriptor is used to perform a translation, the MMU checks the access permissions field of the SD, the type of access being requested by the CPU, and the execution level at which the access is being requested. If the MMU determines that access is not allowed under the given conditions, a fault occurs.

The MMU uses the execution level (kernel, executive, supervisor, user) at which the access is being requested and the contents of the access permissions field to determine whether the given execution level is allowed read/write (RW), read/execute (RE), read-only (RO) or no-access (NA) permissions to the segment. It then checks the type of access requested by the CPU to determine which permissions are needed to allow the access. If the permissions needed for that type of access are not satisfied, a fault occurs. Otherwise, the access is allowed.

The access permissions field is 8 bits wide and is structured as four 2-bit fields, one for each execution level. The type of access allowed to a given execution level is encoded in its 2-bit field.

The address field of the second word of a segment descriptor in an SDT may be used by the MMU in one of the following ways:

1. As the physical base address of a contiguous segment. This is the address in physical memory where the contents of the segment start.

2. As a PDT address for a paged segment. This is the address in physical memory where the page descriptor table starts.

3. As the physical address of another SD, in the case of an indirect SD.

3.6.2.4  *Page descriptors and tables.* For a paged segment, the second word of the segment descriptor is used by the MMU as the address of a page descriptor table. A PDT contains one 4-byte page descriptor for each page in the segment. A PDT may consist of a maximum of 64 page descriptors, but may contain fewer. (See Fig. 3.14.)

P~ (Present). P = = 1 if the page is present, P = = 0 if it is not. If the MMU attempts to fetch a PD during miss-processing and P = = 0, the remainder of the PD information is ignored and a fault occurs.

| 31~~~~~~~~~11 | 10~8 | 7~~6 | 5 | 4 | 3 | 2 | 1 | 0 |
|---|---|---|---|---|---|---|---|---|
| Page~Address | Soft | Res | R | W | Res | L | M | P |

**Fig. 3.14**  Page descriptor format.

R~ (Referenced). The MMU sets R to one when it successfully translates an address for any type of access.

M~ (Modified). The MMU sets M to one, if not already one, when it successfully translates an address for a write access to any byte of the page.

L~ (Last). During translation, if L = = 1 the MMU will access the maximum offset field of the corresponding SD and perform a length check. If L = = 0, the translation proceeds without this action occurring.

It is intended that L = = 1 if the page descriptor corresponds to the last page in a segment whose length is not an integral multiple of 2 kbytes. If L = = 0, the page length is 2 kbytes.

W~ (Fault-On-Write). If access permissions and length are not violated and the access type is a write and W = = 1, a fault occurs. This bit can be used to minimise copying of pages when duplicating a process. Instead of copying every page, each may be shared and have W = = 1. An attempt to write to a shared page by either process then causes a fault and only then does that page have to be duplicated.

Page~ Address. (Page Address) * 2K is the address of the first byte of the page in physical memory.

### 3.6.3 INTERNAL STRUCTURE

The following entities in the MMU may be accessed in the memory mapped peripheral mode:

1. The segment descriptor cache (32 descriptors; directly mapped; total of 64 words).

2. The 2-way set associative page descriptor cache (64 descriptors; 2-way set associative; total of 128 words).

3. Section RAM A. SRAMA contains the addresses of the SDTs, and can be used to flush sections from the descriptor caches.

4. Section RAM B. SRAMB contains the number of entries of each SDT.

5. The fault code register. FLTCR is used to record information about faults that the MMU detects.

6. The fault address register. FLTAR contains the virtual address that was being processed when a fault occurred.

7. The configuration register. CR contains bits that specify configurable aspects of the MMU behaviour.

8. The virtual address register. VAR contains the virtual address to be translated by the MMU, and can be used to flush single entries from the descriptor caches.

### 3.6.3.1 *Descriptor caches.* The segment descriptor cache consists of 32 descriptors, each of which is 64 bits wide. These descriptors have a format that differs from the format of the SDs in SDTs

that were described earlier. Cached SDs contain a tag field and do not contain V, I, P and R bits, among other differences.

The SDC is a directly mapped cache divided into 4 parts that correspond to the 4 sections. It requires a 5-bit index to select an entry and a 10-bit tag for unique identification of the descriptor.

The page descriptor cache consists of 64 64-bit descriptors organised in a two-way set associative fashion. The format of cached PDs is different from the format of PDs in PDTs in memory. Cached PDs contain a tag field and an access permissions field (copied from the SD) and do not contain P and soft bits, among other differences.

The PDC is divided into 4 parts that correspond to the 4 sections. As in the SDC, the index is 5 bits. The tag, however, is 16 bits.

### 3.6.3.2 *Other objects.*

Section RAM A consists of four 32-bit words. Each word is used as the physical base address of a sections segment descriptor table (SDT) during miss-processing.

Section RAM B contains the number of segments in each section, minus one. This is used for segment descriptor table bounds checking during miss-processing. SRAMB consists of four 32-bit words.

The virtual address register contains the virtual address to be translated by the MMU.

The fault code register keeps a log of faults and operational states in the MMU chip. Its contents are overwritten every time a fault occurs.

The FLTAR contains the virtual address that was being processed when the last fault occurred. The FLTAR contents are changed when the CPU writes to it in peripheral mode, and when faults occur.

The configuration register is a 32-bit register containing three one-bit items called $, Ref and Mod. The Ref and Mod bits enable or disable setting of segment R and M bits in memory. During miss-processing and R and M update, the $-bit determines the state of an output pin. This may be tied to an external cache to prevent or allow caching of descriptors in the external cache.

### 3.6.4 OPERATIONS

This section describes several operations that the MMU performs in response to actions by the CPU. Most of the operations are quite complex, yet they all occur with no CPU intervention.

**3.6.4.1** *Translation, miss-processing and R and M update.* Translation is the operation during which the caches are accessed to determine whether or not there are hits (whether the necessary descriptors are in the caches). If necessary descriptors are missing, miss-processing is invoked. If the descriptors are present, or after miss-processing is completed, access permissions and segment length are checked and the physical address is calculated (simultaneously). If there are no faults, R and M updating is invoked. When it completes, the physical address is output.

When a segment or page descriptor needed to translate a virtual address into a physical address is not present in the descriptor caches, the MMU must access descriptor tables in memory to fetch the appropriate descriptors into the descriptor caches. This activity is called miss-processing. Miss-processing to fetch a segment descriptor, a page descriptor or both may be necessary. Faults may occur during this activity. Invalid (V = = 0) or not-present (P = = 0) descriptors are never put into the caches.

The R and M bits of page descriptors are always kept up to date both in the descriptor cache and in memory. The process of checking and setting R and M bits in the caches and in memory is called R and M updating. It may involve miss-processing to fetch a segment descriptor (because the segment descriptor contains the address of the page descriptor in memory).

**3.6.4.2** *Faults.* If the address translation process cannot be completed for some reason, a fault will be triggered. All faults cause the MMU to set the FLTCR fields appropriately, copy the contents of VAR into FLTAR, and signal a fault to the CPU. The FLTCR and FLTAR contents will not be altered in the course of successful (non-faulted) translations and miss-processing. Only another fault or a peripheral mode write can change their contents.

The FLTCR contains three fields: access requested, access Xlevel and fault type. The access requested field contains a code that specifies the type of access (instruction fetch, data fetch, etc.) attempted by the CPU when the fault occurred. The access Xlevel field contains a code that specifies the execution level at which the faulted access was attempted.

The fault type field of the fault code register (FLTCR) may contain many values corresponding to different fault types. They fall into several categories, from the operating system point of view. User mistakes may cause the segment offset, access, access-&-seg-offset, SDT length, PDT length or invalid SD faults. A need for swapping may be signalled by the seg not present, PDT not Present or page not present faults. Serious operating system problems cause the double-page hit, miss proc mem, R-M-update mem or too many indirections faults. The other fault types are object trap, page write and no fault.


### 3.6.4.3 *Memory mapped peripheral mode and flushing.*

The MMU can be used as a memory mapped peripheral. In this mode, many of the internal registers of the MMU and its descriptor caches can be addressed as memory locations. Each of these locations can be read or written.

A peripheral mode access to the MMU occurs when external logic asserts the MMU chip select pin. Various bits of the address sent to the MMU are used to select an object within the MMU and (for some objects) a word within the object.

All objects described in Section 3.6.3 may be accessed in peripheral mode.

Writes to the FLTCR cause the fault type field to be set to no-fault.

When the CPU writes an address into Section RAM A (SRAMA), the MMU will flush all SDC and PDC descriptors that are in the section corresponding to the newly written SRAMA entry. When the CPU writes an address into the MMU virtual address register (VAR), the MMU will flush any segment and page descriptor cache entries corresponding to that virtual address.


## 3.7 Operating system considerations

It is the responsibility of the operating system to initialise the MMU and the overall system by setting up the SDTs and PDTs in physical memory and writing values into MMU registers that provide necessary information, such as table addresses.

The operating system is also responsible for changing SRAM values when process switches occur. This will cause the MMU to flush and fill its caches.

The transfer of descriptors between the MMU caches and physical memory (miss-processing) is handled by the MMU without any operating system intervention.

Operating system action is required when the MMU signals to the CPU that a fault has occurred. There are a number of fault types that relate to errors that the MMU detects in critical data, such as memory faults when the MMU tries to read the SDTs or PDTs. These faults require unusual and perhaps drastic action by the operating system.

Two other types of faults are the page not present fault (for a paged segment) and the segment not present fault (for a contiguous segment). In either case, the MMU is telling the CPU that a required page or segment is not present in physical memory, and must be brought into physical memory. The operating system is responsible for these activities, and must do any I/O that is necessary and adjust the appropriate SDT and/or PDT entries.

The MMU provides hardware support for operating system page or segment replacement algorithms by setting the R (referenced) and M (Modified) bits in the segment and page descriptors whenever a segment or page is referenced or modified. If the operating system periodically clears all of the R bits, for example, it can use the R bits to implement a variation of the LRU replacement algorithm. It could choose to replace segments or pages that still have their R bits clear when swapping is called for, reasoning that those segments or pages have been referenced less recently than the ones with the R bits set.

The operating system will occasionally alter the contents of the descriptor tables in memory. For example, it must do this to set and clear P (present) bits whenever pages or segments are swapped in and out of physical memory. Any alteration to the table contents must be followed by some type of flushing of the MMU caches, to prevent the chaos that would result from tables and caches that contain conflicting information.

### 3.8   WE32106 math acceleration unit architecture

The WE32106 math accelerator unit (MAU)[4] provides the WE32100 microprocessor with complete IEEE standard floating point support as a coprocessor. The MAU supports both coprocessor and peripheral mode operations. Floating point data types of single (32-bit), double (64-bit), and double extended (80-bit) precision are supported. In addition, the 32-bit integer data type and an 18-digit decimal data type are supported for conversions. All four IEEE standard rounding modes are supported (round to nearest, round to zero, round to plus infinity, and round to minus infinity), as well as all five maskable exception types (invalid operation, overflow, underflow, divide by zero, and inexact). In addition, a maskable integer overflow exception is supported for integer and decimal conversions. The WE32106 MAU supports the following instruction operations:

1. *Arithmetic.* Add, Subtract, Multiply, Divide, Remainder, Square Root, Negate, Absolute Value, Compare (4 versions), Move.

2. *Conversions.* Float to Integer, Integer to Float, Float to Decimal, Decimal to Float.

3. *Control and Status.* Read Status Register, Write Status Register, Extract Result on Fault, Load Data Register, No Operation.

The control and status instructions allow the MAU context to be saved and restored on process switches, and also provide valuable debugging information when an operation generates an exception.

The WE32106 MAU supports all required data types, including positive and negative zeros, positive and negative infinities, and trapping and non-trapping NANs (Not a Number). Gradual underflow is also supported, in the form of de-normal numbers in single and double precision, and un-normal numbers in extended precision. Sign, zero and overflow status flags are automatically returned to the WE32100 CPU, and use of the MAU's instructions with the WE32100 CPU is totally transparent to the user in co-processor mode. In addition, the MAU is compatible with all WE32100 chip-set features, including DMA, interrupts and restartability.

The WE32106 MAU contains many hardware optimisations to achieve a high floating point performance. The data path interconnections have been carefully optimised to obtain a high level of performance on the high-runner Add and Subtract operations. The addition of a full barrel switch (BSW) is especially helpful for these operations. The Multiply operation is implemented with a highly encoded form of Booth's algorithm which processes three bits of the result per iteration of a heavily pipelined loop. The Divide operation uses a highly pipelined implementation of the non-restoring divide algorithm. In addition to these internal optimisations, the coprocessor interface to the MAU allows exceptionally high speed transfers of data to/from CPU and memory on a 32-bit data bus. The combined effect of these optimisations is a total execution rate for the familiar Whetstone benchmark in single precision IEEE standard floating point of 1.0 mega Whetstones. This number is for the WE32100 CPU and WE32106 MAU running together in coprocessor mode with zero wait-state memory access at 14 MHz. Double precision execution rates are slightly lower.

### 3.8.1 SUPPORT OF THE IEEE FLOATING POINT STANDARD IN THE WE32106 MAU

The IEEE standard for binary floating point arithmetic facilitates:

● Generation of high quality numerical software.
● Software portability between complying implementations.
● Careful and deterministic handling of the exception conditions and anomalies.

The standard does not impose any restrictions on complying implementations. That is, an implementation can be realised entirely in software, entirely in hardware or in any combination of software and hardware. The WE32106 is a hardware implementation of the standard.

3.8.1.1 *Data formats.* A floating point number consists of three parts: a biased exponent, a significand (or mantissa) and a single bit in the leftmost position of the number that indicates the sign of the significand. The significand consists of implicit or explicit leading bit to the left of the implied binary point and fraction to the right. The standard categorises data formats into basic and extended, with each having two widths, single and double. The conforming implementation must support the single format. The support of the extended format corresponding to the widest supported basic format is also strongly recommended.

The MAU supports single, double, and double extended formats of the IEEE standard.

3.8.1.2 *Data types.* The MAU supports all the required data types. What follows is a brief discussion of these data types.

*Normalised floating point numbers.* This is the working data type that the user will interact with. This data type is identified by the exponent value not being at formats minimum or maximum.

*Denormalised floating point numbers.* These numbers have non-zero mantissa with the exponent corresponding to the format's minimum exponent value. The most significant implicit bit of the mantissa (to the left of the binary point) has a value of zero. A denormalised number is generated when a masked underflow exception occurs. Denormalised numbers provide gradual underflow to zero.

Zeroes: this is a number with the exponent at formats minimum and a zero significand. Zeroes are signed.

Infinities: a number with a zero significand and format's maximum exponent is infinity. Again both positive and negative infinities are encoded.

Not a number (NaN): NaNs are symbolic entities that are intended for diagnostic purposes and to allow enhancements that are outside the scope of the standard. NaNs are the numbers that have format's maximum exponent with a non-zero fraction. NaNs are further classified into two categories, *signalling* and *quiet*. A quiet NaN can be used to detect an error which had propagated through a sequence of operations. It can also be used to indicate usage of uninitiated variables. A quiet NaN propagates through operations without causing any exception. When a signalling NaN is encountered, an exception is taken. If the exception condition is masked, an operation with a signalling NaN as an operand completes normally and produces quiet NaN as a result.

**3.8.1.3** *Operations.* The conforming implementations must provide operations to add, subtract, multiply, divide, square root, remainder, round to integral value, conversions between various floating point integer and decimal formats and compare. The MAU directly supports all of these operations in hardware.

**3.8.1.4** *Rounding.* Rounding takes an infinitely precise number and modifies it to fit in the destination format. The standard requires all floating point operations to produce an intermediate result that is correct to infinite precision with unbounded range, then round it according to the mode of rounding selected. The standard proposes four different rounding modes:

● Round to nearest. In this mode, the representable value closest to the infinitely precise result is delivered. This is the default rounding mode.
● Round towards positive infinity.
● Round towards negative infinity.
● Round towards zero.

The MAU directly implements all four rounding modes.

3.8.1.5 *Exceptions.* The IEEE standards specifies five different types of exceptions: invalid operation, underflow, overflow, divide by zero and inexact. The standard requires individual trap enable/disable control for each exception. The default response is to proceed without the trap. Also, individual status flags are required for each exception. The status flags can be 'sticky' in nature, i.e. once set to indicate exception condition, an explicit operation to reset the flag is necessary. The sticky nature of the flags allows the exception status information to propagate through a sequence of operations when the corresponding trap is disabled. The exception handling in the MAU conforms to the standard as described above.

### 3.8.2 SUMMARY OF IEEE STANDARD

The IEEE standard for binary floating point arithmetic differs from generic floating point arithmetic processors in many ways. Some of the features of the standard that increase the hardware complexity are:

1. The standard recommends three data types: single, double and extended. The number of bits in the exponent is different in each format. This makes conversion from one format to another more complex than other floating point implementations, in which single and double precision formats have identical exponent fields.
2. The special data types such as not a number (NaN), infinity, denormalised numbers, and unnormalised numbers require special hardware to recognise and process.
3. The standard defines five exceptions with individual enable/disable control for each exception and corresponding status flags. The standard is also very specific about the default response to the exception when it is masked and about the information supplied to the exception handler when it is enabled.
4. The definition of the remainder operation requires it to be broken down into several steps in order to avoid locking out interrupts.

### 3.9 DMAC direct memory access controller architecture

The WE32104 DMAC is a 4-channel DMA controller designed specifically for 32-bit applications. A unique 2-bus architecture allows for simple, efficient interconnection of byte oriented peripheral devices, such as UARTs, disk controllers and network interfaces, with a 32-bit processor memory system bus. Isolating the slower peripheral traffic on a separate bus not only simplifies interconnection logic, but greatly reduces contention for the system bus, thereby increasing overall system throughput.

To support its dual bus architecture, the DMAC provides a 32-byte data buffer for each channel. Data read from the byte-wide peripheral bus is packed into larger operands (up to a 16-byte quad-word) before being written to memory. In addition to byte, halfword, and word transfers, the DMAC supports double-word and quad-word transfers on the system bus for improved memory bandwidth, and reduced bus arbitration overhead. A block diagram of the DMAC is shown in Fig. 3.15.

Each of the four channels is independently controlled and can be programmed for burst or cycle-steal transfer mode. In burst mode, the DMAC will hold the system bus as long as needed, while in cycle-steal mode the system bus is relinquished after every bus transfer. Four transfer types are provided: memory-to-peripheral, peripheral-to-memory, memory-to-memory and memory fill. Other programmable options include selection of peripheral device transfer characteristics, enabling interrupts on channel completion, and enabling a channel for chained transfer mode. In chained mode, a linked list of request blocks containing source/destination and transfer count information are loaded in memory by the processor. The DMAC can than execute this list, fetching transfer parameters directly from memory, without further intervention by the host processor.

In burst mode, a 14 MHz DMAC can perform memory-to-memory copies at 11.2 Mbyte/s, and memory-fill operations at 20.3 Mbyte/s. Given that these rates are as much as 5 times greater than can be achieved with equivalent CPU instructions, many system level functions can be coded for higher performance by making use of the DMAC.

For transfers to and from the peripheral bus, the maximum data transfer rate obtainable is 6 Mbyte/s, when the peripheral bus burst feature is employed, and 3.7 Mbyte/s, when a single byte is transferred for each peripheral bus request. Equally important, however, the DMAC only requests the system bus once a quad-word has been packed into its data buffer, performing in one bus cycle what would otherwise require 16 bus cycles. Including the overhead incurred during bus arbitration, bus utilisation is reduced by a factor of ten.

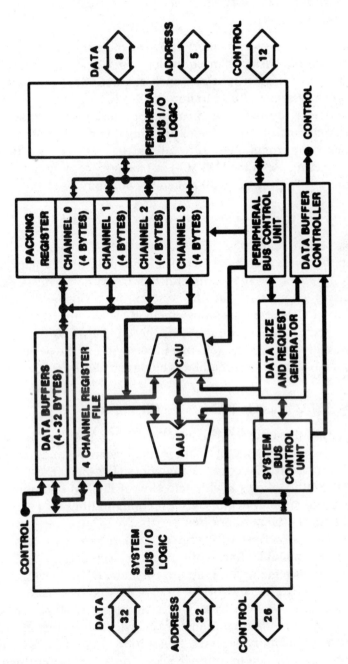

**Fig. 3.15** WE32104 direct memory access controller block diagram.

### 3.9.1   DMAC MEMORY-TO-MEMORY COPY IMPROVES UNIX SYSTEM PERFORMANCE

The DMAC's memory-to-memory copy and memory fill operations are up to 5 times faster than equivalent operations executed by the CPU. UNIX system routines, such as fork, exec, and logical I/O between system and user buffer areas, rely on fast buffer copy and block clear routines which can be optimised by making use of a DMA channel. UNIX system profiling demonstrates that the CPU spends approximately 10% of its time performing these routines. Making use of the DMAC's fast memory copy capabilities would thereby improve overall system throughput by 8%.

### 3.9.2   ADVANTAGES OF 8-BIT PERIPHERAL BUS ON DMAC

The 8-bit peripheral bus on the WE32104 DMAC is ideally suited to 8-bit peripherals such as disk controllers and local area network interfaces. Separating the peripheral bus from the 32-bit system bus reduces contention for the system bus. This allows the WE32100 CPU to execute more efficiently while the DMAC is servicing peripherals. In one model, the CPU had 10 times the system bus allocation compared to a model without the peripheral bus, when a 10 Mbit/s peripheral was being serviced by the DMAC.

### 3.10   WE32103 dynamic RAM controller architecture

The WE32103 dynamic RAM controller (DRC) provides address multiplexing, access and cycle time management, and refresh control for dynamic random access memory (DRAM). The DRC's extreme flexibility allows a wide selection of DRAM components to be used, in varying memory system configurations.

Among the features supported by the WE32103 are: several different modes of refresh (distributed/burst, internally/externally timed), programmable time constants to meet diverse DRAM component requirements, and support for many DRAM sizes, such as 256K by 1, 64K by 4, and 1M by 1 DRAMs. The DRC is capable of addressing up to 16 Mbyte of DRAM using 1 Mbyte chips. Page and nibble mode operation may be selceted for fast double and quad-word memory accesses. In addition, a unique pre-translation mode is provided to improve access time for systems incorporating paged virtual memory. For applications requiring highly reliable operation, a full set of handshake signals is provided for (optional) error detection and correction hardware.

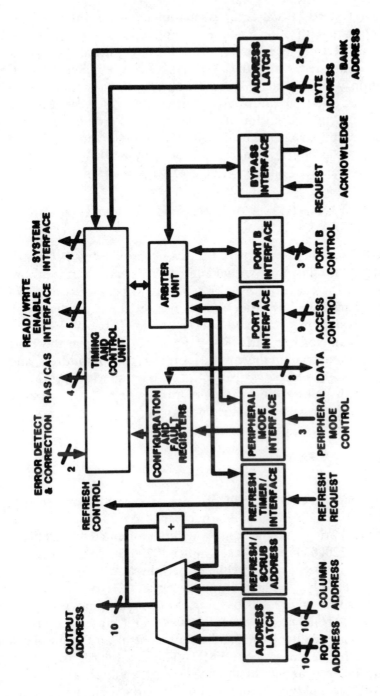

**Fig. 3.16** WE32103 dynamic RAM controller block diagram.

The WE32103 DRC has an asynchronous mode which permits it to operate with other commercial microprocessors. However, enhanced performance can be achieved using synchronous mode, when configured with the WE32100 chip-set. Synchronous operation will, in general, save a wait-state for processor reads and writes. Pre-translation mode further reduces access time by overlapping the row portion of a memory access with the WE32101 MMU's address translation. Finally, fast double and quad-word memory cycles, utilising page and nibble mode DRAMs, are supported to enhance both CPU and DMAC performance.

### 3.10.1   WE32103 DRC PRE-TRANSLATION MODE USING 256K DRAMs

The DRC has the capability to begin a memory access before the MMU has translated the virtual address. This early start is advantageous in systems utilising a paged virtual memory scheme. In such a system, the low order address bits are the page offset, and thus equivalent in virtual and physical address spaces.

If programmed for early RAS, the DRC will drive the page offset contained within the virtual address as the row address, and assert the ROW address strobe (RAS0) in parallel with the MMU's address translation. Utilising the pre-translation feature, one cycle can be saved from the memory access. A block diagram of the DRC is shown in Fig. 3.16.

### 3.11   Summary

The WE32100 chip-set and its first generation predecessor (WE32000) are operational in a number of AT&T systems, spanning time sharing, real time and transaction oriented applications.

The WE32000 chip-set is used in the 3B2 and 3B5 systems. The CPU is also used as an intelligent peripheral controller for the 3B5 system. Other applications include the Teletype DMD 5620 terminal, where the WE32000 is used to execute graphics primitives as well as resident programs. Network interfaces using the WE32000 are available to handle flow control and higher level protocols in the 3B systems. VME-bus based boards have been built to take advantage of the chip-set capabilities, and can be used as basic building blocks for single-board computers or multiple processor systems. Several multiprocessor systems have also been built.

The chip-set is supported by a completed set of UNIX based development support tools that provides easy access to internal signals and status for hardware debugging and development, and symbolic debugging for software development[5].

With the high performance of the MAU, the chip set has a very competitive performance in floating point operations and has opened the door for broader applications (e.g. CAD/CAM) that require floating point arithmetic and high precision. The UNIX Microsystem is expanding to even higher performance parts by going to smaller design rules and enhanced implementations, while maintaining compatibility with the products available today. The early availability of the WE32104 DMAC and the WE32103 DRC underline AT&T's commitment to a complete system solution. The WE32101 MMU provides memory management capabilities unmatched by any product currently on the market.

### Acknowledgements

This chapter was written jointly by many people who worked on the architecture and the design of the chips. Some of the sections were extracted from previous papers[2,3]. I would like to acknowledge the written contributions of the following: A.D. Berenbaum, M.W. Condry, W.A. Dietrich, J.A. Fields, M.L. Fuccio, A.K. Goksel, L.N. Goyal, U.V. Gumaste, M.E. Thierbach and P.A. Voldstad.

### References

1. 'Hardware Configuration and I/O Protocol of the WE32100 Microprocessor Chip Set'. Fuccio, M. L. and Goyal, L. N., *WESCON 1985*.
2. 'The Operating System and Language Support Features of the BELLMAC-32 Microprocessor'. Berenbaum, A. D., Condry, M. and Lu, P. M. *Symp. Arch. Support for Prog. Lang. and Op. Sys.* Palo Alto, Cal., 30–38, 1–3 Mar., 1982.
3. 'Architecture of a VLSI Map for BELLMAC-32 Microprocessor'. Lu, P. M., Dietrich, Jr., W. A., Fuccio, M. L., Goyal, L. N., Chen, C. J., Blahut, D. E., Fields, J. A., Goksel, A. K. and LaRocca, F. D. *Spring COMPCON 1983*, San Francisco, Ca., 213–217, 28 Feb. to 3 Mar., 1983.
4. 'An IEEE Standard Floating Point Chip'. Goksel, A. K., Diodato, Phil W., Fields, John A., Gumaste, Ulhas V., Kung, Chew K., Lin, Kingyao, Lega, Mario E., Maurer, Peter M., Ng, Thomas K., Oh, Yaw T. and Thierbach, Mark E. *ISSCC 1985*, 18 and 19, Feb. 1985.
5. 'Hardware/Software Development System for the WE32100 CPU and MMU'. Clark, M. H., Rango, R. A., Rusnock, K. J. and Stubblebine, W. A. *WESCON 1984*.

# CHAPTER 4
# The Inmos Transputer*

J.R. NEWPORT
*CAP Scientific Ltd*

## 4.1 Introduction

Transputers, manufactured in Britain by Inmos, are high performance single-chip computers with integral processor-to-processor
serial links and optional on-chip memory. However, such a simple
description vastly underrates the potential of this new range of
devices.

The name 'Transputer' is derived from two words: *transistor*
and *computer*. The intention is that just as transistors have been
the building blocks of computers, so Transputers will be the
building blocks of a whole new range of machines from compact
array processors to vast supercomputers.

Attempts to build multiprocessor systems from conventional
microprocessors have always been fraught with problems, not least
of which have been those concerned with inter-processor communication. Bandwidth problems are usually encountered when
more than about 4 processors are linked via a shared bus. This
effect can be clearly seen if total system performance is plotted
against the number of constituent processors (see Fig. 4.1(a)).
Plots will vary slightly, depending on the types of bus and processor
being used, but a point will be reached at which adding further
processors will tie up the bus and then actually reduce total system
performance. This limit is usually reached when between 6 and 8
processors share a common bus.

Transputers have their own built-in serial links, each capable
of concurrently inputting and outputting at up to 10 Mbit/s. A

---

* Inmos and occam are trademarks of the INMOS group of companies. 'Ada'
is a registered trademark of the US Department of Defense.

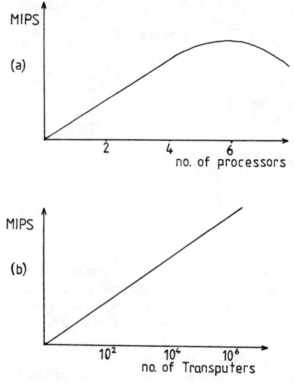

**Fig. 4.1**   (a) Plot of performance against number of processors for a conventional multiprocessor system; (b) the same plot for a multi-Transputer system.

typical Transputer has four such links, giving it a communications capacity of 40 Mbit/s into the device and 40 Mbit/s out. As these links are an integral part of each individual Transputer, the greater the number of Transputers in a network, the greater the total bandwidth of the system. Because communication bandwidth is far less of a problem, it is now found that plotting system performance against the number of constituent processors for a Transputer network gives a near linear graph (see Fig. 4.1(b)).

The size at which closely coupled networks of Transputers, connected by their serial links, becomes impractical has yet to be determined. In theory there is no reason why supercomputers containing thousands or even hundreds of thousands of Transputers should not be constructed.

One area where very high performance figures are required is in Artificial Intelligence. The performance rating of AI machines is measured in logical inferences per second (LIPS), with one logical inference being roughly equivalent to one hundred machine instructions. The target set by the Japanese team developing fifth generation architectures was for a prototype machine capable of one billion (or giga) logical inferences per second by 1991. It is believed that such a machine would, for example, be capable of translating from Japanese to English (and *vice versa*) in real time, using either text or voice input. An array of ten thousand Transputers could potentially deliver a similar performance figure and it could be assembled and be up-and-running before the end of 1986. Software development of a particular application might well extend beyond this date by one or two years, depending on the complexity of the application. However, the hardware for a fifth generation machine could be made available five years ahead of what was considered by many to be highly ambitious goal.

As Inmos have realised that simply providing hardware with a high performance potential does not necessarily produce a high performance system, a new programming language, occam, has been developed hand-in-hand with the Transputer. A number of more well established languages such as Pascal, FORTRAN and C will also be available for use on Transputers, but it is occam which will enable the performance potential of Transputer based systems to be fully realised. Occam provides direct software support for both concurrency and for the 10 Mbit/s inter-processor serial links.

The Transputer architecture combines several features developed for other processors over the years to achieve a performance rating of 10 million instructions per second (10 MIPS). However, the key elements which allow high performance systems to be constructed from Transputer devices are concurrency and communication and the support provided for both these features by the Occam language.

## 4.2   The Transputer generic architecture

As we can see in Fig. 4.2, the Transputer architecture does not define a single device but rather a whole family of Transputers. The T424 32-bit Transputer, with 4 serial links and 4 kbyte of on-chip static RAM, is usually taken as being the standard general purpose Transputer, but various combinations of on-chip facilities are possible. Transputers always include a processor, system services and one or more serial links, but they may have 4 kbyte of on-chip RAM, 2 kbyte, or no on-chip memory at all.

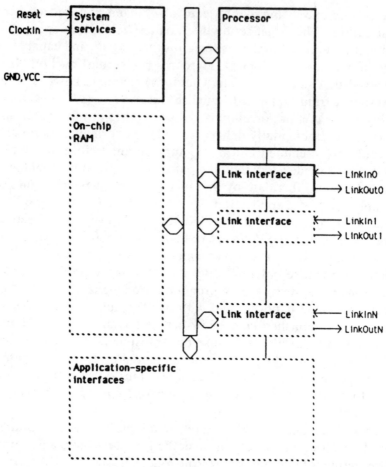

**Fig. 4.2**   Transputer generic architecture (*Courtesy Inmos group of companies*).

The first 32-bit Transputer to become freely available was the T414, released by Inmos in October 1985. The T414 has 4 serial links but only 2 kbyte of on-chip RAM. A 16-bit family of Transputers is also being developed, the first of these being the T212. Released at the same time as the T414, the T212 also has 2 kbyte of on-chip memory.

The second digit in a Transputer's product name indicates the amount of on-chip RAM in units of 2 kbyte. A 4 following the T indicates a 32-bit processor, and a 2 in the same position, a 16-bit processor. However, Inmos have been less logical with the last digit, which they say provides 'product uniqueness' rather than indicating the number of available links on the chip (the T212 has 4 links, not 2, as might be expected). The speed of a particular device in megahertz (MHz) may also be included in the name, following a hyphen, e.g. a T424-20 would run at 20 MHz, and a T424-12 would run at 12.5 MHz (Transputer speeds go up in 2.5 MHz steps from 10 to 20 MHz).

All Transputers have a timer which runs off a 5 MHz external clock. Both the processor clock frequency and the link clock (which controls the transfer rate of the serial links) are derived from the external clock frequency by internal scaling. Future Transputers will be capable of operating their links at much higher speeds but all Transputers will support the 10 Mbit/s standard. Link speed selection pins on each device allow one or more links to be set to the standard speed, thus allowing communication between any two Transputers. A tolerance of +/−0.02% is allowable on the external clock signal for correct operation of the serial links. This means that two communicating Transputers do not have to use the same external clock. Also the tolerance is such that relatively cheap crystal oscillators can be used to provide the signals. Links are intended for use only between Transputers on the same board or between those on adjacent boards on the same backplane. Over long distances (>400 mm) links will require some form of buffering. RS422 driver/receivers can be used to extend the link communication distance.

The link protocol, like the link speed, is standard across the whole range of Transputers. Data is transmitted one byte at a time in packets, with each packet being acknowledged by the receiving Transputer. The acknowledgement packet is sent as soon as the data packet is identified and, since each link is bi-directional, data packets and acknowledgement packets can be communicated concurrently. Acknowledgement packets consist of just two bits, a 1 and a 0. The second bit identifies the packet type. Data packets consist of two 1s followed by a byte of data and terminated with a 0 (see Fig. 4.3).

The T212 and T414 are stepping stones on the way to developing the T222 and T424 respectively (the T424 is currently planned for release in mid 1986). The characteristics of Transputer products in the future will be governed more and more by the specialist needs of the customer. As experience is gained in running development systems, and in many cases by developing actual products incorporating T414 and T424 processors, these specialist needs will become more apparent. Some applications may benefit from having more on-chip RAM while others may require more links. As links and on-chip memory are both contending for space on

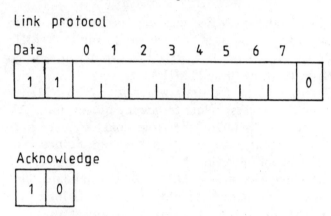

**Fig. 4.3**   Link protocol (*Courtesy Inmos group of companies*).

the same chip there will always be a tradeoff between the two, with the ideal balance depending on the application. In a single-processor system, for example, it may be more useful to have only one or two links for input and output and to have more on-chip RAM, which can be accessed more quickly than off-chip RAM. This would in turn improve the overall processing performance.

Many of the planned applications of the T424 have processors arranged in large two-dimensional arrays, with each T424 connected to its four nearest neighbours via its serial links (see Fig. 4.4). As system designers become more familiar with building Transputer networks, they will start to think 'Why just connect the nearest four neighbours, why not eight?' More adventurous designers are already planning three-dimensional networks, requiring at least six links and even $n$-dimensional networks requiring at least $2n$ links on each Transputer. The problem of building three-dimensional Transputer networks can be solved in the short term by pairing Transputers. Connecting two T424s, using one link each, leaves six links available for connecting to the six nearest neighbours in three dimensions. The need for hypercubes, super-clusters and other novel architectures will be considered in more detail in Section 4.10.

The characteristics of future Transputers will depend on demand, investment and technological advancements. It would be unrealistic to expect a 6-link Transputer with 8 kbyte of on-chip RAM (a T446, if a more logical nomenclature were to be adopted) to be released immediately after the T424. But if the demand exists, a 6-link chip with 2 kbyte may be entirely practical (T416), possibly followed by a version with 4 kbyte of on-chip memory (T426).

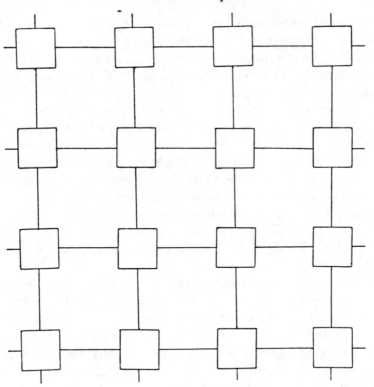

Fig. 4.4 Two-dimensional array of Transputers.

In addition to serial links and on-chip memory, the generic Transputer architecture also provides for the inclusion of application specific interfaces on-chip. Special purpose Transputers for graphics and disk drive control have already been developed and are due for release in December 1985. These are the G412 graphics controller and the M212 disk controller (the M standing for Mass storage). These specialised Transputers provide a convenient means of communicating directly with peripheral devices. Although these are not actually Transputers in their own right, it is worth mentioning the Inmos link adaptors in this section. The C series of devices, C001, C002, etc., are specialised devices which can be attached to a Transputer's serial link to adapt it to an 8-bit parallel link. A third method of interfacing peripherals is to memory map them on to the Transputer's memory bus. A peripheral can be memory mapped anywhere in the off-chip address space and can then be controlled using instructions written in occam.

The hardware floating point Transputer, the F424, is currently under development and should be released some months after the T424. The F424 will not be an add-on coprocessor for the T424, as has been the standard practice for conventional microprocessors such as the Intel 8086/8087 combination, but will be a complete Transputer in its own right. It will retain all the functionality of the T424 in addition to having floating point arithmetic facilities, conforming to the IEEE Standard P754 draft 10.0, implemented on-chip. Operations on both single precision (sign bit, 8-bit exponent and 23-bit fraction) and double precision (sign bit, 11-bit exponent and 52-bit fraction) floating point numbers will be supported. Operations on floating point numbers are expected by Inmos to take approximately 1 μs giving the F424 a peak performance rating of one million floating point operations per second (1 MFLOPS).

Several applications, such as aircraft simulation, signal processing and the analysis of seismic data, require large numbers of floating point operations to be performed in as short a time as possible. Just as fifth generation computer designers have a target of 1000 LIPS, so those involved with the development of array processors and mainframes with floating point accelerators have set a target of 1000 MFLOPS. A machine constructed from one thousand F424 Transputers could potentially provide such a performance figure – one giga FLOPS.

### 4.3   The T424 Transputer

Having considered the generic features of the Transputer family, a specific member of the family, the T424, will now be considered (see Fig. 4.5). The T424 has 4 kbyte of on-chip static RAM with an access time of 50 ns, four 10 Mbit/s bi-directional serial links, a 32-bit wide 25 Mbyte/s external memory interface and of course a processor and system services. This represents approximately 250 000 devices fabricated using a 1.5 μm CMOS process. The T414 chip, the first 32-bit Transputer, occupies a silicon area of just over 9×9 mm and contains 200 000 components. The T424 might be expected to be slightly larger, although the designers will aim to minimise any size increase because of packaging constraints. It is assumed that the T424, like the T414, will be available in a standard 84-pin J-lead chip carrier.

Like most 32-bit processors, the T424 is able directly to address 4 Gbytes (2 to the power of 32) of memory. Memory addresses

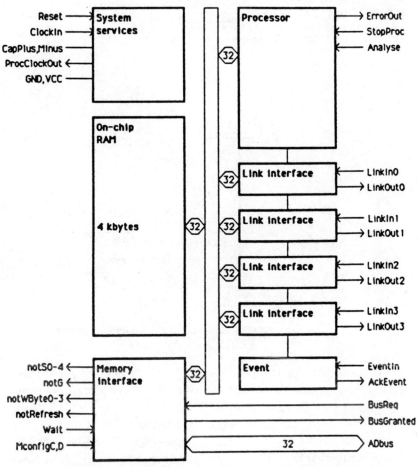

**Fig. 4.5** The T424 (*Courtesy Inmos group of companies*).

are signed, which means that they can be handled just like any other 32-bit integers. Figure 4.6 shows the memory map of the T424's address space. ROM based code is by convention located at the top (most positive) end of the address space, and when configured to bootstrap from ROM, the processor will commence execution from address Hex 7FFF FFFE. The on-chip RAM is organised as 1 kword of 32 bits each, situated at the most negative end of memory, i.e. at addresses Hex 8000 0FFF to Hex 8000 0000. Eighteen words (72 bytes) of on-chip memory, from Hex 8000 0047 to Hex 8000 0000, are used for system purposes, the last 8 words in this range being associated with the four links (one input word and one output word for each link).

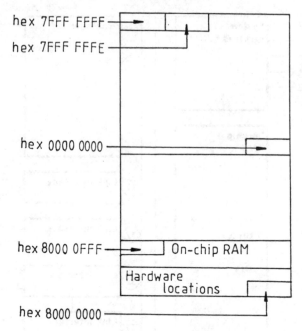

**Fig. 4.6**   T424 memory map (*Courtesy Inmos group of companies*).

The remainder of the on-chip RAM (Hex 8000 0FFF to Hex 8000 0048) is available for applications code and data. Since on-chip memory can be accessed in 50 ns, which is typically half the access time of off-chip RAM, small programs requiring high performance should ideally be located exclusively in on-chip RAM. Where arrays of Transputers interconnected by their serial links are being used, it may be possible to subdivide larger programs and locate them just in on-chip RAM. If this is not possible, the most time critical processes need to be identified so that they can be located within the on-chip memory. The occam language provides facilities for placing code at specific locations within the Transputer's address space. These facilities will be explained further in Section 4.6.

Some microprocessors make use of high speed cache memories which may be on or off-chip. As the processor executes the instructions within a program, dedicated microcode prefetches a block of code including and immediately following the current instruction pointer and places this code in the cache. When the instruction pointer reaches the end of the cache or when a Jump instruction points to an instruction outside the code contained in the cache, the microcode will automatically fetch a new block of code and place it into cache. One advantage of cache memory is that the user does not have to be aware that it exists. On the other hand, Transputer on-chip RAM is treated by the processor in just the same way as off-chip RAM–it simply takes less time to access. This means that the onus is placed on the user to make the best use of the fast RAM. Whether this is considered to be an advantage or a disadvantage will depend on the needs and preferences of the user.

It is useful to remember that a Transputer instruction is only one byte long, but memory is always accessed as words. Therefore, one access to external memory will fetch either four instructions or just one 32-bit data item. Inmos have conducted an experiment to demonstrate the effect of locating either code or data on-chip. The times given in the following table are relative to the case where all the program and all the data are located on-chip, this being taken as 1.

|  | Data intensive | Computation intensive |
|---|---|---|
| All program and data in on-chip RAM | 1 | 1 |
| Program off-chip, data on-chip | 1.3 | 1.1 |
| Program on-chip, data off-chip | 1.5 | 1.2 |
| All off-chip | 1.8 | 1.3 |

These are very important findings, particularly for applications which have large amounts of code but only small amounts of data (less than 4 kbyte). The T424 processor also incorporates an instruction pre-fetcher which holds 8 instructions (2 words). This has been found to be the ideal compromise between reducing code access time and fetching instructions which may not be executed.

The general trend with microprocessors has been to include more and more registers, but the T424 uses just six to execute a sequential program. These consist of an operand register, an instruction pointer, a workspace pointer and three registers which make up an evaluation stack. In addition to these six, there are two further registers which are used by the chip's priority scheduler to timeshare between parallel processes located on the same Transputer. Although occam allows any number of priority levels, only two are supported on the T424 and T414, these being priority 0 and priority 1, with 0 being the higher. If one or more priority 0 process has been placed on one Transputer, one will be selected to proceed by the scheduler and will then run until completion or until it has to wait for communication or for a timer input. High

priority processes should therefore be kept relatively short, otherwise they will tend to monopolise the processor. Priority 1 processes will only be scheduled when no priority 0 processes can
proceed. Priority 1 processes are time sliced so that no one process
is kept waiting too long. Time slice periods on early versions of
the Transputer lasted 4096 cycles of the 5 MHz input clock. In
later devices, however, this has been extended to 5120 cycles of
the input clock, which corresponds to a time of just over 1 ms.


## 4.4 The T424 instruction set

Transputers are a form of reduced instruction set computer
(RISCs). The characteristics and advantages of using a RISC are
well documented and are covered in some detail in Chapter 2. In
brief, it has been found that programs running on complex instruction set computers (CISCs) use only a small percentage of these
instructions on a regular basis. Some of the remaining instructions
are used only in rare situations. RISC machine designers concentrate their efforts in supporting the more frequently used instructions, with less frequently used functions being implemented either
by using combinations of instructions or by adding modifiers or
extenders. Some of these functions may well require more machine
cycles to execute on a RISC than on a CISC. However, on the
whole, RISCs achieve high performance and efficiency by requiring
less effort to decode instructions and requiring fewer registers.

Generally speaking, designing a compiler for a RISC is a relatively straight forward task. The compiler is presented with a
relatively simple and predictable task and the resulting object code
tends to be compact and efficient. Although a relatively simple
task for a machine, generating code for a RISC tends to be both
tedious and error prone when performed by a human programmer.
This could well be a contributory factor in Inmos' decision not to
release details such as instruction code values or even the complete
range of instructions offered on particular Transputers. Occam is
intended to be the lowest level language used on any Transputer
and Inmos do not support the use of machine code by the user.
There are in fact more sound reasons behind this apparently strict
policy decision than being worried about error prone hand-coded
programs. VLSI technology is advancing rapidly and techniques
are being developed whereby new features can be quickly incorporated into a chip's hardware design. By supporting occam as the
standard language for all the members in the Transputer family,
a new device can be developed with a totally new instruction set

and with, for example, a significant increase in performance. All the user would have to do would be to buy the new compiler for the device and he could run all his old occam programs. Minor changes to a program may well be required to optimise the performance when porting between Transputers. This would be particularly true if the new device incorporated more on-chip RAM or had more serial links. Having a separate compiler for each device is far less trouble than maintaining separate versions of the same programs in what would effectively be different languages. The following information is therefore included purely as a matter of interest as the reader is unlikely to need to program in Transputer machine code. No values are given for the various functions and instructions since these may vary, even between different versions of the same device.

All instructions on the Transputer are just one byte long and are split into two fields. The four most significant bits contain the function and the four least significant bits the data (see Fig. 4.7). Four bit fields allow up to 16 local data items to be manipulated by up to 16 instructions. Thirteen of these values are used to represent the most frequently used functions. These are known as *one address instructions* as the operand is used by the instruction as a value. These instructions are:

Load local
Store local
Load local pointer
Load non-local
Store non-local
Load non-local pointer
Adjust workspace

Load constant
Add constant
Add to memory
Jump
Conditional jump
Call

Two additional instructions, Prefix and Negative Prefix, can be used to extend the operand of any instruction to any length. All instructions start by loading the four data bits from the instruction's data field into the least significant four bits in the operand register as shown in Fig. 4.7. All instructions except Prefix and Negative Prefix end by clearing the operand register ready for the next instruction. The Prefix instruction loads its four data bits into the operand register and then shifts them four places to the left (i.e. four places more significant). The Negative Prefix instruction is similar except that it complements the operand register before shifting it up. Using a single prefixing instruction, any operand from −256 to 255 can be represented. By using several prefixing

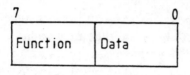

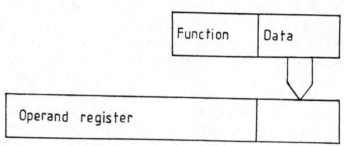

**Fig. 4.7** T424 instruction format (*Courtesy Inmos group of companies*).

instructions, any operand in the full 32-bit range can be represented.

The other type of instructions are the zero address instructions. These use the operand to define operations on values already in the evaluation stack:

| | | |
|---|---|---|
| Add | Shift left | Read timer |
| Subtract | Shift right | Test error |
| Multiply | | Reverse |
| Divide | Move message | Return |
| Remainder | Input message | Minimum integer |
| Long add | Output message | Initialise |
| Long subtract | | |
| Long multiply | Load byte | Start process |
| Long divide | Store byte | End process |
| Normalise | Byte count | Alt start |
| | Word count | Enable channel |
| Difference | Byte subscript | Enable timer |
| Greater than | Word subscript | Disable channel |
| Equal zero | Check subscript | Disable timer |
| | Extend to word | Alt wait |
| And | Check partword | |
| Or | Extend to double | |

## 4.5   The history and philosophy of the occam language

Occam was named after William of Occam, a fourteenth century English philosopher who studied at Oxford. William was credited a Latin quotation known as Occam's Razor:

*Entia non sunt multiplicanda praeter necessitatem*

Which states that entities are not be multiplied beyond necessity. At the second meeting of the Occam Users' Group, held appropriately in William of Occam's home town of Oxford, one speaker made the point that he had extreme doubts about a philosopher who contrived such a complex way of saying:

KEEP THINGS SIMPLE

This less formal translation of Occam's Razor presents a much clearer view of the philosophy behind the language. The simplicity of occam is a reflection of the simplicity of the underlying instruction set. The occam language and the Transputer have been developed hand-in-hand to produce a language which combines the performance benefits of an assembly language with the readability, programmer productivity and maintainability aspects of a higher level language.

In terms of complexity, occam can be seen as being at the other end of the spectrum to Ada, the US DoD's new standard language for embedded systems. The designers of Ada were set an extremely difficult task in that they were given an extensive list of essential features which the new standard language was to support. Not only did the Ada language have to support programming features such as structured constructs and strong typing, it was also required to support the principles of software engineering, such as abstraction, information hiding and modularity. It is arguable whether these higher level software management aspects should be addressed by the features of the language itself. Some suggestions as to how large occam systems might be developed and managed will be given in a later section.

One indication of the complexity of a programming language is to measure the size of the language's definition. As a benchmark by which to judge the other two languages, Algol 60 can be defined in 43 pages of text, with 50 lines of text to one page, and Pascal can be defined in 38 pages. Occam can be defined in just 18 pages. When its far reaching brief is taken into consideration, it will come as no surprise to discover that Ada requires a definition of 275 pages. Although this is by no means an absolute measure of language complexity, it provides a useful comparison. If nothing else it gives an idea of the size of the problem facing the Ada compiler writer.

Apart from being named after a historical figure, rather than being an abbreviation, both occam and Ada have one important feature in common: both languages support concurrent processing. Not only do they both support concurrent processing but in each language the model of concurrency was based on the work carried out by Professor Hoare at Oxford University, on communicating sequential processes. Professor Hoare was closely involved in the definition stage of the occam language, which was developed at Inmos by David May.

Concurrency has been recognised as the key feature in freeing the system designer from the physical limitations of the available hardware. The performance of sequentially executed software is limited to the speed of the single processor on which it runs. Only by subdividing that software into tasks which can execute independently, and in parallel on separate processors, can the performance of the total system be increased. Running totally independent software in parallel has never presented a problem. A company with an expanding workforce divided equally between two factories which finds its computer can no longer run payroll program in the required time simply buys a second computer. Real time systems in critical applications present much greater problems. Let us suppose that a particular processor has been chosen on which to run an air traffic control system. The system is required to track up to one hundred aircraft at a time. Because of extra functions, however, and safety checks specified in the requirement, performance calculations indicate that one of the chosen processors can only track one aircraft at a time. Should one aircraft be plotted on each processor and their outputs combined in some way? Obviously not. The software processes modelling each aircraft need to be able to examine the states of processes modelling other aircraft. This may be performed either directly, or via control processes which plan the aircraft's future movements and predict when aircraft may approach each other too closely. The essential features which should be supported by a real time language should therefore be concurrency and communication.

Ada provides objects known as *tasks* to support concurrency, but these are just one of many object types from which Ada programs can be constructed. In occam, the object which supports concurrency is the *process*, which is in fact the only object type within the occam language. Occam programs are constructed exclusively of hierarchical levels of processes. At the lowest level, the language is built up from just three primitive process types:

*assignment, input* and *output.* Input and output primitives directly support communication between named processes via channels.

At the start of this section, it was stated that the philosophy behind the occam language was to keep things simple. It can now be seen that this is achieved by recognising that a real time language needs to support just two essential features:

*concurrency* and *communication*

### 4.6 The occam language

Occam programs are constructed of hierarchical levels of processes. At the lowest level, the language is built up from just three primitive process types: *assignment, input* and *output.* The symbol used for assignment is : = as in several other high level languages. In occam, however, no symbol is required to terminate a primitive process, but only one primitive may appear on each line. For example:

    x := 1

assigns the value of the expression to the right of the := symbol to the previously declared variable on the left, in this case assigning the literal value 1 to the variable x.

The symbol ? is used to indicate input, e.g.:

    c ? x

inputs a value from a previously declared channel, c, and assigns this value to the variable x.

The symbol ! is used to indicate an output. For example:

    c ! y

outputs the value contained in y to channel c.

Primitive processes may be built up into higher level processes by the use of constructs. The sequential construct, SEQ, indicates that the processes which follow it are to be executed sequentially. Component processes are indented by two characters with respect to the construct.

    SEQ
        c1 ? x
        x := x + 1
        c2 ! x

In the above example there is no alternative other than to execute the three processes sequentially. The value must be input from c1 and assigned to x before it is incremented, before it is output to c2. However, if two values are input from different channels into different variables, then the two inputs could conceptually execute in parallel. This condition is catered for in the occam language and is implemented by the parallel construct, PAR.

```
PAR
    c1 ? x
    c2 ? y
```

If x and y were to be summed and the result assigned to x then obviously this could not be evaluated until after both inputs had occurred. Similarly if expresssions containing the new value of x were to be output, they would have to follow the summing process. The program below consists of three sequential processes, the first consisting of two parallel input processes, the second being a primitive process (an assignment) and the third consisting of two parallel output processes.

```
SEQ
    PAR
        c1 ? x
        c2 ? x
    x := x + y
    PAR
        c3 ! x + 1
        c4 ! x - 1
```

The positions of the three constituent processes of the sequential construct can be seen to be aligned with each other and indented two places with respect to the SEQ. In this way, more and more complex processes can be constructed. However, in order to increase the readability and maintainability of a program, it is good practice to have named processes, or PROCs, each of which has only a few levels of constituent processes. The above process could be named as follows:

```
PROC P1 (CHAN c1, c2, c3, c4) =
    VAR x :
    VAR y :
    SEQ
        PAR
            c1 ? x
            c2 ? y
        x := x + y
```

```
PAR
   c3 ! x + 1
   c4 ! x - 1
SKIP :
```

SKIP simply terminates with no effect. (Note that the end of a named PROC must also be indicated by a : symbol.) Named processes communicate by means of channels which connect two processes together. When the processes at either end of a particular channel are on the same Transputer, communication occurs by means of a memory-to-memory data transfer. If the processes are located on different Transputers, communication occurs via a standard Inmos link. In either case the processes will be concurrent and the communication will be synchronised, with the transfer occurring when both the inputting and outputting processes are ready.

The locating of processes onto specified Transputers is controlled by placement commands. Both separately compiled processes and components of a PAR construct can be individually located in this way. PLACE is also used to associate named channels connecting processes on separate Transputers with actual serial links.

PRI PAR applies a priority to the component processes of a PAR construct. This only applies to the outermost PAR. The first of the parallel processes is given the highest priority, priority 0, the second is given priority 1 and so on. The number of priority levels depends on the implementation of the priority scheduler on a particular Transputer. The T414 and T424 support two priority levels, 0 and 1.

Replication can be used with both SEQ constructs to create conventional loops and with PARs to construct arrays of concurrent processes.

```
SEQ i = 0 FOR n
   P

PAR i = 0 FOR n
   Pi
```

The first example will loop n times, the second will create n parallel processes, P0 to Pn-1.

The IF construct allows one of a number of processes to execute depending on the condition which precedes it:

```
IF
    x > 0
        x := x - 1
    x > 0
        x := x + 1
    x = 0
        SKIP
```

The ALT construct can be particularly useful where signals might appear on one of a number of alternative channels:

```
ALT
    c1 ? ANY
        count1 := count1 + 1
    c2 ? ANY
        count2 := count2 + 1
    c3 ? ANY
        count3 := count3 + 1
```

The use of ANY indicates that the actual value of the signals is not important, only the presence of a signal on that particular channel is of interest.

Repetition is implemented by the use of WHILE:

```
WHILE (x - 1) > 0
    x := x - 1
```

The WHILE TRUE condition allows processes to run continuously once started:

```
PROC square (CHAN Xin, SquareOut) =
    WHILE TRUE
        VAR x:
        SEQ
            Xin ? x
            SquareOut ! x*x :
```

(This example also shows the syntax for declaring channel parameters, Xin and SquareOut.) All implementations of occam support a number of basic types:

CHAN, TIMER, BOOL, BYTE and INT

Other implementations may also support the signed integers INT16, INT32 and INT64; and the IEEE Standard P754 draft 10.0 floating point number types REAL32 and REAL64.

Expressions may be constructed using the following operators:

Arithmetic operator: $+,-,*,/,\backslash$
$(\backslash$ is a remainder)
Modulo arithmetics: PLUS,MINUS,TIMES,DIVIDE
Relational: $=,<>,>,<,>=,<=$
Boolean operators: AND,OR,NOT
Bit operators: BITAND,BITOR,$>$ $<$,BITNOT
$(>$ $<$ is exclusive OR)
Shift operators: $<<,>>$

All transputers incorporate a timer which can be read into a variable of type integer:

tim ? t

Delayed inputs are also supported and are of the form:

tim ? AFTER t0

## 4.7 Transputer system development

In an ideal world, the user provides the system designer with a requirement and a performance specification but he does not specify a particular hardware configuration. It should be left to the designer to specify what hardware is required to implement his design and to deliver the required performance. Terminology varies from application to application and from company to company, but software development is usually broken down into three phases:

● Requirements specification
● Design
● Implementation.

As no one is so naive as to expect an implemented system to work first time and to continue to work for years to come, two further phases need to be considered:

● Testing and debugging
● Maintenance.

The initial phase, requirements specification, is simply the process of taking the user's requirements and presenting them in a form which is unambiguous and is understood by both the user and the developer. In the not too distant future, machines exhibiting some degree of artificial intelligence will be capable of executing the requirement specification directly, but until that time is reached a design phase is still necessary in order to generate code which can be compiled and run.

Experience with developing many large software systems has shown that in order to produce code which has any chance of being both correct and maintainable, the use of a rigorous development method is essential. The most promising design methods applicable to the design of concurrent occam software are those based on dataflow diagrams and software modelling. Dataflow diagrams represent software designs as networks of processes connected by data streams (see Fig. 4.8). This representation maps directly onto occam's model of processes connected by channels. Some design methods, notably Jackson System Development (JSD), use software processes to model processes in the real world. JSD goes on to consider a network of these processes, each of which is considered to execute conceptually on its own individual processor. If there are more processes than processors on the target hardware then the processes are 'inverted', which is a means of transforming a process so that it can be called like a procedure. The Transputer's hardware scheduler can run occam processes directly. This removes the need for the inversion phase in JSD.

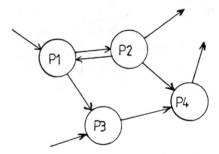

**Fig. 4.8**   Occam processes shown as dataflow diagram.

Whichever design method is adopted, a high degree of automation will be required, particularly if large software designs are to be implemented on Transputer networks. Some software tools already exist, but as yet they are basic and stand alone. It was mentioned earlier that it is arguable whether a language itself should provide facilities to check the correctness of code, to handle run-time errors and configuration control. When a fully integrated software toolset incorporating all the necessary facilities has been developed there will be no need to duplicate these in the programming language. The fact that occam provides only a limited number of facilities for software management and error checking will not therefore be a problem.

The area in which occam offers several positive advantages over other languages is in its flexibility at the implementation phase. When a design for a system has been developed it can be implemented in occam on any host computer for which a compiler has been produced. Once tested, this same occam code can be recompiled and run on a single Transputer or on an array of interconnected Transputers. By using the PLACED operator, processes can be located on specified Transputers. A performance estimator is available from Inmos which runs on the host machine (DEC Vax 11/780 series are currently supported as host machines) and allows the performance on the target hardware to be predicted. Therefore the number of Transputers necessary to meet the performance specification can be determined before the software is run on the target hardware. If the performance requirement is increased by the user, it is a relatively simple task to retarget the software onto a larger array of Transputers.

The Transputer and occam would seem to offer an extremely attractive combination of hardware and software for developing concurrent systems. However, there are still several problems to be solved. For real time software development, generating syntactically correct code is not the end of the story. One of the features of real time software is that code tested on the host can still deadlock when it is run on the target hardware. The only way in which deadlocks can be avoided is to provide mechanisms to guard against them in all possible situations in which they could occur. It is occam's interprocess channels which present the greatest potential for deadlocks occurring. If for any reason a process is unable to output to a channel, the process at the other end of the channel will hang, which could cause a chain reaction and hang a complete system. Occam provides no assistance in avoiding or recovering from such a deadlock. At the third meeting of the Occam Users' Group meeting (23–24 September, 1985) channel associated deadlocks were highlighted as being the problem requiring most urgent attention. This should not present a major problem to the development of Transputer based systems, but it is an area which requires some fairly urgent research effort.

Let us now look ahead, hopefully months rather than years, to when a toolset capable of handling the design of a moderately large system implemented in occam has been developed. An occam program has been tested on the host, is located on a single Transputer and runs a particular application in three seconds. The performance specification, however, states a requirement for it to run in one second. Seeing that the top level of process hierarchy consists of three processes in a parallel construct, the developer changes the PAR to a PLACED PAR, and locates the three processes on three separate Transputers coupled by their serial links. The same application is run and to the dismay of the developer it takes – two seconds to run!

The answer to this problem is quite simple: one of the three parallel processes in the program takes twice as long to execute as the other two processes added together. This process therefore represents the critical path and needs to be decomposed into smaller processes. This trivial example highlights the need to consider what might be called the first law of concurrent processing:

Share the workload evenly between the available processors.

The next section will consider some of the other problems which need to be addressed when designing and implementing concurrent occam software on Transputer networks.


### 4.8   Sharing the load

The secret of realising the full performance potential of any multiprocessor system lies in the even distribution of the workload. Parallelism is the most obvious and the most attractive means of sharing the workload between processors, but frequently a parallel solution to a problem is simply not possible. Consider the occam program:

```
SEQ
   P1
   P2
   P3
```

The processes P1, P2 and P3 contain totally dissimilar sequences of primitive processes. P3 uses the end results of P2 and P2 uses the end results of P1; therefore the above construct is the only possible way of implementing the program. How can the workload of such a sequential program be shared between multiprocessors? The answer is to pipeline the program's processes. Pipelining involves locating sequential processes on a linear arrangement of processors.

In Fig. 4.9 each of the software processes, P1, P2 and P3, is located on its own processor. P1 starts, inputs a data item D1, processes this data and outputs an interim result to P2 and then terminates. P2 starts, processes the interim result from P1, outputs its own interim result to P3 and terminates. P3 starts, runs and outputs the overall program's final result R, and terminates.

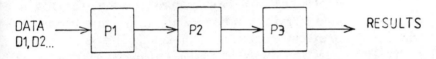

**Fig. 4.9**    Transputer arranged as a pipeline.

It will immediately be apparent that only one of these processes is executing at any one time. In fact if all three processes could be located within the on-chip memory of a single Transputer, they would execute just as quickly on that one processor as they would on three. The areas in which pipelines are useful are where continuous streams of data need to be processed. Consider a stream of data items D1, D2, D3, D4, . . . , D$n$, being input into the above pipeline. This time, when P1 has processed D1 it outputs the interim result to P2, but does not terminate. Instead it repeats the sequence with data item D2. In the second time period, P2 is processing the derivative of D1 while P1 is processing D2. Therefore both P1 and P2 are operating in parallel. If the workload has been equally divided between the processes then each set of data will remain in each processor an equal length of time, *T*. After time 3*T*, D1 will have been processed to produce a result R1 at the end of the pipeline and all the processors will continue to execute as long as new data items can be input into P1.

It can now be seen that two techniques exist to share the workload: pipelining and parallelism. Let us now consider how the two techniques can be combined. Returning to the earlier problem of how to distribute three unequal processes which are capable of operating in parallel, how can the workload be evenly distributed between three processors if P1 runs in 4 time units and P2 and P3 each run in one time unit?

```
PAR
  P1
  P2
  P3
```

Running these processes on a single Transputer takes 6 time units. We would therefore expect to run the same software on three Transputers in 2 time units. As P1 takes 4 time units to execute, it has to be subdivided. If P1 consists of a set of sequential processes, which may be primitive or complex, it can be split into two processes, P1a and P1b, which take roughly the same length of time to execute. These two processes can now be pipelined together and located on two of the available processors. The Occam processes P2 and P3 will then be located on the third processor where they can execute conceptually in parallel and be scheduled by the Transputer's hardware scheduler. Of course, as this is now a pipelined solution, it will only execute efficiently if streams of data items are being processed.

A technique has been developed in recent years which implements pipelines in two dimensions; this is known as *systolic processing*. Systolic processing is ideal for implementing on two-dimensional arrays of Transputers, where each Transputer is connected to its four nearest neighbours via their serial links. Figure 4.10 shows an array of Transputers with pipelines running from top to bottom and from left to right. Processes in each Transputer input the data from the left channel and the top channel, process the data and pass data or interim results to the right and bottom channels. Such an array could be used for matrix multiplication where the two inputs are multiplied together and added to a running total:

```
SEQ
  PAR
    top  ? x
    left ? y
  PAR
    total := total + (x * y)
    bottom ! x
    right ! y
```

In the above occam code, x, y and 'total' have been declared as variables with 'total' initialised to zero. Top, bottom, left and right have been declared as channels. It will be seen that x and y are output in parallel with the evaluation of the expression assigned

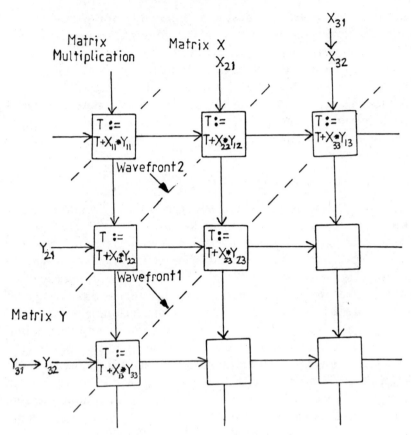

**Fig. 4.10** Wavefront and systolic processing.

to 'total'. In this way, neighbouring processors below and to the right are not kept waiting unnecessarily. It has been stated earlier that the components of a parallel construct, implemented on a single processor, will only execute 'conceptually' in parallel. However, in this particular case the two output processes are handled by link interfaces which are able to operate independently of the main processor. As soon as the processor has initiated the two outputs, the communication with the neighbouring Transputers proceeds in parallel with the evaluation of the expression. Parallel communication processes will actually have a slight effect on the overall processor performance. Inmos claim that the performance of the processes not directly involved with communication will only be reduced by 8%, even when the links are operating at their peak rates.

Figure 4.10 shows how data injected into pipelines in two dimensions creates diagonal wavefronts of data items. In this example, the wavefronts pass across the processor array from top left to bottom right. Because of this analogy, matrix manipulations implemented in this way are referred to as *wavefront processing*. The name 'systolic' is derived from the analogy between the pulsing of data through the array and the systolic beat of the heart. Although systolic processing is not usually appropriate to software problems in general, for particular mathematical applications it can be highly efficient.

### 4.9 Design of concurrent systems

Any application which at present runs on a conventional array processor can usually be implemented on an array of Transputers. Some excellent work has been carried out in the area of wavefront and systolic processing (particularly by S.Y. Kung who originally adopted the word 'systolic') and these techniques are particularly well suited for implementation on two-dimensional arrays of Transputers. However, Transputer system development should not be thought of as the means of transforming every application into a systolic process on a two-dimensional array of processors.

System design with the Transputer presents a totally different level of problem than most designers will have been used to. In the past, devising mechanisms for interprocessor communication, task scheduling and process synchronisation has taken up a large proportion of the system designer's time, effort and creative skills. On the Transputer, the majority of these problems are handled by the occam language and the Transputer itself. Freed from the need to consider these more mundane problems, the system designer can address himself to the particular problems associated with concurrency and the architecture of large systems.

The design of concurrent systems will be a totally new experience to most designers, simply because concurrent machines have been a rarity until quite recently. The design of a sequential program, running on a conventional Von Neumann type machine, can be compared to the task of a design engineer who has to consider a single factory production line. He must ensure that all the necessary specialist workers, machines and resources are available to process items on that one production line. Taking a similar analogy, the design of a concurrent computer system is like the design of a complete factory. Here the designer must not only provide all the specialist workers, machines and resources required by all the factory's production lines, he must provide them all in the right numbers. If particular machines, resources or skills are to be shared between production lines, then the designer must ensure that bottlenecks are not created. More importantly, he must avoid critical shared resources being monopolised in such a way that the whole factory grinds to a standstill. The complexity of such a task is such that the designer may not be able to solve all the problems on the drawing board. Some problems may only become apparent after the factory is in operation. In just the same way, concurrent computer systems will always require some degree of debugging before they are fully operational.

Besides considering the special problems of concurrency, many Transputer system designers will also have to address the problems of designing extremely large arrays of processors. Some of these problems will be considered in the following section.

**4.10   System architecture**

To the conventional designer, some of the more esoteric architectures being put forward for the Transputer may seem unnecessarily complex. In fact the reaction of many to such ideas as multi-dimensional hypercubes is to classify them in the field of science fiction rather than in the area of practical system design. There are, however, sound reasons for actually using these novel architectures in real systems.

Transputers provide a means of distributing software across a number of processors, but it should still be remembered that a communication overhead will always exist, particularly when the communication needs to pass across more than one Transputer. As a general policy the designer should aim to minimise inter-processor communication wherever possible. If at all possible, certain groups of closely coupled software processes should reside on the same processor. These groups are identified by analysing dataflow representations of the software design. Processes connected by frequent or high volume data flows are said to be *closely coupled*. This group of processes might typically form a sub-system of an embedded computer system, such as an aircraft's autopilot or a section of a signal processing algorithm, taking in relatively small amounts of data and returning results. If performance studies indicate that a group of tightly coupled processes will have to run on more than one processor, then in order to minimise communication overheads every processor supporting this sub-system should be connected directly to all the other processors supporting that same task. This configuration will be familiar to any network analyst. If *n* processors are required to provide the necessary performance for the sub-system then, if possible, each processor should have *n* − 1 links to connect directly to all the other processors and one link to connect to other sub-systems or to the outside world. This makes a total of (*n* − 1) + 1 = *n* links required for each processor in the sub-system. Therefore the number of processors which can be networked to form a cluster is equal to the number of links which each has available. T424 Transputers should therefore be linked in clusters of four (see Fig. 4.11).

Students of chemistry, or anyone who has used a molecular modelling kit, will know that connecting objects to their nearest neighbours by four regularly distributed links forms a three-dimensional tetrahedral structure (see Fig. 4.12.) It is this structure which gives the diamond crystal its strength. It is also the ideal way of connecting a large network of 4-linked Transputers to minimise communication overheads. The problem with such a network is that it does not lend itself to being tracked onto a two-dimensional printed circuitboard. Figure 4.13 is a three-dimensional representation of Fig. 4.14. It can be seen that this is different to the diamond structure in Fig. 4.12 in that it is not totally regular but is built up from clusters of four processors each. Although this network structure has been arrived at in a methodical and purely logical manner, it is still hard to believe that this structure provides a lower communication overhead than that of the North–South East–West connection of the array shown in Fig.

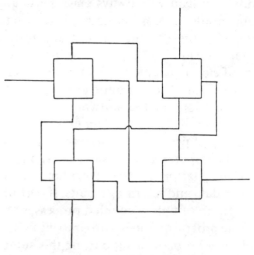

**Fig. 4.11**   Four interconnected Transputers.

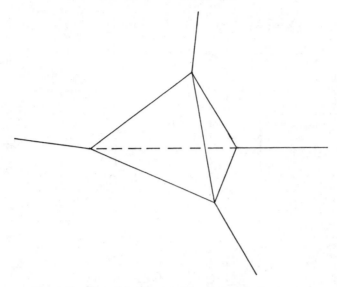

**Fig. 4.12**  Network connected in diamond structure.

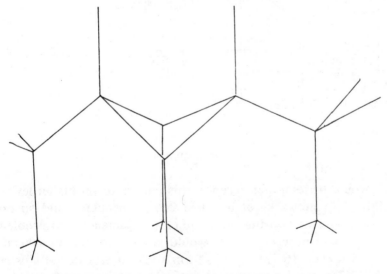

**Fig. 4.13**  Three-dimensional representation of connections shown in Fig. 4.11.

4.4. A quick check, however, using the array in Fig. 4.4, shows that a signal passing from a Transputer at a corner of the conventional array to the Transputer at the opposite corner of the array has to pass along at least six links. In the array shown in Fig. 4.14, the signal only requires three links to pass between the processors in the same relative positions. In fact three is the maximum number of links used to connect any two processors in this network.

**Fig. 4.14**   Sixteen interconnected Transputers.

It would be tempting to repeat this pattern to yet higher levels, building up networks of 64, then 256 Transputers, and so on. Unfortunately the wiring would quickly become a major problem and the inter-processor links would soon exceed their 400 mm limit. However, 16 Transputers form a very useful size of cluster. If 16 T424s can be fitted onto a single circuitboard the cluster becomes even more practical.

Two-dimensional Transputer networks in which each processor is connected to its four nearest neighbours, as shown in Fig. 4.4, can in fact be quite useful for implementing algorithms involving matrix manipulation. This array is also applicable to many image processing tasks where the Transputers can be used either to process an incoming image or to generate graphics, with each processor being allocated a number of pixels to control. Some image processing algorithms require that each modelling process communicates with its eight nearest neighbours rather than four. This does not require a particularly novel architecture, just that it would be preferable for each processor to have eight links rather than four so that all diagonals could be interconnected.

Joining two Transputers using one link from each produces a dual processor with six available links:

$$(2 \times 4) - 2 = 6$$

Having six links allows cubic Transputer networks to be constructed in three dimensions. Connecting three Transputers in a linear structure provides a triple processor with eight spare links. This allows a four-dimensional network to be constructed. Multidimensional 'hypercubes' are not imaginary network structures, they can actually be built. However, the multi-layer printed circuit-board tracking problems created by actually trying to build one can become a nightmare. In theory, an $n$-dimensional hypercube can be constructed from clusters containing $n - 1$ Transputers and having $2n$ links each, where $n$ can be any number. In practice it would seem to be far more sensible to wait until Transputers with six, eight or ten links are manufactured. Building three-dimensional networks is worth considering, particularly where three-dimensional processes are being modelled, but the practicality of building hypercubes must be questioned. Small sided hypercubes may well find uses as superclusters to host a closely coupled sub-system. For example, a four-dimensional cube of side 2 would contain $2^4 = 16$ nodes, with each node containing three Transputers. Such a supercluster, or mini-hypercube, may well find practical uses, but interconnecting 48 Transputers in such a complex architecture is not a trivial task.

The argument for hypercubes is that they reduce communication latency. Consider two networks, each containing 48 Transputers; a $6 \times 8$ two-dimensional array and a $2 \times 2 \times 2 \times 2$ triple Transputer noded hypercube. Taking the worst case of trying to communicate between Transputers at opposite corners of each network, on the two-dimensional array the message is relayed by eleven Transputers, on the four-dimensional network it can be relayed by anything from two Transputers to ten, depending on the orientation of each node. On average, therefore, communication within a hypercube is faster. Deadlock prediction on such a structure, however, will be impossible until an automatic deadlock analyser is developed.

## 4.11  Future developments

We have seen that the generic architecture of the Transputer allows a whole family of components to be developed, each having its own area of specialist application. The Transputer's unique characteristics offer many other exciting possibilities. Many designs for two-dimensional arrays of Transputers look remarkably similar to the way in which the chips are laid out on the silicon wafer on which they are manufactured. It seems a great waste of time, effort and money to split these wafers, package up the individual chips and to design and manufacture a printed circuitboard so that the chips can be interconnected in the same layout in which they were manufactured. It would seem far more sensible to connect the Transputers to their neighbours while they are still on the wafer. Wafer scale integration, as this is known, has already being tried out with memory devices, which like the Transputer can be connected in regular networks.

Wafer scale integration has two major problems to overcome. First, the yield of working chips from a silicon wafer is rarely 100%. Simply connecting each Transputer to all its neighbours would almost inevitably include faulty Transputers in the network.

**Fig. 4.15**  T414 Transputer on wafer (*Courtesy Inmos group of companies*).

Second, there are the problems of getting electrical power in and getting heat out. Power must be routed to each chip and the one watt of heat generated by each Transputer must be removed.

Obviously, on the first point, every effort must be made to improve production techniques to achieve the maximum possible yield of correctly working chips. In the longer term, however, software could be developed to configure the arrays to bypass faulty chips. If the software could dynamically configure the networks and continually monitor the condition of each processor, chips which failed in operation could also be bypassed. The long term solution to the power problem is to develop new semiconductors which require less power. As an added bonus, these materials may present a lower impedance which would allow signals to be passed around the chips more quickly, thereby increasing the performance of each individual processor.

The short term solution to achieving wafer scale integration of Transputer arrays would be to indentify all occurrences of two-by-two arrays of working chips on a wafer. This process could be carried out by a computer aided device which had been fed with the position of all the working chips by the automatic testing equipment. Slicing the chip to cut out an irregular pattern of

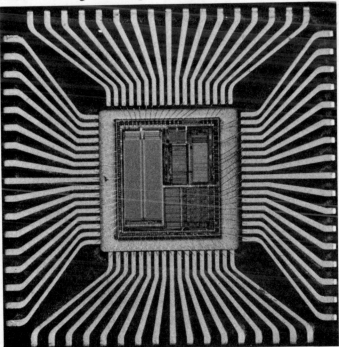

**Fig. 4.16**  T414 Transputer (*Courtesy Inmos group of companies*).

two-by-two arrays may be more difficult but should still be possible. It may also be possible to package the working chips in these two-by-two arrays.

Again in the longer term, connection of processors across the wafer would probably be by some form of parallel link, probably 32-bits wide, which would considerably increase the wafer's internal bandwidth. For the first wafer scale Transputer products, the standard serial links would provide a simple means of connecting processors, without the need to modify their internal architecture.

Having two-by-two arrays of Transputers on each wafer would reduce the problems of getting power to each processor, as all four would be accessible from the edge of the wafer. Waste heat might present a more difficult problem and some way of cooling the chip would be required, possibly by integrating heat pipes and heat sinks into the wafer's packaging. As these problems are gradually overcome, it will be possible to produce larger and larger arrays of integrated Transputers. A wafer just 10 cm square, using 1985 technology, could operate at one billion operations per second and would also incorporate 100 kbyte of fast memory.

For those designers requiring more than four links on their Transputers, the quad T424 wafer scale integrated package could well provide the answer to their problems. In addition to a performance rating of 40 MIPS, a quad T424 would have eight serial links with a total bandwidth of 80 Mbit/s. In addition to the performance advantage, it may actually be that a quad T424 could be developed in a shorter timescale than a single Transputer with eight links.

It should at this point be made perfectly clear that all these ideas for future products are, at the moment, pure speculation. Various representatives from Inmos have, over the last year or so, mentioned the possibility of wafer scale products, but there is no actual commitment to develop these devices. Their development, like that of the individual devices in the Transputer family, will depend on demand, investment in research and development and on being able to overcome the large number of technical problems which will inevitably be encountered.

What is certain is that as the Transputer is used in more and more real applications, the need for many variations of the device will emerge. The Transputer is the most significant development since the microprocessor. This microprocessor sized device, with the power of a small mainframe computer, provides us with a building block to replace most of today's machines. General purpose processors, array processors, supercomputers and machines which have not been possible until now, such as the fifth generation machines, can all be assembled from Transputers. Most importantly, the Transputer exists here and now. In developing new products from this device, we are limited only by our imaginations.

## References

1. *The Occam Programming Manual*, Prentice-Hall Int., 1982.
2. *Towards Fifth-Generation computers*, Simons, G.L., NCC Publications, 1983.
3. *Transputer Reference Manual*, Inmos, 1985.
4. Kung, S.Y., IEEE ASSP magazine, July, 1985.
5. *System Development*, Jackson, M.A., Prentice-Hall Int., 1983.

# CHAPTER 5
# Intel's 80386

NICK JOHN
*Customer Marketing Manager,
Microcomputer Group, Intel International*

## 5.1 Introduction

The 32-bit microprocessor is accelerating the convergence of the minicomputer and microprocessor bases of application, originally fuelled by the 16-bit microprocessor. Many of the more demanding of today's 16-bit microprocessor applications are evolving to need greater levels of performance and more address space. Additionally, today's systems designers are incorporating features that have never before been available on 16-bit or 32-bit microprocessors into emerging application areas such as machine vision, advanced robotic systems and voice recognition.

A large proportion of microprocessor based designs have reached a stage where the software factor is the chief component of overall development cost, as well as being a key factor in bringing product benefits to market. Tomorrow's multi-user business systems and multi-tasking engineering workstations require a high level of software sophistication to be effective.

This critical importance of software imposes correspondingly strenuous requirements on high end 32-bit or 16-bit microprocessors.

Initially a 32-bit microprocessor must allow the development of highly efficient compilers in order that operating systems and applications may mirror the performance of the microprocessor. The microprocessor must also offer an enhanced feature set to support the requirements of the systems designer. Applications such as financial transaction systems must offer the ability to protect confidential data. Workstations and high end business systems require large logical address space support for each individual program. Finally, in all application areas, the capability to allow the migration of existing software and the upward compatibility with previous microprocessors is of paramount importance.

The powerful instruction set, high performance and flexibility of the Intel 80386 make it a superior choice for a diverse set of execution environments such as central office switching systems, industrial controllers and engineering workstations.

In this chapter we will look in detail at the 80386 32-bit microprocessor, especially its implications for both software writers and systems designers.

## 5.2  Programming model

Following directly from the performance requirements of advanced software, one of the primary objectives in designing the 80386 was to make it an excellent target for code generation. Two important aspects of the machine help achieve this goal. One is the complete

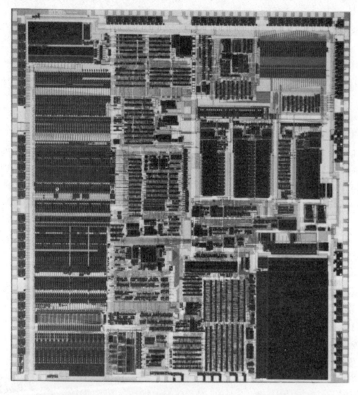

With over 275 000 transistors and a 1.5 μm CHMOS-III process, Intel's 80386 microprocessor combines a 32-bit processor and memory management functions on one chip.

set of 32-bit general purpose registers which may be used, without restriction, either for performing calculations or for forming memory addresses. The other is the rich set of data types that the machine supports.

### 5.2.1 REGISTER SET

The 80386 microprocessor has various on-chip sets of registers to support its advanced features. Figure 5.1 illustrates these register sets.

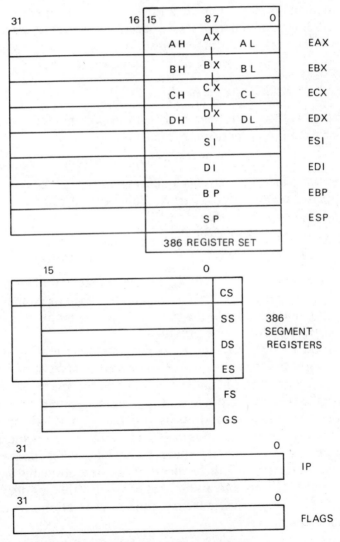

**Fig. 5.1** 80386 base architecture registers.

Eight *general purpose registers* (EAX, EBX, ECX, EDX, ESP, EBP, ESI and EDI) are used to perform calculations and memory addressing; this provides an optimal set of registers to implement all the most commonly used addressing modes, as well as a large set of register variables, without wasting silicon on unnecessary registers. Three *control registers* and the *flags register* control machine behaviour and report the status of various operations. Six additional segment registers (CX, SS, DS, ES, FS and GS) can be used to structure the large 64-terabyte (trillion byte) address space into separate logical spaces called *segments*; each program can then have six logical address spaces mapped at one time, including four separate data spaces. Furthermore, six *debug registers* control the setting of up to four *code or data breakpoints* to provide previously unavailable debug capabilities.

### 5.2.1.1  *Addressing operands*

Probably the simplest method of storing an operand is in a register. For example, to perform the calculation:

$$Power = Voltage \times Current$$

the following instruction sequence might be used, assuming Current is already stored in EBX, Voltage is already stored in ESI, and Power is to be stored in EDI:

```
MOV  EDI, ESI    :    Save Voltage
IMUL EDI, EBX    :    Power = EDI × Current
```

Such a scheme is very effective when register variables are desired (as in C language) from a compiler writer's viewpoint. The orthogonal qualities of the 80386 addressing modes allow multiple register variables to be provided.

Next to a register, the most common source of an operand is memory. In its simplest form, the *effective address*, or byte index, of an operand within a given logical address space can be directly specified in an instruction. However, it is often the case that a particular memory address is not known until the program is actually executing, such as in dynamic array accesses and execution of relocatable code. In these cases, effective addresses can be formed by summing the contents of one or, optionally, two general purpose registers and an optimal constant value, or displacement.

The register based effective address generation scheme can be summarised as:

[Base Register] + [Index Register] * [Scale] + [Displacement]

Here the Base Register is any general purpose register and the Index Register is any general register other than ESP. Since ESP always points to the current stack, it can be easily used for stack relative addressing. The scale specification is a constant value, either 1, 2, 4 or 8, by which the index may be multiplied. The displacement field is also a constant: its value may range anywhere from $-2^{31}$ to $2^{31}-1$. Table 5.1 details the 32-bit addressing modes of the 80386.

Since the base, index and displacement are optional, and the scale is also optional when an index is present, the 80386 offers eleven distinct 32-bit addressing modes. This set of modes includes all the most commonly used modes in advanced high level language compilers. Let us consider the uses of some of these modes.

Assume that parameters are passed to a subroutine by pushing them onto a stack. Then the last parameter could be pushed onto the stack from register EAX by using the base displacement mode, specifying:

MOV DWORD PTR [ESP+4], EAX ; 2 clocks

**Table 5.1** 386 addressing modes

| Base | Index | | | | Displacement |
|------|-------|---|---|---|--------------|
| EAX<br>ECX<br>EDX<br>EBX  +<br>ESP<br>EBP<br>ESI<br>EDI | EAX<br>ECX<br>EDX<br>EBX  *<br>EBP<br>ESI<br>EDI | $\begin{bmatrix}1\\2\\4\\8\end{bmatrix}$ | + | | $\begin{bmatrix}0\\ \text{8-bit displacement}\\ \text{32-bit displacement}\end{bmatrix}$ |

|       |   |       |   |       |   |      | MODE |
|-------|---|-------|---|-------|---|------|------|
|       |   |       |   |       |   | Disp | Displacement-only |
| Base  |   |       |   |       |   |      | Base |
| Base  |   |       |   |       | + | Disp | Base displacement |
|       |   | Index |   |       |   |      | Index |
|       |   | Index | * | Scale |   |      | Scaled index |
|       |   | Index |   |       | + | Disp | Index displacement |
|       |   | Index | * | Scale | + | Disp | Scaled index displacement |
| Base  | + | Index |   |       |   |      | Based index |
| Base  | + | Index | * | Scale |   |      | Based scaled index |
| Base  | + | Index |   |       | + | Disp | Based index displacement |
| Base  | + | Index | * | Scale | + | Disp | Based scaled index displacement |
| Register |   |    |   |       |   |      | Register operand |
| Immediate |  |    |   |       |   |      | Immediate operand |

Similarly, assuming the pointer Next Record is stored in register EAX, the statement:

Next Record = Next Record. Link;

could be translated as:

MOV EAX, DWORD PTR [EAX + LinkOffset] ; 4 clocks

This allows an offset into a structure to be used with no additional overhead. Finally, let us assume that V points to a dynamically allocated integer vector, and that we are to initialise v[i + 2] to the variable stored in EDI, the statement:

MOV DWORD PTR [ESI + EDI * 4 + 8], 5 ; 3 clocks

uses the based scaled index displacement mode and performs the desired initialisation. The use of scaled indexing to generate a byte index into an integer (4 byte) array eliminates the need for another instruction to generate the byte index. Additionally, all 8086 family 16-bit addressing modes are also supported by the 80386 to retain compatibility with the 16-bit members of the 8086 family (i.e. 8086, 8088 and 80286).

Note the total clock counts for each of the instructions. A key reason for the high performance of the 80386 is that effective address formation for a given instruction is started during the last clock of the previous instruction when executing straight line code. Since it takes only one clock to form an effective address in all cases where an index is not specified, the effective address formation time is almost always hidden. And, due to the 80386's on-chip Memory Management Unit (MMU), the effective address formation time includes the logical to physical address translation via the segmentation and paging units. Thus, there is virtually no address generation and translation delay on the 386. The only exception occurs when an index is used. For this case, two clocks are needed for effective address generation, resulting in an effective delay of one clock.

## 5.2.2  DATA TYPES

The support of data types by the 80386 is geared to cover all of the fundamental types to be found in most high level languages. The 80386 allows basic operation over all of these data types. These are illustrated and described in more detail in Fig. 5.2.

| | Ordinal | Integer | BCD | Floating point | String | Bit string |
|---|---|---|---|---|---|---|
| Move<br>To/from memory<br>Convert precision | × | × | 1 | 2 | × | × |
| Arithmetic<br>Add, subtract,<br>multiply, divide,<br>negate | × | × | 1 | 2 | | |
| Logicals<br>And, Or, Xor,<br>shift | × | × | | | | |
| Compare | × | × | 1 | 2 | × | × |
| Transcendentals | | | | 2 | | |

1. ASCII adjust and decimal adjust instructions are provided to implement efficient loops. BCD is supported directly by the 287 and 387 numeric coprocessors.
2. Available directly using the 287 or 387 numeric coprocessors.

**Fig. 5.2**  Instruction set datatype support.

### 5.2.2.1  Ordinal

An ordinal is an unsigned number on the range 0 through 4 294 967 295 ($2^{32} - 1$). As with integers, 32-bit, 16-bit and 8-bit variants of ordinals are available.

### 5.2.2.2  Pointer

A pointer describes a memory address. All pointers have two components: a 16-bit *selector* which names the logical address space, and a 32-bit *effective address*, or *offset*, which specifies the byte index within the logical address space. Since all addresses can be generated using an implied selector, the full 48-bit selector : offset pair can often be abbreviated to the 32-bit offset, which can address a linear 4 gigabyte address space. A compact version features a 16-bit selector and a 16-bit offset, which also supports iAPX86 family software compatibility.

### 5.2.2.3  Integer

An integer is a 2's complement signed number in the range $-2\ 147\ 483\ 648$ through $2\ 147\ 483\ 647$ ($-2^{31}$ to $2^{31} - 1$). For numbers which do not have such a large magnitude, 16-bit and 8-bit signed integers are also supported. An example of an integer operation is the instruction sequence:

IMUL EBX, V[EDX * 4] ; Signed EBX = EBX * V[EDX]

Here, the contents of EBX are multiplied by the EDXth element of the integer array V and the result stored in EBX.

## 5.2.2.4    BCD

Primitives to help construct both packed and unpacked decimal arithmetic operations are supported by the 80386. In addition, the 287 and 387 numerics processors provide direct support for arithmetic on 80-bit packed decimal operations.

Now consider the C program fragment:

```
struct (Present: 1;
        DPL    :   2;
        Seg    :   1;
        ECRA   :   4;
       )accessRights;
regVar  =accessRights.DPL;
```

Assuming regVar is a register variable stored in ESI, this code can be translated directly into 80386 instructions as the sequence:

```
MOV CL, 2                              ; setup field length
MOV EAX, 5                             ; setup field offset
XBTS ESI, accessRights, EAX, CL
```

## 5.2.2.5    *Floating point*

The 386 supports both the 80287 and 80387 numerics coprocessors. These coprocessors extend the data types supported by the 80386 to include 64-bit long integer, 18-digit BCD integer, 32-bit single real, 64-bit double real and 80-bit extended real. The 287 and 387 also make available a comprehensive set of numerics instructions to allow use of these data types.

## 5.2.2.6    *Multi-precision operations*

The 80386 supports 64-bit operations. Integer and ordinal multiply and divide operations are supported with 64-bit products and dividends. Multi-precision add and subtract operations are also easily implemented via the use of the add-with-carry and subtract-with-carry operations of the 80386.

In addition to arithmetic, the 80386 also supports 64-bit shift operators with 32-bit results. This operation is useful for creating high performance loops for processing unaligned memory based operands.

As an example, let us see how to construct a routine to move a bit string from one location to another, as might be desired in a bit-mapped graphics application. Assume here that register ESI

stores a double-word aligned source address, register CL stores
the bit offset to the start of the bit string, and EDI has the address
of the destination address.

```
        LODS    EAX,    [ESI]:    grab 1st word of string, increment src
                                  ptr
        MOV     EDX,    EAX;      EDX = first DWORD
        LODS    EAX,    [ESI];    grab next DWORD of string,
                                  increment src ptr
loop:   SHRD    EAX,    EDX, CL;  align DWORD: EDX = EAX:EDX
                                  shifted by CL bits
        XCHG    EDX,    EAX;      swap EAX with EDX
        STOS    [EDI],  EAX;      Store aligned data, incr EDI
        DEC     EBX     ;         Decrement transfer count
        JA      loop    ;         Repeat loop if count > 0
```

This routine assumes that the destination is double-word aligned.
To allow an arbitrary bit field for the destination, we need only
to move sufficient bits from the source to the destination to align
the destination. After this is done, the code shown above can be
used.

### 5.2.2.7   *Bit fields*

Contiguous sequences of bits up to 31 bits in length can be
fetched/stored from/to a larger bit string, which can be up to 4
gigabits in size, and single-bit values can be tested and modified.
An example of the usage of a bit field is the instruction sequence:

```
waitLp:   LOCK BTS   sema, 2
          JC         waitLp
```

This implements a semaphore by performing an atomic (locked)
test and set on bit 2 of the byte *sema* and waiting until the bit is clear.

### 5.2.3   ADDRESS TRANSLATION

The 80386 provides a mechanism for memory addressing that is
both powerful and comprehensive. The major contributor to this
high level of functionality is provided by the 80386's on-chip
Memory Management Unit (MMU).

Starting at the user program, the addresses manipulated at the
instruction set level are logical addresses. These consist of a selector: offset pair – the selector specifies a logical address space, the

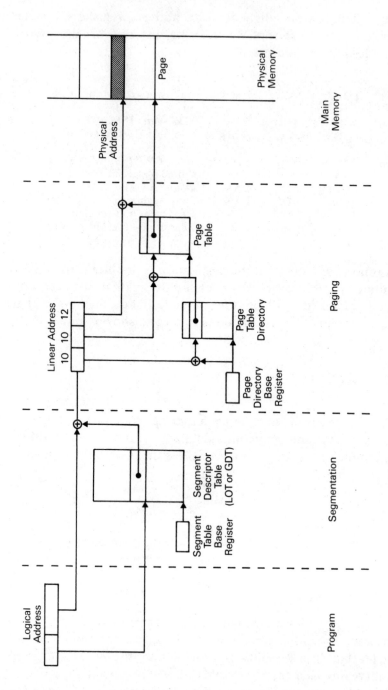

**Fig. 5.3**  Linear to physical address translation.

offset specifies the byte address within the logical address space. Since offsets are 32-bit quantities in the 80386, each logical address space provides 32 bits of linear addressability. The segmentation mechanism of the 80386 performs the table look-up and addition necessary to translate the logical address pair viewed by a program into a linear address.

A linear address space has 32 bits of addressability. This address space is mapped into physical addresses through the paging mechanism of the on-chip MMU. Physical addresses are what actually appear at the pins of the 80386 address bus. Figure 5.3 illustrates the two levels of page tables that are used in the 80386 linear-to-physical address translation. The linear address is divided into three fields: a *page directory table index*, a *page table index* and a *byte index* into a page. The page directory table index is a 10-bit field which selects one of 1024 page tables. The selected page table is then indexed by the (10-bit) page table index, thus pointing at one of 1024 pages. The actual page is a 4096-byte memory block which is finally indexed by the 12-bit byte index. The byte thus located specifies the least significant byte of the operand being addressed.

The entries in the segmentation tables are 64-bit quantities called *segment descriptors*. These descriptors contain the base linear address of a logical address space, or segment, and other information about the address space. The entries in the page directory and page tables are 32-bit quantities called *page descriptors* which store the base physical addresses of pages, along with other information, such as the traditional dirty, accessed and present bits to allow for the implementation of replacement policies in a demand paged system. The information contained in the segment and page descriptors provides many other advanced features that are described in Section 5.3.

Note that the paging mechanism of the 80386 is configurable. If desired, paging need not be used, in which case the address output by the segmentation unit is the physical address.

## 5.3 Operating system model

Now that we have seen the application's view of the 80386, let us take a look at how the 80386 supports the operating systems that manage the application environment. Since operating system capability requirements are becoming more and more sophisticated, operating system support has been given a great deal of attention throughout the development of the 80386. By including many of the features required by an advanced operating system on-chip, the 80386 provides the framework to design fast, simple and standard operating systems. The 80386 operating support is totally transparent to the application view of the machine. The operating system support functions provided on-chip by the 80386 are:

Two level memory management/protection:
● Segmentation system with 4 gigabyte segments.
● Paging system with 4 kbyte pages.
● Hardware enforced segment/page/task isolation and protection.

Multi-tasking support:
● Fast hardware task switch.
● Multiple execution and addressing environment on a per task/per segment basis (dynamic transitions).

### 5.3.1 MEMORY MANAGEMENT

Multi-user/multi-tasking operating systems must provide the means to allocate efficiently system memory to all applications. In addition to allocating memory, the OS must provide a means to isolate and protect each application from all others. Both segmentation and paging can be used to enforce this isolation. The following sections will describe both the address relocation and memory protection features of paging and segmentation.

### 5.3.1.1 *Protected segmentation*

The 80386 implements a descriptor based segmented memory management system. Each task may have many segments defined (up to 16 384 at a time) to describe its logical memory view. The descriptor for each segment, as shown in Fig. 5.4, completely defines the segment. The descriptor is stored in system memory in one of two current descriptor tables available to each task; a

| 31 | | | | | 0 |
|---|---|---|---|---|---|
| +0 | Segment base 15 .. 0 | | | Segment limit 15 .. 0 | |
| +4 | Base 31 .. 24 | Semantic control | Limit 19 .. 16 | Access control | Base 23 .. 16 |

**Fig. 5.4**  Segment descriptor format.

descriptor resides in either the system wide *global descriptor table* (GDT), or the per task *local descriptor table* (LDT). A particular table and descriptor within that table is selected by a segment *selector*, shown in Fig. 5.5.

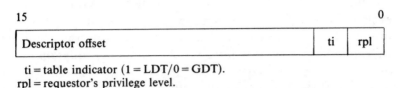

ti = table indicator (1 = LDT/0 = GDT).
rpl = requestor's privilege level.

**Fig. 5.5**   Segment selector format.

The *access control* field of the descriptor provides for many different types of segments to be used. For instance, a read-only data segment can be defined to hold sensitive system configuration data, or an execute-only code segment can be created to ensure that a program will not be corrupted. Other system types are available to improve execution speed, such as the task state segment type. The operating system has the freedom to create segments dynamically as required by the executing applications. In addition to relocation and protection, descriptors provide several *semantic controls* for each segment; this capability is described later. Further, the combination of 16 384 segments per task with the 32-bit offsets of the 80386 provides a logical address space of 64-terabytes for each task.

### 5.3.1.2   Segmented protection

In addition to providing logical-to-linear address translation, the 80386 segmentation mechanism supplies the capability to incorporate various degrees of protection in a system design. Program address integrity is always present in the form of the *base* and *limit* fields of a descriptor. An application generated offset will cause access to the linear address (base + offset). If the offset is greater than the limit of the segment, a protection violation will occur. A semantic control bit, called the *granularity bit* (G-bit), determines the interpretation of the limit field within the descriptor: a value of 0 indicates an absolute limit (byte granular limit), while 1 indicates the segment limit is the limit field * 4 K (page granular limit).

Another 80386 protection capability is program level protection, based on privilege levels. The access control of each segment descriptor contains a *descriptor privilege level* (DPL), which identifies the privilege of the segment. All privileges are in the range of 0–3, with 0 being the most privileged. At any point in time, the 80386 is operating at some *current privilege level* (CPL) which is determined by the privilege level of the executing code segment.

Figure 5.6 illustrates the partitioning of a system into privilege levels. As a rule, when executing at a given privilege level, a program may access segments which are no more privileged than itself. In addition, a program may call upon other programs which are at least as privileged as itself. Interlevel transfers are provided by a special descriptor called a *call gate*, which provides a controlled entry point to more privileged routines.

Figure 5.6 also illustrates the 80386's intertask protection capability. This capability arises from the option to define a separate local descriptor table (LDT) for each task. Using a separate LDT results in a logically isolated address space for each task.

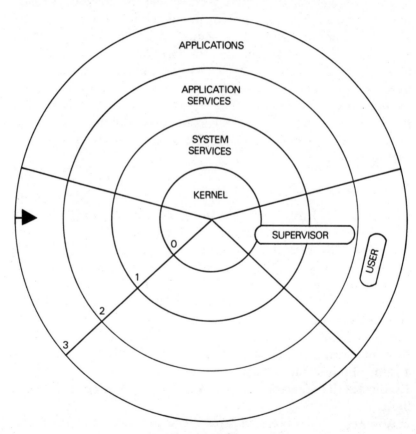

**Fig. 5.6**  Privilege levels.

### 5.3.1.3 Semantic controls

Several other control bits are of interest. The *default size* bit (D-bit) for code segments determines whether 32-bit (D = 1) or 16-bit (D = 0) operations are to be assumed. The *expand down* bit (E-bit) for data segments defines whether a data segment is an expand down or expand up stack (the limit field is also suitably interpreted). Note that all of these semantic controls are changeable from one segment to the next, so it is possible to switch dynamically between 16-bit and 32-bit code. In this manner, the processor conforms to the mode of processing that was selected for each segment and task, allowing easy switches between unchanged 8086 or 80286 code and new 32-bit code.

### 5.3.1.4 Paged memory management

The 80386 incorporates a 2-level page translation mechanism that allows mapping any 4K linear memory address page into any arbitrary 4K physical memory frame. The 2-level page map for the current task is located in memory by a pointer in control register 3 (CR3), or *page directory base register*. All page tables are located on page boundaries for efficient table manipulation. For each page in the logical memory space, a page descriptor is defined (see Fig. 5.7). The page descriptor contains the physical address corresponding to each logical page, as well as other page status information.

To speed the linear-to-physical address translation, the 80386 contains a page descriptor cache, otherwise known as a *translation*

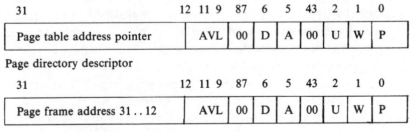

Page directory descriptor

Page table descriptor

AVL = Available for use.
D   = Dirty.
A   = Accessed.
U   = User (1) / supervisor (0).
W   = Writable (1) / read-only (0).
P   = Present.

**Fig. 5.7** Page table and directory descriptors.

*lookaside buffer* (TLB). The TLB's 32 entries result in a greater than 98% hit rate on translations, which means that over 98% of the time the translation has no effect on performance. The 386 TLB is illustrated in Fig. 5.8.

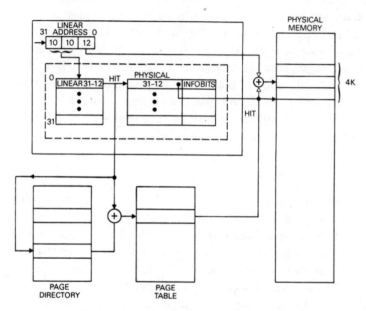

**Fig. 5.8**   Translation lookaside buffer.

Table 5.2 shows the different degrees of protection that can be attributed to each page, which is provided by the *user bit*. The page protection levels map to the segmentation protection levels, with the user level mapping to a CPL of 3 and the supervisor level mapping to CPLs 0 through 2. Also, two status bits are available to track page usage. The *accessed bit* is true if a page or page directory has been accessed by the MMU. The *dirty bit* is true if the page or directory has been written.

The 386's paging support thus provides a powerful base for implementing the key operating system services necessary to support paged virtual memory management: memory page frame allocation, memory page frame replacement, and virtual page storage on secondary memory.

### 5.3.1.5   *Using 80386 memory management*

The flexibility of the 80386's MMU, described above in detail, provides the user with the tools for designing address space architectures directly suited to different applications. Manipulation of

**Table 5.2**   User/supervisor page protection

| Page directory descriptor | | Page frame descriptor | | Access | |
|---|---|---|---|---|---|
| U/S | W/R | U/S | W/R | User | Supervisor |
| 0 | 0 | 0 | 0 | None | Read/write |
| 0 | 0 | 0 | 1 | None | Read/write |
| 0 | 0 | 1 | 0 | None | Read/write |
| 0 | 0 | 1 | 1 | None | Read/write |
| 0 | 1 | 0 | 0 | None | Read/write |
| 0 | 1 | 0 | 1 | None | Read/write |
| 0 | 1 | 1 | 0 | None | Read/write |
| 0 | 1 | 1 | 1 | None | Read/write |
| 1 | 0 | 0 | 0 | None | Read/write |
| 1 | 0 | 0 | 1 | None | Read/write |
| 1 | 0 | 1 | 0 | Read-only | Read/write |
| 1 | 0 | 1 | 1 | Read-only | Read/write |
| 1 | 1 | 0 | 0 | None | Read/write |
| 1 | 1 | 0 | 1 | None | Read/write |
| 1 | 1 | 1 | 0 | Read-only | Read/write |
| 1 | 1 | 1 | 1 | Read/write | Read/write |

the segmentation and paging mechanisms allows the four major address spaces illustrated in Fig. 5.9 to be directly implemented:

● Linear model (effectively no paging or segmentation).
● Paged linear model (paged relocation).
● Segmented and paged model (uses the full power of the 80386).
● Segmented model (paged relocation).

For example, the segmented and paged model is the model used in UNIX* System V. In UNIX System V, each task has a code segment, data segment and stack segment; the 80386's segmentation unit provides the per-task segments, while the paging unit allows effective management of the working set to be kept in main memory.

The segmented model is very useful when segment sizes are not large, and when compatibility with previous iAPX 86 family processors is desired. Additionally, the protection scheme provided by the 80386 segmentation mechanism is very important when system security and/or reliability are desired benefits.

The linear model allows very compact operating systems to be implemented since segmentation and paging can be configured

* UNIX is a trademark of AT&T.

Segmented Model

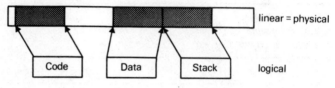

Segmented & Paged Model

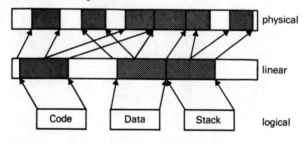

Linear Model

Linear Paged Model

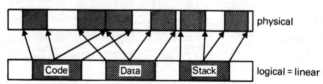

**Fig. 5.9**    80386 address spaces.

out of the system; the program address is the physical address in this model. This is typically the preferred design in many real time applications.

Finally, some designers prefer a completely flat logical architecture with paging used to manage physical memory. The 80386 also provides this memory view in the paged linear model and, since the 80386's paging mechanism is on-chip, the performance of the 80386 is superior to off-chip MMU architecture using this model.

### 5.3.2 MULTI-TASKING AND MULTIPLE ENVIRONMENTS

Recall that one of the special segment types provided on the 80386 is the *task state segment*, or TSS. This segment type is a repository for all task state information, which allows a hardware assist to be used to switch tasks extremely quickly by storing and reloading information from old and new TSSs in one instruction. The 80386 maintains upward compatibility with the 80286's task switch mechanism by providing both 80286 and 80386 TSS format support – 80286 and 80386 formats are different since the 80286 is a 16-bit processor. Additionally, the 80386 TSS includes the state of the page directory base register, allowing a different page map to be used for each task.

### 5.3.3 VIRTUAL 8086 EXECUTION

The 80386 includes a model to emulate the operation of the 8086/8088 processor within its protected virtual mode environment. This capability is controlled by the *virtual mode bit* (VM-bit) in the *flags register*. The most significant attribute of this model is the loading and use of segment registers. In a virtual 8086 code segment, segment register semantics are the same as in the 8086. Thus, unchanged 8086 code (even code that includes the unrecommended practice of using segment registers for temporary storage) can be executed in the protected mode of the 80386. This makes possible the easy leverage of the approximately $4 billion of software that now exists for the 8086/8088.

When in virtual 86 mode, the 80386 looks just like an 8086 to the applications program – the value in the segment selector register is shifted left by 4 bits to compute the actual segment base. As in the 8086, and in the 80286 and 80386 real modes, the size of each segment is 64K. Even though the 80386 is capable of generating offsets greater than 64K, this memory is not accessible. Interrupts cause an automatic switch out of virtual 86 mode, where the operating system interrupt handler can field the interrupt and hand it off to the 8086 program, if appropriate.

Each virtual 8086 code section will generate linear addresses in a 0–1 megabyte address range. In order to provide separate adress spaces for each of these, a separate page directory must be used for each task. The paging mechanism can also be used to simulate the address wrap at 1 megabyte that was on the 8086. And the

80386 protection scheme is still alive and well in virtual 86 mode as programs in virtual 86 mode always execute in the least privileged level, level 3.

### 5.3.4 MULTI-TASKED ENVIRONMENTS

One of the most powerful aspects of the 80386 is realised when the semantic control, flexible address space architecture and multi-tasking assist mechanisms are combined. For example, applications written for each of the following environments could exist as concurrent tasks in the 386 – in fact, there could be multiple instances of each environment executing concurrently:

● Segmented and paged model executing 32-bit Unix System V code and data with 64 terabytes of address space available.
● Segmented and paged model executing 16-bit 80286 object code from previous products based on the 286 – the paging provides physical memory management and is transparent to applications.
● Segmented and paged model executing 8088 object code, such as PC programs, in 16-bit virtual 8086 mode.
● Paged linear model executing 32-bit code ported from linear Unix environments, such as Berkeley 4.2 Unix.

Since all the semantic control bits of the 386 are switched when a task switch is performed, a new environment can be entered with one instruction. With these mechanisms, the systems designer has a high degree of flexibility and power with which to design an optimal system for his application.

In the remaining sections of this chapter we will look in more detail at the hardware subsystems surrounding the 80386, allowing the systems designer the ability to harness the internal power of the 80386.

### 5.4  80386 external bus

The external bus of the 80386 has been optimised to allow efficient access to external memory and I/O. Only two clock cycles are required for the processor to perform a full 32-bit bus access, thus permitting a sustained bus throughput of up to 32 Mbyte/s at 16 MHz. This high speed bus is ideal for use with cache memory to obtain maximum bus bandwidth with cost effective components.

The 80386 has a 32-bit data bus and a 32-bit physical address bus. The instruction set can access data in byte, word or double-word format. If a word or double-word access is not aligned and crosses two double-words on the 32-bit external bus, the 80386 will automatically generate two bus cycles to perform the access.

The 80386 also accommodates slower memory and peripheral subsystems. A READY input to the processor is used to indicate that the bus access has been completed. The external subsystem can hold READY inactive to make the 80386 processor stretch the bus cycle with any number of wait-state clock cycles until the subsystem has completed the access.

Most 32-bit memory systems, regardless of individual processor, require only the upper address bits and use individual-enables for the four lower bytes rather than the two least significant address bits A1 and A0. The 80386, therefore, directly generates the upper address bits (A31:2) and the individual byte-enables instead of the two least significant address bits in order to interface simply and efficiently to memory. The alternative method of generating all 32 address lines along with signals to indicate access size (byte, word or double-word) requires an identical number of processor pins and makes the external interface logic slower and significantly more complex. If, however, the two least significant address bits must be generated, they can easily be decoded from the byte-enables with four gates. Generally the only time the least significant address bits are required is when a standard system bus is used.

One of the most significant considerations in the design of the 80386 bus was the accommodation of a wide variety of peripherals and memory types. In order to simplify the bus interface logic, only one signal is used to indicate the start of a bus cycle (Address Status – ADS), then individual signals are used to indicate write/read (W/R) memory/IO (M/IO), and data/code (D/C). Additionally, the LOCK signal indicates that a critical bus operation is being performed to other bus masters who are consequently not allowed to gain access to the bus while that critical operation is underway. It can be used in multi-processing systems to implement reliably test-and-set semaphores or to access other critical data. LOCK is automatically activated by the 80386 for the exchange instruction (XCHG), during descriptor and page table updates and during interrupt acknowledge cycles. (The programmer can, of course, explicitly activate the LOCK signal during certain instructions.)

Not only are the 80386 bus signals carefully chosen to make interfacing to memory and I/O as simple as possible, but the entire bus is designed to allow very high performance with cost effective memory. Like some other microprocessors, the 80386 uses separate address and data buses (each uses a separate set of pins rather than being multiplexed onto the same pins), which allows the bus to run faster. But the 80386 goes one step further by also externally pipelining the address and data bus. If desired, the address for the next bus cycle can be pipelined. The next address can be output by the 80386 before the current bus cycle has completed. This allows all address output delays and buffer delays to overlap completely the current bus cycle and provides more access time for the memory and I/O systems, without any effect on performance. Therefore, very high bus performance can be obtained from slower and less expensive memory and I/O components.

For maximum flexibility, external hardware has complete control of when and if the next 80386 bus cycle address is pipelined. If the address is non-pipelined (Fig. 5.10), it stays valid through the end of a bus cycle. When the external hardware activates the 80386 next-address pin (NA), the address bus is pipelined (Fig. 5.11), and the address for the next bus cycle becomes available before the current bus cycle ends.

### 5.4.1  SRAM AND CACHE SUBSYSTEMS

Although DRAM memory can be used with very high performance, even higher bus bandwidth can be obtained using static RAMs (SRAMs). At 16 MHz, 55 ns SRAMs are fast enough to complete an access within two clocks without interleaving and without address pipelining. This means that all bus accesses can be completed with zero wait states. The 80386 optimally accommodates these very fast memories by not forcing the address to be pipelined.

In the case when the address of the next bus cycle is not known until after the current cycle has finished (such as indirect jumps or data dependent accesses) or following an idle bus cycle, if the 80386 did force the address to be pipelined one clock before the next bus cycle started, then the access would actually be delayed by a clock. Instead, the 80386 can generate bus cycles either with or without address pipelining. Permitting pipelining is most optimal for slower memories, such as DRAMs, while not forcing pipelining to be used is most optimal for fast memories, such as SRAMs. Unlike other microprocessors, the 80386 is flexible enough to use a simple memory interface that provides all the benefits of both pipelined and non-pipelined address buses.

Therefore, the 80386 does not pipeline the address when it is not available soon enough, and if the memory subsystem can

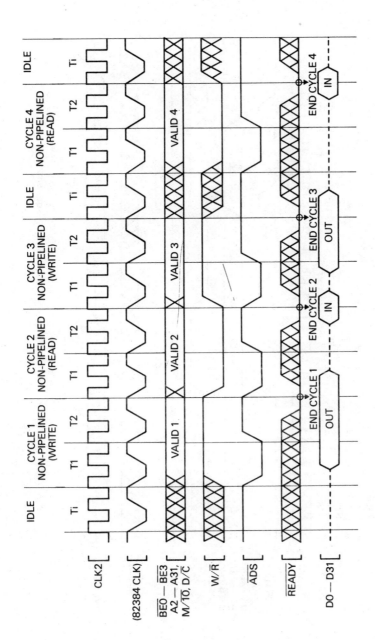

**Fig. 5.10** Bus cycles with non-pipelined address (zero wait states).

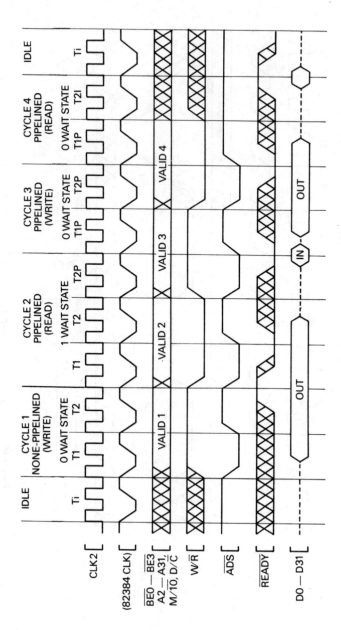

**Fig. 5.11**  80386 bus cycles with and without pipelining and wait states.

complete the access in two clocks, it simply activates $\overline{\text{READY}}$, so no penalty is paid for the lack of a pipelined address.

Although SRAMs provide the highest bus performance, DRAMs can provide much more memory space for much less cost and board space.

A caching system can be used to take advantage of the best features of both. A cache system can be built which allows the most often accessed code and data to be stored in the fast SRAMs, and place less often used code and data to be stored in the slower DRAMs. This lowers overall memory cost while still providing near zero wait state performance.

Figure 5.12 shows a cache subsystem that can complete zero wait state bus cycles with or without a pipelined address. For a 12 MHz system it uses 95 ns data RAMs and 75 ns tag RAMs. For a 16 MHz system it uses 55 ns data RAMs and 35 ns tag RAMs. To keep the cache control simple and cost effective, a direct, 4-byte block, write-through cache is used.

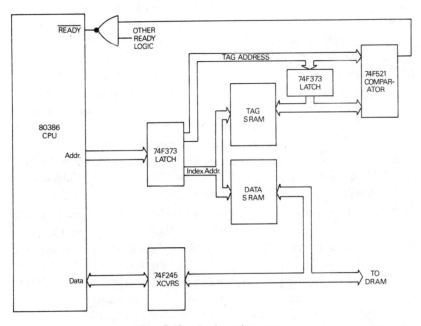

**Fig. 5.12**   Cache subsystem.

With 32 kbytes of cache, this cache will have an approximate hit rate of 86%, which means that 86% of the time the data or code is in the cache and bus accesses require zero wait states. With 64 kbytes of cache the hit rate increases to near 92%.

### 5.4.1.1    Cache effectiveness

In many cases, high performance processor-based designs require a vast amount of high speed memory so that the processor can run large programs or quickly access a vast amount of data. The designer of a high performance system has the challenge of providing this large amount of high speed memory at a reasonable cost.

For maximum performance, a large application on a high speed microprocessor, such as the 16 MHz 80386, may require several megabytes of zero wait state memory (requiring the complete memory access time, including buffer delays and set-up times, to be under 125 ns). While SRAMs can provide the necessary speed, they become prohibitively expensive for most applications when a large amount of memory is required (many of today's applications cannot afford more than 64K of SRAM). At the other end of the spectrum, DRAMs provide large amounts of low cost memory, but today's inexpensive DRAMs are too slow to allow the microprocessor to run without wait states (a typical application today may have several megabytes of 150 ns DRAMs).

The most cost effective solution in many cases is to design a cache memory. A cache memory is simply a high speed memory (typically SRAM) that is placed between the processor and a larger, lower speed memory (typically DRAM). Most computer programs have a habit of reaccessing the same memory locations soon after the first reference to these locations. For the first reference to a location, the processor generally has to wait for the access from the lower speed memory. While the processor is performing this access, the cache also places the data in its memory. Then, when the processor needs to access this same location again, it can simply complete an access to the high speed cache memory. Because the cache memory has less space than the larger low speed memory, the cache cannot possibly contain all the information in the low speed memory. Therefore, when the cache becomes full, and it needs to store the contents of a new memory location, it must replace the contents of an old location with the contents of the new location. The goal of a cache is to keep the locations that the processor will most probably need in the cache so that accesses to these locations can use the fast cache memory rather than the slower DRAM memory.

Most caches keep the most recently used information (code and data) available in high speed memory because most programs exhibit locality of reference, which means the probability is high that this information will again be accessed in the near future. The percentage of the processor accesses that find the information already located in the cache is called the *cache hit rate*.

The hit rate of a cache is a very important indicator of the effectiveness of the cache. The higher the hit rate, the more often the required data or code is found in the cache, and a fast cache access is used instead of a slower low speed memory access. There are many factors that determine the hit rate of a cache, such as the amount of memory in the cache and the method of determining which location should be replaced when the cache is full, but the hit rate indicates the overall effectiveness of the cache.

In nearly all microprocessor caching systems, the low speed DRAM access is not started until after it is determined that the required data or code is not found in the cache, which is usually one or two clocks after the bus cycle started. Therefore, when the data or code is not found in the cache and a DRAM cycle is required, the DRAM cycle actually takes longer than if no cache has been used, because it started later. If the hit rate is low enough, meaning cache misses are prevalent, then use of a cache can actually decrease overall performance. A cache with a hit rate of under 50-60% is of very questionable value. Caches less than 4 K in size are not generally useful.

Not only does a low hit rate indicate that a cache is relatively ineffective, but a cache with a very low hit rate can actually degrade performance. The most cost effective way to increase hit rate is to increase the size of the cache. Therefore, rather than including a limited cache on-chip, the 80386 bus supports an external 2-clock cache, whose size and hit rate, and thus overall effectiveness, can be made as large as desired.

The fast 80386 bus allows external memory references to be made in the same number of clocks as other microprocessors require to access on-chip caches.

While current silicon technology prevents useful general purpose caches to be placed on the processor chip, relatively small on-chip MMU caches can be very effective. The 80386 caches both segment and page descriptors. By placing a 32-entry TLB (translation lookaside buffer) page descriptor cache on the 80386, a hit rate of over 98% has been achieved.

## 5.5 Peripherals

The 80386 bus structure has been simplified, minimising the logic connect overhead for the interface to common peripherals and ROM/EPROMs. Discrete logic, PALS or gate arrays can be configured as efficient, customised interfaces to the specific set of peripherals required.

The 80386 has an input called Bus Size 16 Bit (BS16) which simplifies the use of the processor on either a 32-bit or a 16-bit bus. This allows control of the external bus width for the current bus cycle. When active, only the lower 16 data pins are used (D15:0) and unaligned or 32-bit accesses are broken up into multiple 16-bit word accesses. When BS16 is inactive, the 80386 uses its full 32-bit data bus (D31:0) to perform byte, word or double-word accesses. (Because the 80386 has instructions to perform byte, word and double-word accesses, 8-, 16- and 32-bit peripherals can be connected directly to the local bus.)

This 16-bit bus capability reduces system cost and consumes less local bus interconnect, giving the additional advantage of placing peripherals at 16-bit word boundaries to duplicate the I/O address used in other 16-bit systems offering software compatibility with 8086 and 80286 systems.

A bus cycle that uses only the lower two data bus bytes (cycle with BE2 and BE3 inactive) always uses only D15:0 and, therefore, BS16 is ignored. A Read bus cycle with BE0 and BE1 inactive would normally use D31:16 to read the data, but if BS16 is active the data is read from D15:0. A Write cycle with BE0 and BE1 inactive will always duplicate the write data on D31:16 onto D15:0 so that either 16 bits may be utilised by the hardware and BS16 is again ignored by the 80386. All remaining accesses are automatically converted by the 80386 into two bus cycles. This facilitates direct connection of external 16-bit buses to D15:0. The 80386 will perform both 16-bit and 32-bit accesses without wasted cycles in either case.

## 5.6 Direct memory access

The move data between the RAM and peripherals it is possible to interrupt the processor, have it save its state, perform the transfer and then restore the processor state. However, it is much more efficient to move large amounts of sequential data with a controller optimised for the task, a *direct memory access* (DMA) controller, so as to not disturb the processor's execution. The 80386 provides hold (HOLD) and hold acknowledge (HLDA) pins which permit a DMA controller or another processor to tri-state the 80386 bus signals and take over the bus to perform such transfers.

A very common use of DMA is to perform transfers between memory and mass storage, such as in the swapping of virtual memory.

The 80386 permits segments of various sizes, from one byte up to $2^{32}$ (4 gigabytes), which is quite sufficient for nearly any code or data structure. With a possibility of such large segments, it is very easy for the programmer to place his data and code into segments, but it would often be very difficult, if not impossible, for the operating system implementing virtual memory to find space in physical RAM to swap in the entire segment. Therefore, the 80386 also implements paging underneath segmentation. If it is used, a segment can be split up into several regularly sized pages, possibly with each page corresponding to the size of a block of mass storage. This not only allows portions of segments to reside in RAM, but also permits segments to be split up into several parts to fit into any free, but not necessarily contiguous, RAM and eliminates memory fragmentation problems.

While segmentation allows the software programmer to place his code and data into natural and efficient structures and provides the operating system with valuable information on which portions of memory are good candidates for swapping, paging underneath segmentation allows efficient hardware implementation of virtual memory.

In implementing a demand paged system, a standard DMA controller can be used to move one or more sequential blocks (pages) of data between the RAM and mass storage. After each series of sequential blocks is moved, the DMA controller normally interrupts the processor and waits for further commands from the processor.

If several blocks are being moved into several non-sequential pages, the DMA must stop after each page and interrupt the processor. The processor must then send new commands to the DMA controller for the next page. This will decrease the processor performance because the processor must stop and handle an interrupt after each page. Also, the overall data transfer from mass storage transfer may be slower. Mass storage is usually implemented as a spinning disk in which sequential blocks pass under the read/write head. If there is not enough time between the end of one page and the beginning of the next for the DMA to interrupt the processor and the processor to reprogram the DMA, then the next page will be missed and the DMA will have to wait for the disk to go around again before transferring the next page.

The Intel 82258 Advanced DMA controller chip can be used to solve both these problems: fewer interrupts to the processor and quicker multi-page transfers. The processor can generate a list of source of destination blocks for the DMA, for example, to swap a series of non-contiguous pages. Then the 82258 can use its data chaining feature automatically to swap all the pages, without interrupting the processor and without reprogramming the 82258 between each non-contiguous page. Therefore, the 82258 provides excellent performance in a demand paged environment.

### 5.7 Design example: engineering workstation

An engineering workstation typically requires high computational power and a very large memory space to perform such tasks as design simulation and verification. In addition, the ability to run multiple programs at the same time allows the designer to maximise his effectiveness because he can work on one part of the design while simulating another part in the background. In many cases, the ability of the workstation quickly to create and manipulate detailed graphical pictures of the design is also essential to allow the designer to enter and view his work efficiently. Finally, because most designers work in teams rather than individually, it is important that their workstations can easily communicate with each other.

Figure 5.13 illustrates a complete 80386 system design which meets all these needs. Its fast processing speed and large physical and virtual address space allow large simulations to be performed efficiently. For high performance with large amounts of cost effective DRAM, a cache is used to allow near zero wait state operation. The 80386 segmentation and paging capabilities, together with 82258 advanced DMA and the intelligent fixed disk controller (82062), combine to form a powerful and efficient implementation of virtual memory. The 80386 on-chip memory management not only provides efficient translations for virtual memory, but also offers protection and multi-tasking capabilities.

While the computational speed and flexibility of the 80386 allows it to perform all the calculation, graphics and communication functions for some workstations, even greater performance can be

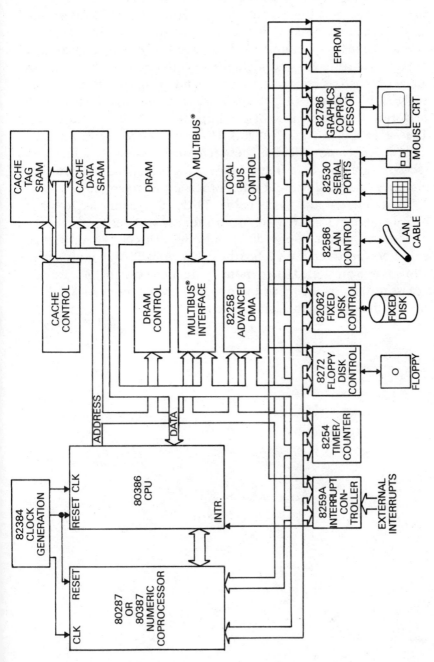

**Fig. 5.13** Engineering workstation.

obtained when specialised coprocessors are used. The 80287 or 80387 Numeric Processor can be used to provide fast floating point arithmetic, allowing complex and accurate simulations to complete quickly. Intel's upcoming 82786 Graphics/Display coprocessor can quickly generate and manipulate complex text and graphics images as well as create an efficient windowing environment. The 80386 simply supplies high level graphics commands and the 82786 performs the tedious task of pixel updates and display functions. The 82586 Local Area Network (LAN) coprocessor can handle high speed communication between workstations: sending and receiving multiple data frames, generating protocols, and performing error checking without microprocessor intervention.

To round out the system, the 80386 also connects to slave peripherals including two serial ports for the keyboard and a mouse or modem, and a floppy disk controller. This 80386 subsystem could be constructed on a board with a MULTIBUS interface to allow it to be installed in an industry standard system and provide access to the processors and peripheral devices on other MULTI-BUS boards within the same system.

# CHAPTER 6
# The Motorola 68020

CYNDY ZOCH
*Motorola Inc., USA*

## 6.1 Introduction

The MC68020 is the first 32-bit microprocessor based on Motorola's M68000 family. It is implemented with 32-bit registers and data paths, 32-bit addresses, a rich instruction set, and versatile addressing modes.

The MC68020 is object code compatible with the other members of the M68000 family (the MC68000, MC68008, MC68010 and the MC68012). It has the added features of an on-chip instruction cache, high level language support via new addressing modes, and a flexible coprocessor interface. In addition, the MC68020 supports a dynamic bus sizing mechanism that allows it to determine port size on a cycle-by-cycle basis.

This chapter will first cover the processing technology and the architecture of the MC68020, followed by a discussion on data organisation. Next, the addressing capabilities, instruction set and hardware signals will be examined. Then, some of the special features of the MC68020 will be detailed, including the dynamic bus sizing mechanism, the on-chip instruction cache, and the coprocessor interface. The next three sections will cover memory management, development system support, and software support. Finally, the chapter will close with a look at performance.

## 6.2 Processing

The MC68020 is a product of 60 man-years of design effort. The processor is manufactured using a High-density Complementary Metal Oxide Semiconductor (HCMOS) process which provides

*32-Bit Microprocessors*

an important combination of high speed performance and low power consumption. More specifically, the MC68020 runs at a clock speed of 16.67 MHz and has a maximum power dissipation of 1.75 W. The processor consists of 200 000 actual transistors in a die 0.375 × 0.350 in and is packaged in a 114-pin grid array.

### 6.3 Architecture

Figure 6.1 shows a functional block diagram of the MC68020. The processor can be divided into three main sections: the bus control-

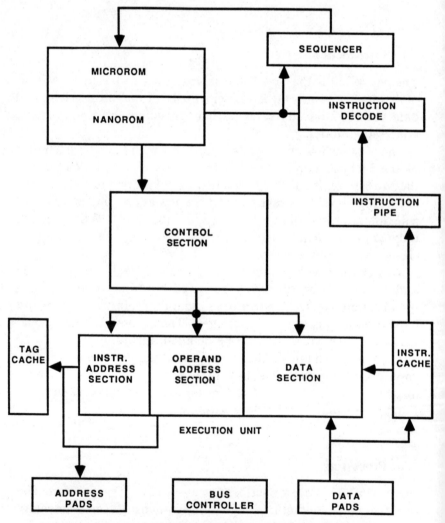

**Fig. 6.1** MC68020 functional block diagram.

ler, the micromachine, and the miscellaneous area. These major sections operate in a completely autonomous fashion.

The bus controller comprises the address and data pads and the multiplexors necessary for dynamic bus sizing support. In addition, the bus controller contains the instruction cache and associated control circuitry, a macro bus controller and two micro bus controllers. The macro bus controller schedules bus cycles on a priority basis, while the two micro bus controllers control the bus cycles; one for instruction accesses and the other for operand accesses.

The micromachine consists of an instruction pipe, decode PLAs, ROM control store, an execution unit, and miscellaneous control stores. The execution unit contains an instruction address section, an operand address section, and a data section. The ROM control store comprises the microrom and the nanorom, which provide microcode control. The decode PLAs are used to provide the information necessary to sequence through the microcode. The instruction pipe consists of three stages (see Fig. 6.2) and provides for decode of instructions. Instructions that have been prefetched from either the on-chip cache or from external memory are loaded into stage B. The instructions are then sequenced from stage B to stage D. Stage D contains a fully decoded instruction ready for execution. If the instruction had contained an extension word, it would be available in stage C at the time the op code would be in stage D.

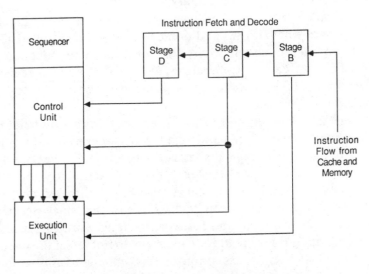

**Fig. 6.2** MC68020 pipeline.

## 6.4  Data organisation

### 6.4.1  OPERANDS

The MC68020 supports seven basic data types: bits, bit fields, BCD digits, byte integers, word integers, long word integers, and quad word integers. A bit field consists of from 1 to 32 bits, a byte is 8 bits, a word is 16 bits, a long word is 32 bits and a quad word is 64 bits wide. In addition, the MC68020 supports variable byte length operands necessary for the coprocessor interface (i.e. co-processors can define operand lengths required for its particular application).

### 6.4.2  PROGRAMMING MODEL

As with the other processors in the M68000 family, the MC68020 operates in one of two modes – user or supervisor. The user mode is intended to provide an environment for application programs. The supervisor mode has access to additional instructions, registers and privileges and is intended to be used by the operating system.

The user and supervisor programming models for the MC68020 are shown in Fig. 6.3(a) and (b) respectively. The user programming model features eight 32-bit data registers, eight 32-bit address registers, one of which (A7) is used as the user stack pointer, a 32-bit program counter, and an 8-bit condition code register. In addition to the above registers, the supervisor programming model also includes two 32-bit supervisory stack pointers (one called *master* and the other called *interrupt*), a 16-bit status register (the low byte of which is the condition code register mentioned above), a 32-bit vector base register, two 3-bit alternate function code registers, a cache control register, and a cache address register. A description of each of these registers is given in the following paragraphs.

The eight data registers (D0–D7) are used for bit, bit field, BCD, byte, word, long word, and quad word operations. In general, operations on data registers affect the condition codes, but do not cause the result in the register to be sign extended to the full 32 bits. The seven address registers (A0–A6) and the user, master and interrupt stack pointers can be used as software stack pointers, as base address registers and for word or long word operations. In general, operations on address registers do not affect the condition codes (CMPA is an exception to this statement) and cause the result to be sign extended to the full 32 bits. In addition, both data

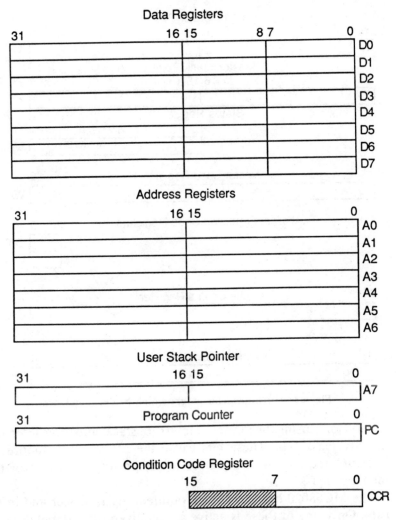

**Fig. 6.3** (a) User programming model.

and address registers (D0–D7 and A0–A7) can be used as index registers.

The status register (SR) contains two bytes: the user byte (condition code register) and the system byte. The system byte is accessible only in the supervisor mode. The user byte contains bits for the following conditions: extend (X), negative (N), zero (Z), overflow (V), and carry (C). The system byte has two trace mode bits that allow tracing on every instruction or only on change of program flow, an S bit that indicates whether the processor is in the user or supervisor mode, an M bit that indicates whether the

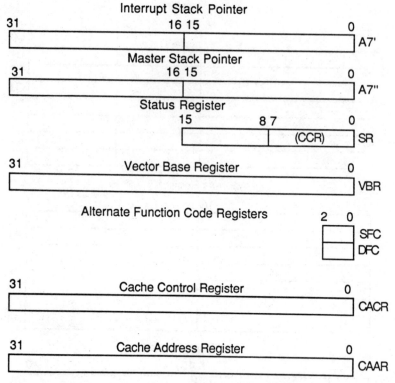

**Fig. 6.3**   (b) Supervisor programming model supplement.

supervisor is using the master or interrupt stack, and three interrupt priority mask bits. These bits cause the MC68020 to ignore all interrupt requests with equal or lower priority than that of the interrupt mask.

The MC68020 has three stack pointers: user, master and interrupt. Only one of these is active at any given time, depending on the state of the M and S bits in the status register. The user stack pointer (USP) operates in the same way in the MC68020 as it does for other M68000 family processors. It is active only when the S bit in the status register is cleared. If both the S bit and M bit are set to 1, the master stack pointer (MSP) is the active stack. If the S bit is set to 1 and the M bit is cleared, the interrupt stack pointer (ISP) is the active stack. This final scenario corresponds to the supervisor mode in the MC68000, MC68008, MC68010 and MC68012. The master and interrupt stacks interact with each other during interrupts. If both the M and S bits in the status register are set (master stack operation) and an interrupt is recognised, the exception vector offset, program counter, and the status register

Bit Data

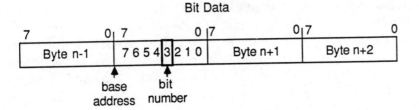

Bit Field Data  base bit

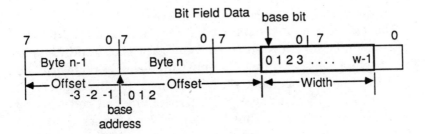

Byte Integer Data

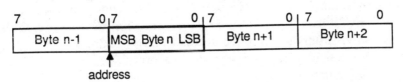

Word Integer Data

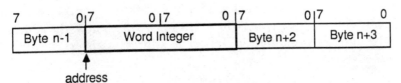

**Fig. 6.3** (b) cont.

are saved on the master stack. In addition, the M bit will be cleared and a copy of this stack frame (called a *throwaway stack frame*) is created on the interrupt stack. If any other interrupts occur while processing this interrupt, the corresponding state information will be stacked only on the interrupt stack. Thus, the two stack pointers work very well in multi-tasking environments. Each task can have its own master stack pointer and exceptions that apply only to that task stacked there. If an interrupt occurs, the information is stacked on both the master stack and the interrupt stack because it may apply to both the task and the operating system (as in the case of a task switch). The information for interrupts that occur while processing this interrupt would be stacked only on the interrupt stack because it would apply only to the operating system.

The vector base register (VBR) contains the base address of the 1 kbyte exception vector table and is used to relocate the vector table anywhere within the 4 gigabyte address space of the MC68020. As a result, the MC68020 supports multiple vector tables such as might be required in a multi-tasking environment. Upon reset, the vector base register is set to zero.

The two alternate function code registers (source, SFC and destination DFC) allow the supervisor to access any address space (see Section 6.4.4) and are used only with the MOVES instruction. In some earlier members of the M68000 family, namely the MC68000 and the MC68008, the alternate function code registers were not implemented. Thus, all supervisor accesses were made to either supervisor program or data space. When a MOVES instruction is executed on the MC68020, the contents of the alternate function code registers are put on the function code lines (FC0–FC2) for either the source or destination operand. This allows the supervisor to have access to other address spaces. The MOVES instruction is privileged, thus prohibiting the user from accessing supervisor space.

The two cache registers (control, CACR and address, CAAR) are provided to allow software manipulation of the on-chip instruction cache. The cache control register contains bits for clearing the cache, freezing the cache, enabling the cache, and clearing a specific entry in the cache. When clearing a cache entry, the address of the entry is contained in the cache address register.

### 6.4.3  MEMORY ORGANISATION

As with all members of the M68000 family, memory for the MC68020 is organised so that the lower addresses correspond to the higher order bytes. For example, the address N of a long word is also the address of the most significant byte of the higher order word. Thus, the address of the least significant byte of the lower order word is N+3.

Figure 6.4 shows how the data types supported by the MC68020 are organised in memory. These data types can be accessed on any byte boundary. The MC68020 does not require that data operands be on even byte boundaries. This feature is called *mis-*

Long Word Integer Data

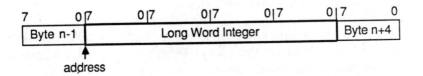

Packed Binary-Coded Data

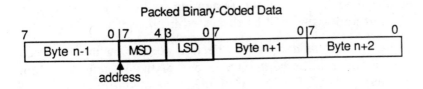

Unpacked Binary-Coded Data

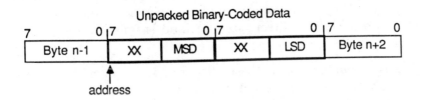

XX = User-Defined Value

**Fig. 6.4** Memory data organisation.

*alignment* and will be discussed in Section 6.8. However, maximum performance is achieved whenever data is aligned to the same byte boundary as its operand size. Instructions are not allowed to be misaligned. All instructions must always be aligned to even byte boundaries. The MC68020 forces an address error exception any time the program counter contains an odd address.

### 6.4.4 PROGRAM AND DATA REFERENCES

Memory is divided into two classes in the MC68020: program and data. Program references are references to that part of memory that contains instructions. Data references are references to that part of memory that contains data. In general, operand reads are from the data space and all operand writes are to the data space, except when caused by the MOVES (move address space) instruction.

## 6.5   Addressing capabilities

### 6.5.1   EFFECTIVE ADDRESSING MODES

The location of an operand used in the execution of an instruction can be specified in one of three ways. First, the location (or address) can be contained in a register. Second, the instruction, by definition, can imply the use of a specific register that contains the location of the operand. Third, the address of the operand can be specified by one of the remaining addressing modes. These types of addressing will be discussed in this section.

*Register direct modes.* These effective addressing modes specify that the operand is contained in one of the 16 general purpose registers (A0–A7, D0–D7) or in one of the 6 control registers (SR, VBR, SFC, DFC, CACR and CAAR).

Data register direct – the operand is found in the data register specified by the register field of the operation word.
Address register direct – the operand is found in the address register specified by the register field.

*Register indirect modes.* These effective addressing modes specify that the operand is located at a memory address based on the contents of an address register.

Address register indirect – the address of the operand is contained in the address register specified by the register field.
Address register indirect with postincrement – the address of the operand is contained in the address register specified by the register field. The contents of the address register are then incremented by 1, 2 or 4 depending on whether the operand size is a byte, word or long word. An exception to this is when the address register is the stack pointer and the operand size is a byte. In this case, the stack pointer will be incremented by two to keep the stack pointer aligned on an even byte boundary.
Address register indirect with predecrement – the address register specified by the register field is first decremented by 1, 2 or 4 depending on the size of the operand. This decremented value is then used as the address of the operand. Stacks are handled as in the previous paragraph with decrement substituted for increment.
Address register indirect with displacement – the address of the operand is the sum of the contents of the address register

specified by the register field and a sign extended 16-bit displacement. This displacement is contained in an extension word following the op word.

*Register indirect with index modes.* These addressing modes specify that the address of the operand is derived from a calculation involving an address register, an index register and a displacement. The format of the index operand is 'Xn.SIZE*SCALE'. Xn can be any data or address register. SIZE specifies the index size and can be either word or long word. SCALE allows the contents of the index register to be multiplied by 1, 2, 4 or 8. Index operands and displacements are always sign extended to 32 bits before being used in the calculation.

Address register indirect with index (8-bit displacement) – the address of the operand is the sum of the contents of the address register specified by the register field, the sign extended contents of the index register (sized and scaled), and a sign extended 8-bit displacement. This mode requires one word of extension that specifies the index register and the 8-bit displacement.
Address register indirect with index (base displacement) – the address of the operand is the sum of the contents of the address register specified by the register field, the sign extended contents of an index register, and a sign extended 16- or 32-bit displacement. Note that with this addressing mode, a 'data register indirect' addressing mode can be obtained by using a data register as the index register and not specifying an address register.

*Memory indirect addressing modes.* These addressing modes use four user-specified values in determining the value of the operand. They are: an address register to be used as a base register; a base displacement, which is added to the base register; an index register; and an outer displacement that is added to the address operand. These addressing modes call for intermediate addresses to be fetched from memory before continuing with the effective address calculation. The index operand can be added in after the intermediate address fetch (post-indexed) or before the intermediate address fetch (pre-indexed).

All four user-specified values are optional. The base and outer displacements may be null, word or long word values. If a displacement is null (or an element is suppressed), its value is taken as zero in the effective address calculation.

Memory indirect post-indexed – an intermediate indirect memory address is calculated by adding together the base register and the base displacement. This address is used for an indirect memory access of a long word. This long word is then added to the index operand (Xn.SIZE*SCALE) and the outer displacement, if any, to yield the effective address.

Memory indirect pre-indexed – the index operand (XN.SIZE*SCALE) is added to the base register and the base displacement. This intermediate sum is then used for an indirect access of a long word. The outer displacement, if any, is then added to this long word to yield the effective address.

*Program counter indirect with displacement mode.* The address of the operand is the sum of the address in the program counter (PC) and a sign extended 16-bit displacement. The displacement is contained in an extension word following the op code. The value in the program counter is the address of the extension word. All references that use this addressing mode are classified as program references.

*Program counter indirect with index modes.* These addressing modes are analogous to the register indirect with index modes described earlier, with the PC used as the base register. As before, the index operand (sized and scaled) and a displacement are used in the calculation of the effective address. Once again, displacements and index operands are always sign extended to 32 bits prior to being used in the effective address calculation.

PC indirect with index (8-bit displacement) – the address of the operand is the sum of the address in the program counter, the sign extended integer in the lower order 8 bits of the extension word, and the sized and scaled index operand. The value in the PC is the address of the extension word. The user must specify the displacement, the PC and the index register when using this addressing mode.

PC indirect with index (base displacement) – the address of the operand is the sum of the address in the program counter, the sized and scaled contents of the index register, and the sign extended base displacement. This addressing mode requires additional extension words that contain the index register indication and the 16- or 32-bit displacement. All three parameters are optional in this mode.

*Program counter memory indirect modes.* These addressing modes are analogous to the memory indirect addressing modes described earlier, with the program counter being used as the base register. The intermediate memory access can be either post-indexed or pre-indexed. All four user-specified values are optional.

Program counter memory indirect post-indexed – an intermediate indirect memory address is calculated by adding the PC (used as a base register) and a base displacement. This address is used for an indirect access of a long word, followed by the addition of the index operand (sized and scaled) with the fetched address. Finally, the outer displacement, if any, is added to yield the final effective address.

Program counter memory indirect pre-indexed – the sized and scaled index operand is added to the program counter and the base displacement. This sum is used for an indirect access of a long word. The outer displacement, if any, is then added to yield the final effective address.

*Absolute address modes.* These addressing modes specify the address of the operand in the extension words.

Absolute short address – the address of the operand is contained in the extension word. The 16-bit address is sign extended to 32 bits before it is used. This mode requires one word of extension.

Absolute long address – this addressing mode requires two words of extension. The address of the operand is obtained by the concatenation of the extension words. The first extension word contains the higher order part of the address and the second extension word contains the lower order part.

*Immediate data.* This addressing mode requires one or two words of extension, depending on the size of the operation.

Byte operation – operand is in the lower order byte of the extension word.

Word operation – operand is in the extension word.

Long word operation – operand is in two extension words; high order 16 bits are in the first extension word; low order 16 bits are in the second extension word.

### 6.6   Instruction set summary

This section contains an overview of the MC68020 instruction set.

The instructions can be categorised as follows:

| | |
|---|---|
| Data movement | Bit field manipulation |
| Integer arithmetic | Binary coded decimal arithmetic |
| Logical | Program control |
| Shift and rotate | System control |
| Bit manipulation | Multiprocessor control |

The following paragraphs describe the MC68020 instruction set by categories.

### 6.6.1 DATA MOVEMENT

The basic means of accomplishing address and data transfer and storage is through the move (MOVE) instruction. Data movement instructions allow byte, word and long word operands to be transferred from memory to memory, memory to register, register to memory, and register to register. Address movement instructions (MOVE and MOVEA) allow word and long word operand transfers on legal address boundaries. In addition to the move instruction, there are several special data movement instructions: move multiple registers (MOVEM), move peripheral data (MOVEP), move quick (MOVEQ), exchange registers (EXG), load effective address (LEA), push effective address (PEA), link stack (LINK), and unlink stack (UNLK).

### 6.6.2 INTEGER ARITHMETIC OPERATIONS

The integer arithmetic instructions consist of the four basic operations of add (ADD), subtract (SUB), multiply (MULT) and divide (DIV) as well as clear (CLR), negate (NEG) and arithmetic compare (CMP, CMPM). Both data and address operations can be performed with the ADD, SUB and CMP instructions. Address operations are limited to legal address size operands (16 or 32 bits), while data operands can accept all operand sizes. The CLR and NEG instructions may be used on all data operand sizes.

The MC68020 has a multiply and divide instruction for both signed and unsigned integers. Multiplying word size operands results in a long word product and multiplying long word operands results in either a long word or quad word product. A long word dividend with a word divisor produces a word quotient with a word remainder, and a long word or a quad word dividend with a long word divisor produces a long word quotient with a long word remainder.

The MC68020 has a set of extended instructions to accomplish multi-precision and mixed size arithmetic operations. They are: add extended (ADDX), subtract extended (SUBX), sign extend (EXT) and negate binary with extend (NEGX).

### 6.6.3 LOGICAL OPERATIONS

The logical operation instructions include AND (AND), inclusive OR (OR), exclusive OR (EOR), and one's complement (NOT). These instructions may be used with all sizes of data operands. A similar set of immediate instructions (ANDI, ORI and EORI) performs the logical operations on all sizes of immediate data. The test instruction (TST) arithmetically compares the operand with zero. The result is reflected in the condition codes.

### 6.6.4 SHIFT AND ROTATE OPERATIONS

The MC68020 can perform shifts in both directions via the arithmetic shift (ASL and ASR) and the logical shift (LSL and LSR) instructions. In addition, the processor also has four rotate instructions (with and without extend): ROR, ROL, ROXR and ROXL.

All shift and rotate instructions can be performed on either a data register or memory. Register shifts and rotates support all operand sizes and allow a shift count to be specified in the instruction operation word or in another register. Memory shifts and rotates operate on word operands only and allow only single-bit shifts and rotates.

The last instruction in the shift and rotate category is the swap register halves instruction (SWAP). This instruction exchanges the upper and lower words of a data register.

### 6.6.5 BIT MANIPULATION OPERATIONS

The bit manipulation instructions are bit test (BTST), bit test and change (BCHG), bit test and clear (BCLR), and bit test and set (BSET). All bit manipulation instructions can be performed on either a data register or memory with the bit number being specified in either the immediate field of the instruction or in a data register. Register operands are always 32 bits wide while memory operands are 8 bits wide.

### 6.6.6 BIT FIELD OPERATIONS

The bit field instructions include four that are analogous to the bit manipulation instructions discussed in the previous section, namely, bit field test (BFTST), bit field test and change (BFCHG), bit field test and clear (BFCLR), and bit field test and set (BFSET). In addition, there is a bit field insert instruction (BFINS) that inserts a value in a bit field; bit field extract, signed and unsigned (BFEXTS and BFEXTU), which extracts a value from a bit field; and bit field find first one (BFFFO) which finds the first bit that has been set in a bit field. These instructions operate on bit fields of variable length up to 32 bits.

### 6.6.7 BINARY CODED DECIMAL OPERATIONS

Multi-precision arithmetic operations on binary coded decimal (BCD) numbers are accomplished through the following instructions: add decimal with extend (ABCD), subtract decimal with extend (SBCD), and negate decimal with extend (NBCD). The pack (PACK) and unpack (UNPK) instructions are used for conversion of byte encoded numeric data, such as ASCII or EBCDIC strings, to BCD and *vice versa*.

### 6.6.8 PROGRAM CONTROL OPERATIONS

Program control operations are accomplished using a set of conditional and unconditional branch instructions and return instructions. The conditions on which a branch can occur are:

| | |
|---|---|
| carry clear | low or same |
| carry set | less than |
| equal | minus |
| never true | not equal |
| greater or equal | plus |
| greater than | always true |
| high | overflow clear |
| less or equal | overflow set |

In addition, this category includes branch always (BRA), branch to subroutine (BSR), call module (CALLM), jump (JMP), jump to subroutine (JSR), return and deallocate parameters (RTD), return from module (RTM), return and restore condition codes (RTR), and return from subroutine (RTS).

### 6.6.9 SYSTEM CONTROL OPERATIONS

System control operations are accomplished via privileged instructions, trap generating instructions, and instructions that use or explicitly modify the condition code register. The privileged instructions perform ANDing, exclusive ORing, and ORing of immediate data to the status register (ANDI, EORI and ORI, respectively) as well as moving information to and from the status register, the user stack pointer and the control registers. Another version of the MOVE instruction, MOVES, uses the source and destination function code registers to determine which address space to move data into or out of. Other privileged instructions are RESET (which causes the RESET* line to assert), RTE (return from exception), and STOP (which causes the MC68020 to stop processing information). Included in the trap generating instruction category are the BKPT (breakpoint), CHK (check), CHK2 (check 2), ILLEGAL, TRAP, TRAPcc, and TRAPV. The BKPT instruction causes the MC68020 to execute a breakpoint acknowledge cycle, during which the processor latches data bits D31 through D24 and uses that value as the op word. The CHK and CHK2 instructions compare a register value against some specified upper and/or lower bounds and either generates an exception or continues instruction execution based on the results of the compare. The ILLEGAL and TRAP instructions force the MC68020 to generate an illegal instruction exception or a trap exception, respectively. TRAPcc and TRAPV cause the MC68020 to take a trap if the condition is true (TRAPcc) or if an underflow occurred (TRAPV). The instructions affecting the condition code register are ANDI, EORI, ORI and MOVE. The first three instructions either AND, exclusive OR, or OR immediate data with the condition code register, while the last instruction moves data into and out of the register.

### 6.6.10 MULTIPROCESSOR CONTROL OPERATIONS

Multiprocessor support is provided in the MC68020 via the TAS, CAS and CAS2 instructions. These three instructions execute indivisible read–modify–write bus cycles. To indicate this to the external world, the RMC* signal is asserted throughout the execution of the instruction (see Section 6.7).

The test and set (TAS) instruction is used to support semaphore operations. It first reads a byte from memory and checks the most significant bit of that operand, setting the condition codes accordingly. Then it sets the most significant bit of that byte in memory, regardless of its previous state. The program can then execute a conditional branch based on the state of the conditon codes. If the bit has been set previously, this indicates that another processor owns that semaphore and this processor must wait before it can attempt to use the resource associated with that semaphore. If the bit has been cleared then the processor executing the TAS instruction has already claimed ownership by setting the most significant bit. The compare and swap (CAS and CAS2) instructions are used to update system counters, history information and globally shared pointers. Three operands are defined within the CAS instruction: the effective address of the operand, the compare register and the update register. The operand specified by the effective address is first read and compared to the value in the compare register. If the values are equal, then the value contained in the update register is written to the effective address. If the values are not equal, then the operand value is loaded into the compare register. The CAS2 instruction works in exactly the same way, except that it uses two sets of three operands each. This instruction is handy for manipulating doubly-linked lists.

Also included in the multiprocessor operation category are the coprocessor instructions. These instructions will be discussed in detail in Section 6.10.

### 6.7  Signal description

This section contains a brief description of the input and output signals on the MC68020. It is organised by signal function as shown in Fig. 6.5. The term 'assert' is used to indicate that a signal is active, regardless of whether or not that level is represented by a high or low voltage. In the same manner, the term 'negate' is used to indicate that a signal is inactive.

*Function code signals* ($FC0-FC2$). These three-state output signals are used to identify the processor state (supervisor or user) and the address space of the bus cycle currently executing as described in Table 6.1.

*Address bus* ($A0-A31$). During the execution of all bus cycles except CPU-space references, these three-state outputs provide the address for a bus cycle. During CPU-space references, the address bus provides CPU related information. The MC68020 can linearly address 4 gigabytes ($2^{32}$) of data.

*Data bus* ($D0-D31$). These three-state, bidirectional signals provide the data path between the MC68020 and the other devices in

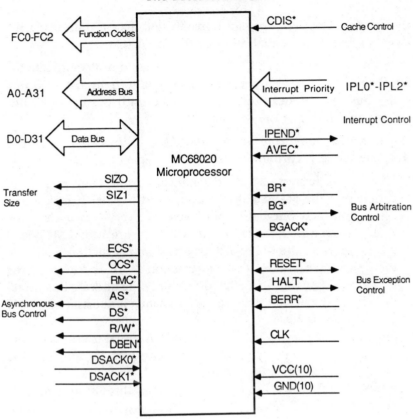

**Fig. 6.5** Functional signal groups.

**Table 6.1** Function code assignments

| FC2 | FC1 | FC0 | Cycle Type |
|-----|-----|-----|------------|
| 0 | 0 | 0 | (Undefined, Reserved)* |
| 0 | 0 | 1 | User Data Space |
| 0 | 1 | 0 | User Program Space |
| 0 | 1 | 1 | (Undefined, Reserved)* |
| 1 | 0 | 0 | (Undefined, Reserved)* |
| 1 | 0 | 1 | Supervisor Data Space |
| 1 | 1 | 0 | Supervisor Program Space |
| 1 | 1 | 1 | CPU Space |

*Address Space 3 is reserved for user definition, while 0 and 4 are reserved for future use by Motorola.

the system. The data bus can transmit and accept data using the dynamic bus sizing capabilities of the MC68020.

*Transfer size* (*SIZ*0, *SIZ*1). These three-state outputs indicate the number of bytes of an operand that remain to be transferred in a given bus cycle. These outputs are used with the dynamic bus sizing capabilities of the MC68020.

*Asynchronous bus control signals.* The following paragraphs describe the asynchronous bus control signals on the MC68020.

External cycle start (ECS*). This output provides an early indication that the MC68020 is starting a bus cycle. It is asserted during the first one-half clock cycle of every bus cycle. This signal must be qualified later with AS* to insure a valid MC68020 bus cycle, since the MC68020 may start an instruction fetch and then abort the access if the instruction word is found in the on-chip cache. The MC68020 drives only the address bus, function code signals and the size outputs when it aborts a bus cycle due to a cache hit.

Operand cycle start (OCS*). This output signal is asserted only during the first bus cycle of an operand transfer and has the same timing as the ECS* signal.

Read–modify–write cycle (RMC*). This three-state signal is asserted for the duration of a read–modify–write cycle. It should be used as a bus lock to insure the integrity of instructions that use read–modify–write cycles.

Address strobe (AS*). This three-state signal is used to indicate that valid addresses, function code, size and read/write information is on the bus.

Data strobe (DS*). During a read cycle, this three-state signal indicates that the selected peripheral should drive the data bus. During a write cycle, this signal indicates that the MC68020 has placed valid data on the data bus.

Read/write (R/W*). This three-state signal is used to indicate the direction of data transfer. A high level indicates that a read cycle is in progress and a low level indicates that a write cycle is being executed.

Data buffer enable (DBEN*). This three-state signal provides an enable to external data buffers. It allows the R/W* line to transition without causing external buffer contention. This signal is not necesssary in all systems.

Data transfer and size acknowledge (DSACK0*, DSACK1*). These inputs indicate to the MC68020 that a data transfer is complete and the amount of data that the external device has accepted or provided. During a read cycle, when the MC68020 recognises the assertion of DSACKx*, it latches the data and terminates the bus cycle. During a write cycle, upon recognition of DSACKx*, the processor terminates the bus cycle. Further explanation of the DSACKx* encodings can be found in Section 6.8.

*Cache disable (CDIS*).* This input signal dynamically disables the on-chip cache. The cache will be disabled internally after the CDIS* signal has been asserted and synchronised internally. Similarly, the cache will be enabled after the CDIS* line has been negated and this condition internally synchronised. See Section 6.9.2 for more information.

*Interrupt control signals.* The following paragraphs describe the interrupt control signals for the MC68020.

Interrupt priority level (IPL0*–IPL2*). These inputs indicate the priority level of the device requesting an interrupt. Level seven has the highest priority and is non-maskable; level zero indicates that no interrupt is requested.
Interrupt pending (IPEND*). This output is used to indicate that the priority level on the IPL2* through IPL0* lines is higher than the priority level in the interrupt mask of the status register, or that a non-maskable interrupt has been recognised.
Autovector (AVEC*). This input may be asserted during an interrupt acknowledge cycle, indicating that an interrupt vector number should be generated internally.

*Bus arbitration signals.* The following paragraphs describe the pins used in determining when other devices in a system may become the bus master.

Bus request (BR*). This input is asserted by a device indicating that it wishes to become the bus master. This signal should be wire-ORed with the other request signals from all other potential bus masters.
Bus grant (BG*). This output signal indicates that the MC68020 will relinquish the bus at the end of the currently executing bus cycle.
Bus grant acknowledge (BGACK*). This input signal indicates to the MC68020 that some other device has assumed ownership of the bus. The device must keep this signal asserted until it has

completed its transactions. This signal should not be asserted until the following conditions have been met:

1. BG* has been received.
2. AS* has been negated, indicating that the MC68020 is not running a bus cycle.
3. DSACK0* and DSACK1* are negated, indicating that no other device is currently driving the bus.
4. BGACK* is negated, indicating that no other bus master has the bus.

*Bus exception control signals.* The following paragraphs describe the bus exception control signals for the MC68020.

Reset (RESET*). This bidirectional, open-drained signal is used as the system reset signal. If asserted as an input, RESET* causes the processor to enter reset exception processing. As an output, the MC68020 asserts RESET* (in response to executing the RESET instruction) to reset external devices but is not affected internally.

Halt (HALT*). This bidirectional, open-drained signal indicates whether the processor is in the halted or run state. When HALT* is asserted as an input, the MC68020 stops all bus activity at the end of the currently executing bus cycle and places all control signals in their inactive state. The processor will, however, continue to drive the function code lines and the address bus.

The MC68020 asserts HALT* as a result of a double bus fault condition to indicate to the other devices in the system that it has stopped executing instructions.

Bus error (BERR*). This input signal is used to indicate to the MC68020 that there is a problem with the currently executing bus cycle. These problems could be the result of:

1. Non-responding devices.
2. Failure to acquire an interrupt vector.
3. Illegal accesses as determined by a memory management unit.
4. Other application dependent errors.

The BERR* signal interacts with the HALT* signal to determine if the current bus cycle should be re-run or aborted.

*Clock (CLK).* This TTL-compatible signal is internally buffered to generate the internal clocks required by the MC68020. It should not be gated off at any time.

**Table 6.2**  Signal summary

| Signal Function | Signal Name | Input/ Output | Active State | Three-State |
|---|---|---|---|---|
| Function Codes | FC0-FC2 | Output | High | Yes |
| Address Bus | A0-A31 | Output | High | Yes |
| Data Bus | D0-D31 | I/O | High | Yes |
| Size | SIZ0-SIZ1 | Output | High | Yes |
| External Cycle Start | ECS* | Output | Low | No |
| Operand Cycle Start | OCS* | Output | Low | No |
| Read-Modify-Write Cycle | RMC* | Output | Low | Yes |
| Address Strobe | AS* | Output | Low | Yes |
| Data Strobe | DS* | Output | Low | Yes |
| Read/Write | R/W* | Output | High/Low | Yes |
| Data Buffer Enable | DBEN* | Output | Low | Yes |
| Data Transfer/Size Acknowledge | DSACK0-1* | Input | Low | - |
| Cache Disable | CDIS* | Input | Low | - |
| Interrupt Priority Level | IPL0-IPL2* | Input | Low | - |
| Interrupt Pending | IPEND* | Output | Low | No |
| Autovector | AVEC* | Input | Low | - |
| Bus Request | BR* | Input | Low | - |
| Bus Grant | BG* | Output | Low | No |
| Bus Grant Acknowledge | BGACK* | Input | Low | - |
| Reset | RESET* | I/O | Low | No* |
| Halt | HALT* | I/O | Low | No* |
| Bus Error | BERR* | Input | Low | - |
| Clock | CLK | Input | - | - |
| Power Supply | VCC | Input | - | - |
| Ground | GND | Input | - | - |

*Open Drain

*Signal summary.* Table 6.2 provides a summary of the MC68020 signals discussed in the previous paragraphs.

## 6.8  Operand transfer mechanism

### 6.8.1  DYNAMIC BUS SIZING

The MC68020 supports an operand transfer mechanism called *dynamic bus sizing* that allows it to determine port size (8, 16 or 32 bits) on a bus cycle by bus cycle basis. During a bus cycle, a port will signal its data bus width and transfer status (complete or not complete) to the MC68020 via the DSACK0* and DSACK1* input lines. These DSACKx* inputs perform the same function as the DTACK* input of the other M68000 family processors, as well as indicating port size. Table 6.3 describes the DSACKx* encodings and their meanings.

As an example, if the MC68020 is attempting to read a 32-bit value from a port, it need not know the port size before it initiates the transfer. If the port responds with a DSACK1*/DSACK0* = 00, indicating that it is a 32-bit wide port, the MC68020 will latch in all 32 bits of the data bus and complete the transfer (i.e. negate the address and data strobes and control signals). If the port indicates that it is 16 bits wide (DSACK1*/DSACK0* = 01), the processor will latch the 16 bits on D31–D16 and begin another bus cycle. When the port asserts DSACKx*, the MC68020 will again latch the data on D31 through D16, thus picking up the full 32 bits. Similar events would occur if the port were 8 bits wide, except that four bus cycles would be required to latch in four bytes on D31 through D24.

In order to locate valid data, the MC68020 makes certain assumptions about where the ports are located with respect to its data bus. 32-bit ports should reside on D31 through D0, 16-bit ports on D31 through D16, and 8-bit ports on D31 through D24. Having the ports aligned in this manner minimises the number of bus cycles required to transfer data.

The MC68020 contains an internal multiplexor that allows it to route the four bytes of the data bus to their correct position. This multiplexor provides the mechanism by which the MC68020 supports dynamic bus sizing and operand misalignment. For example, the most significant byte of an operand, OP0, can be routed to bits D31 through D24, as in normal (aligned) operation, or it can be routed to any other byte position in order to support misalign-

Table 6.3  $\overline{\text{DSACK}}$ codes and results

| DSACK1 | DSACK0 | Result |
|--------|--------|--------|
| H | H | Insert wait states in current bus cycle |
| H | L | Complete cycle - Data bus port size is 8 bits |
| L | H | Complete cycle - Data bus port size is 16 bits |
| L | L | Complete cycle - Data bus port size is 32 bits |

ment. The same applies to the other operand bytes. The byte position the operand occupies is determined by the size lines (SIZ0 and SIZ1) and the two least significant address lines (A1 and A0).

The SIZ1 and SIZ0 lines indicate the number of bytes remaining to be transferred during the current transaction. The number of bytes that are actually transferred depends on port size and operand alignment and will be less than or equal to the value indicated by the SIZx lines. Table 6.4 shows the SIZx output encodings.

The address lines A1 and A0 also affect the operation of the multiplexor. During an operand transfer, A31 through A2 give the long word base address of the operand to be accessed and A1 and A0 give the byte offset from that address. Table 6.5 shows the address offset encodings.

Table 6.6 describes the use of the SIZ0, SIZ1, A0 and A1 lines in defining the transfer pattern from the MC68020's internal multiplexor to the external data bus. For example, suppose the MC68020 needs to move the value $01234567 to the 8-bit port located at address $8000. When the processor begins to execute this instruction, it does not know to what size port it is sending the information,

Table 6.4   SIZE output encodings

| SIZ1 | SIZ0 | Size |
|------|------|------|
| 0 | 1 | Byte |
| 1 | 0 | Word |
| 1 | 1 | 3 Byte |
| 0 | 0 | Long Word |

Table 6.5   Address offset encodings

| A1 | A0 | Offset |
|----|----|--------|
| 0 | 0 | +0 Bytes |
| 0 | 1 | +1 Byte |
| 1 | 0 | +2 Bytes |
| 1 | 1 | +3 Bytes |

**Table 6.6**   MC68020 internal to external data bus multiplexor

| Transfer Size | Size | | Address | | Source/Destination External Data Bus Connection | | | |
|---|---|---|---|---|---|---|---|---|
| | SIZ1 | SIZ0 | A1 | A0 | D31:D24 | D23:D16 | D15:D8 | D7:D0 |
| Byte | 0 | 1 | x | x | OP3 | OP3 | OP3 | OP3 |
| Word | 1 | 0 | x | 0 | OP2 | OP3 | OP2 | OP3 |
| | 1 | 0 | x | 1 | OP2 | OP2 | OP3 | OP2 |
| 3 Byte | 1 | 1 | 0 | 0 | OP1 | OP2 | OP3 | OP0 |
| | 1 | 1 | 0 | 1 | OP1 | OP1 | OP2 | OP3 |
| | 1 | 1 | 1 | 0 | OP1 | OP2 | OP1 | OP2 |
| | 1 | 1 | 1 | 1 | OP1 | OP1 | OP2 | OP1 |
| Long Word | 0 | 0 | 0 | 0 | OP0 | OP1 | OP2 | OP3 |
| | 0 | 0 | 0 | 1 | OP0 | OP0 | OP1 | OP2 |
| | 0 | 0 | 1 | 0 | OP0 | OP1 | OP0 | OP1 |
| | 0 | 0 | 1 | 1 | OP0 | OP0 | OP1* | OP0 |

\* On write cycles, this byte is output; on read cycles, this byte is ignored.
x = don't care

so it attempts to write the full operand, in this case 32 bits, during the first bus cycle. The size lines are both low to indicate that a long word is to be transferred and A1 and A0 are low to indicate that the long word is aligned. The 8-bit port will latch bits D31 through D24 and assert a DSACK1*/DSACK0* of 10, first to indicate that it has received the data, and second, to tell the MC68020 that it is only an 8-bit port. As a result of this '8-bit DSACK', the MC68020 initiates another bus cycle with the next most significant byte of data multiplexed to the uppermost byte of its data bus (D31–D24). The size lines indicate that three bytes remain to be transferred and A1 and A0 are incremented by one to indicate that the next byte in the memory map is being addressed. Again the port latches in the data on D31 through D24 and signals back an 8-bit DSACK. This process continues until the long word transfer is complete.

### 6.8.2 OPERAND MISALIGNMENT

The MC68020 also supports misaligned data operand transfers. The transfer of an operand to/from memory is considered to be misaligned if the address does not fall on an equivalent operand size boundary. Transferring a word to an odd address or a long word to something other than a long word boundary are both examples of misaligned transfers.

The MC68020 places no restrictions on data alignment. However, some performance degradation may occur due to the extra bus cycles the MC68020 must run when word or long word accesses are not made to word or long word boundaries. Note that instructions must always reside on even byte boundaries to insure compatibility with the other members of the M68000 family and to optimise performance for instruction prefetches. Any time an instruction prefetch is attempted from an odd word address, the MC68020 forces an address error exception. This occurs any time an instruction leaves the program counter set to an odd address.

As an example of a misaligned read, suppose the MC68020 is reading a word from location $4001 and storing it in data register D0, where address $4001 corresponds to a 16-bit port. The SIZ1 and SIZ0 lines are 1 and 0 respectively indicating that a word needs to be transferred. The 16-bit port outputs the word at location $4000 ($0123) on bits 31 through 16 of the MC68020 data bus and signals back a DSACK1*/DSACK0* of 01. This encoding indicates to the processor that valid data is present on the data bus and that the port is 16 bits wide. The MC68020 latches in the data, ignores all bytes except for the one at D23–D16 and stores this byte ($23) in a temporary register. It then executes another bus cycle, with the size lines indicating a byte transfer, and the address incremented by one. The 16-bit port then outputs the word at location $4002 ($4567) and returns a 16-bit DSACK*. The MC68020 latches in the data, ignores bits 23 through 0 and stores the value on D31 through D24 ($45), along with the byte stored in the temporary register during the previous cycle, in the lower word of the data register D0.

### 6.8.3 ADVANTAGES OF DYNAMIC BUS SIZING

The dynamic bus sizing capability of the MC68020 gives system designers considerable flexibility; they can pick and choose the size of the ports in the system as they wish. For example, system RAM is accessed numerous times and therefore extra transfers to and from it should be minimised to obtain maximum performance. Thus, in an MC68020 system, the RAM is typically 32 bits wide. However, the same is not necessarily true for ROM. Since existing EPROMs are only 8 bits wide, 16-bit ROM ports require splitting the ROM program into odd and even bytes and 32-bit ROM ports require splitting the program into four pieces. If the ROM contains a monitor routine where execution speed is not a major factor in the performance of the system, then the designer might choose to make it only 8 bits wide. This would eliminate the need to split the routine into every two or every four bytes every time a new EPROM needed to be burned. Also, changes to the routine could be made much more easily and quickly. Programmers are relieved from any constraints imposed by the hardware. Because each size port has a unique handshake via the DSACK* lines, the system, in essence, becomes 'software independent'. In other words, the programmer can send any size data to any port in the system.

## 6.9   Cache

### 6.9.1   CACHE BASICS

A cache memory differs from main memory in a number of regards. First, a cache is smaller and has a much faster access time than main memory. Second, the processor accesses cache memory differently than it accesses main memory. When main memory is accessed by the processor, it outputs the data value contained at the specified address. Cache memory, however, first must compare the incoming address to the address (or addresses) stored in the cache. If the addresses match, then a 'hit' is said to have occurred and the corresponding data is allowed to be read from the cache. If the addresses do not match, a 'miss' is said to have occurred and an access from main memory is allowed to complete. When a miss occurs, the data retrieved from main memory is also provided to the cache so that the next time this specific address is accessed, a hit may occur in the cache.

The following sections describe the types of caches that are or could be implemented with the MC68020. The first section dis-

cusses the MC68020 on-chip cache and the second covers two
ways of designing an external data cache for an MC68020 system.

### 6.9.2   ON CHIP

The MC68020 contains an on-chip instruction cache that improves
the performance of the microprocessor by decreasing instruction
access time and reducing the processor's external bus activity.

Instruction words that are stored in the cache are accessed much
more quickly than if they had been stored in external memory. In
addition, while the MC68020 is accessing the instruction cache, it
can make a simultaneous data fetch on the external bus.

An improvement in bus bandwidth can be obtained using the
cache. If the MC68020 finds an instruction word in the cache, it
does not need to make an external access, thus freeing the bus for
other bus masters in the system.

The MC68020 on-chip cache is a direct-mapped cache containing 64 long word entries. Each entry consists of a tag field, a valid
bit, and instruction words (32 bits). The tag field comprises the
upper 24 address bits and the FC2 value. Thus the 4 gigabyte
address space of the MC68020 is partitioned into blocks of 256
bytes in size.

Whenever the MC68020 makes an instruction fetch, it begins
two simultaneous accesses, the normal one to external memory
(assuming the external bus is free) and the one to the cache
(assuming the cache is enabled). The processor checks the cache
to see if the instruction is present in the cache. To do this, a portion
of the tag field is used as an index into the cache to select one of
the 64 entries. Next, the remainder of the tag for that entry is
compared to the address of the instruction and the FC2 line. If
they agree and the valid bit is set, a 'hit' is said to have occurred.
Bit A1 is used to select the appropriate word from the cache and
the cycle ends. This all occurs within two clock cycles as opposed
to the normal three clock cycles required for an external access.
Externally, the processor may drive the address lines, size, function
code, and ECS* lines before aborting the cycle due to a cache hit.
Note that address strobe is not asserted if there is a hit in the cache.

If the tag of the entry does not agree with the address of the
instruction or if the valid bit is cleared, a 'miss' occurs and the
external cycle is allowed to complete. If the cache is not frozen
(via the freeze bit in the cache control register), the new instruction
is written into the cache and the valid bit set. Note that both words

corresponding to that address are replaced because the MC68020 always fetches long words.

Upon reset, the processor clears the cache by clearing the valid bits for every entry. In addition, the enable and freeze bits in the cache control register are cleared.

### 6.9.3  OFF CHIP

An external cache can be designed for an MC68020 system to provide even more performance. The cache could be either on the logical or on the physical side of the address bus and it could be implemented as an instruction and data cache or data-only cache.

The following paragraphs will discuss the important points of designing a logical data cache for an MC68020 system. It is not meant to provide the reader with a tested design, nor is it meant to imply that this is the best or only design possible. Instead, it should be used to determine what timing specifications are important when designing an external cache for an MC68020 system.

Typically, for main memory, the critical timing specification is from addresses valid to data valid. For a cache memory, the most important timing specification in order to minimise wait states is from addresses valid to decision (hit or miss) required. The decision would trigger the event that causes the bus cycle to terminate. On an MC68020 system, the event could either be DSACKx* asserted or BERR* and HALT* asserted. Each of these methods will be looked into, including timing information and advantages and disadvantages.

In the first method, the assertion of DSACKx* is delayed until it is known whether or not a hit has occurred in the cache. Thus, DSACKx* is a product of the HIT* signal of the cache circuitry. If a hit occurs, the access to main memory (which may be happening simultaneously to the cache access) must be aborted before the memory could start driving the data bus. If a miss occurs, then the cycle to main memory is allowed to complete. Figure 6.6 shows the worst case timing requirements at 16.67 MHz for a no-wait state cache design (assuming a hit) using this method. Note that the amount of time available to determine whether there will be a hit or miss is 55 nanoseconds minimum (the time from addresses valid to DSACKx* asserted). If a hit does occur, data needs to be available at least 5 nanoseconds prior to the falling edge of S4. If the designer is unwilling to invest in the fast RAMs required to achieve a no-wait state cache, wait states can be added for a longer decision time at a performance degradation.

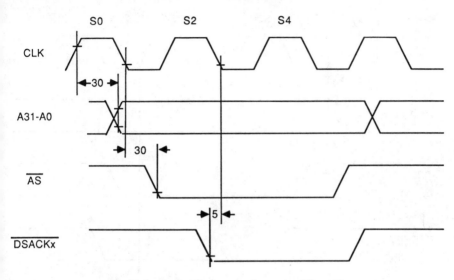

**Fig. 6.6**    Cache timing requirements (Case 1).

In the second method, it is assumed that the cache will always have the correct data (i.e. never incur a miss). Therefore, DSACKx* may be asserted before it is known if the desired address is available in the cache. If a hit does occur, the access will run with no-wait states. If a miss occurs, the BERR* and HALT* lines to the MC68020 must be asserted to indicate to the processor that the cycle should not be terminated normally. This is known as *late retry*. When BERR* and HALT* are negated, the MC68020 reruns the faulted bus cycle. Some external hardware is required to prevent a cache access for this second bus cycle from occurring and to handle the case where bus arbitration occurs between the two bus cycles. A smart design takes advantage of the time between these bus cycles (faulted and retry) and starts the access to main memory when it becomes obvious that the cache access is going to miss. See Fig. 6.7 for the timing requirements (assuming a miss) for this type of cache design. The only requirement for the assertion of DSACKx* is that it be present at least 5 nanoseconds before the falling edge of S2. BERR* and HALT* need to be asserted at least 20 nanoseconds prior to the falling edge of S4 in order for them to be recognised by the MC68020. Therefore, the designer has 100 nanoseconds (from addresses valid to BERR*/HALT* asserted) to determine if a cache hit is going to occur. If it is determined that a miss will occur, the data bus drivers from the data RAMs need to be blocked to prevent them from driving the bus and the

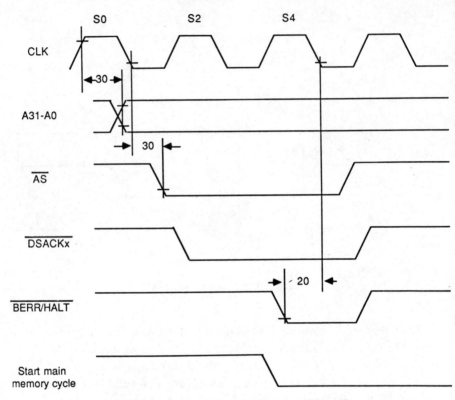

**Fig. 6.7**   Cache timing requirements (Case 2).

access to main memory is started at approximately the same time the BERR* and HALT* lines are asserted.

In the first type of design, the cache requires faster RAMs in order to run with no-wait states. In the second type, slower RAMs could be used, while obtaining the same performance. The cache accesses in this second case always run with zero wait states and memory accesses due to cache misses effectively run with two fewer wait states than a normal main memory access would (i.e. no cache in the system).

## 6.10  Coprocessors

### 6.10.1  COPROCESSOR INTERFACE

The MC68020 supports a coprocessor interface that allows it to extend its functions. While a general purpose machine performs well in several different areas of application, it might not perform as well in one area as a processor designed specifically for that application. Coprocessors allow a main processor to be enhanced for a particular application without losing the generality of the main processor architecture.

In addition, coprocessors allow system designers to 'custom tailor' their designs by selecting only those coprocessors that suit the needs of their system. This eliminates the need for designers to pay for extra hardware that they frequently have to buy in order to obtain the specific hardware that they do require.

A coprocessor is defined as anything that implements the coprocessor interface, whether it be one device, several devices, or a whole board. It provides extensions to the main processor's programming model by adding new registers and new instructions and data types.

The coprocessor implementation is completely transparent to the user. The programmer is not required to have a knowledge of the coprocessor protocol. In fact, he/she need never know that the coprocessor is separate from the MC68020. It appears as an extension to the MC68020 hardware.

Communication between the MC68020 and the coprocessor is initiated by the MC68020 as a result of a coprocessor instruction. The processor begins by writing a command to the coprocessor and waiting for the response. The algorithm necessary for this communication is contained in the microcode of the MC68020. Thus, the user does not have the burden of sending out the command word and polling for a response from the coprocessor. It is only necessary to use the coprocessor instructions, designated by the 'ones' in the most significant bits of the op code (bits 15–12 = 1111). Figure 6.8 shows the format of a coprocessor instruction word or F-line op word. Bits 11 through 9 are defined as the CP-ID (coprocessor identification field). Each coprocessor in a system has a unique ID. Thus, up to eight coprocessors are supported in a system. When the main processor initiates communication with the coprocessor, the CP-ID is placed on address lines A15–A13. While the coprocessor may not necessarily decode these bits internally, they can be used within the address decode to provide the chip selects for the coprocessors. Bits 8 through 6 specify the type of instruction being executed: general, branch,

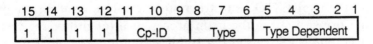

| 15 | 14 | 13 | 12 | 11 | 10 | 9 | 8 | 7 | 6 | 5 | 4 | 3 | 2 | 1 |
|----|----|----|----|----|----|---|---|---|---|---|---|---|---|---|
| 1 | 1 | 1 | 1 | Cp-ID | | | Type | | | Type Dependent | | | | |

**Fig. 6.8**  F-line coprocessor instruction operation word.

conditional, save or restore. These instruction types will be discussed in a later paragraph.

A coprocessor can also be used as a peripheral with a microprocessor other than the MC68020, such as the MC68000, the MC8008 or the MC68010. If an F-line instruction is executed in an M68000, non-MC68020 system, the processor takes the F-line exception, thus allowing the coprocessor interface to be emulated in software.

The coprocessor interface operates with normal M68000 bus cycles; no special signals are required to connect the coprocessor up to an M68000 processor. When running as a coprocessor with the MC68020, the function code lines, along with address lines A11 through A9, are used to generate the chip select for the coprocessor. All coprocessor accesses are made in CPU space. When accessed as a peripheral, a chip select needs to be generated based on the address lines, just like any other peripheral. Figures 6.9(a) and (b) show a block diagram of a coprocessor in an MC68020 and an MC68000 system, respectively. Note that the main processor and coprocessor need not run off the same clock nor do they need to run at the same clock speed.

A processor communicates with the coprocessor via the coprocessor interface registers, shown in Fig. 6.10. Those with asterisks indicate the registers that are required to implement each of the instruction types. Note that all addresses are in CPU space. The following paragraphs describe the coprocessor interface register set.

*Response register* – a 16-bit read-only register by which the coprocessor requests action of the main processor.

*Control register* – a 16-bit write-only register through which the main processor acknowledges coprocessor requested exception processing. In addition, the main processor uses this register to abort instruction execution.

*Save register* – a 16-bit readable/writable register. The main processor reads this register to initiate a cpSAVE instruction. The coprocessor then returns status and state frame format information to the main processor through this register.

*Restore register* – a 16-bit readable/writable register. The main processor writes a coprocessor format word to this register to initiate a cpRESTORE instruction. The coprocessor then returns the format word to the main processor through this register.

*Operation word register* – a 16-bit write-only register. The main processor writes the F-line operation word to this register in

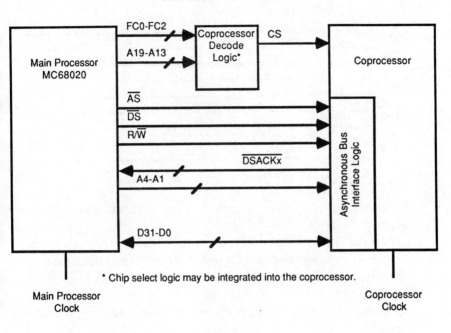

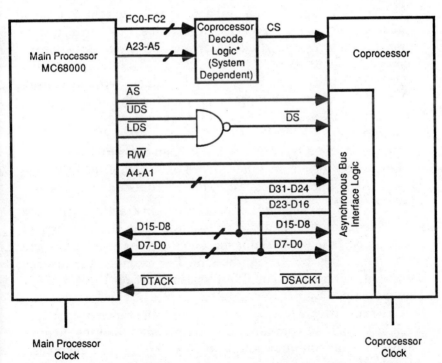

**Fig. 6.9**    (a) MC68020 interface to coprocessor on a 32-bit data bus: (b) MC68000 interface to coprocessor on a 16-bit data bus.

| | 31 | 15 | 0 |
|---|---|---|---|
| $00 | Response* | Control* | |
| $04 | Save* | Restore* | |
| $08 | Operation Word | Command* | |
| $0C | (Reserved) | Condition* | |
| $10 | Operand* | | |
| $14 | Register Select | (Reserved) | |
| $18 | Instruction Address | | |
| $1C | Operand Address | | |

**Fig. 6.10**    Coprocessor interface register set map.

response to a transfer operation word request from the coprocessor.

*Command register* – a 16-bit write-only register through which the main processor initiates an instruction in the general instruction category (discussed later).

*Condition register* – a 16-bit write-only register through which the main processor initiates an instruction in the coprocessor conditional category.

*Register select register* – a 16-bit read-only register. The main processor reads this register to determine which registers to transfer upon receiving a transfer register(s) request from the coprocessor.

*Instruction address register* – a 32-bit readable/writable register through which the main processor transfers the address of the instruction it is currently executing upon a request from the coprocessor.

*Operand address register* – a 32-bit readable/writable register. The transfer of an operand address is accomplished through this register upon the request of the coprocessor.

There are three categories of coprocessor instructions. They are general, conditional, and system control. The general class of instructions is used to describe most coprocessor instructions and is defined mainly by the coprocessor. For example, the floating point add, subtract and multiply instructions on the MC68881 Floating Point Coprocessor are all examples of a general instruction. The conditional instructions include both branch instructions (such as branch on condition) and other conditional instructions (such as set on condition and trap on condition). In each case, the main processor passes the condition selector to the coprocessor for evaluation. The coprocessor then indicates a true or false condition back to the main processor which can then continue with the execution of the instruction. The system control instructions include two instructions that permit operating system task switching. They are cpSAVE and cpRESTORE. The cpSAVE instruction causes the coprocessor to pass a format word and internal state information to the main processor which then stores it in memory. The cpRESTORE instruction causes the coprocessor to load its internal state with the information passed to it from the main processor. Both instructions are privileged and thus can only be executed while executing in the supervisor mode.

More information about the M68000 coprocessor interface can be found in the *MC68020 User's Manual.*

### 6.10.2   MC68881 FLOATING POINT COPROCESSOR

The MC68881 Floating Point Coprocessor, processed in HCMOS, was designed primarily for use as a coprocessor with the MC68020, but can also be operated as a peripheral in non-MC68020 systems. It fully supports the IEEE P754 floating point standard (draft 10.0). In addition, it provides a full set of trigonometric and logarithmic functions not defined by the IEEE standard. It performs all internal calculations to 80 bits of precision.

The MC68881 architecture appears as a logical extension of the M68000 architecture. When coupled to the MC68020 as a coprocessor, the MC68881 registers can be regarded by the programmer as residing on the MC68020 die. Figure 6.11 shows the programmer's model for the MC68881. It contains eight 80-bit floating point registers (FP0–FP7) that are analogous to the integer data registers (D0–D7) on the MC68020, a 32-bit control register, a 32-bit status register, and a 32-bit instruction address register. The control register contains enable bits for each class of exception trap and mode bits for selecting rounding and precision modes. The status register contains floating point condition codes, quotient bits, and exception status information. The instruction address register contains the address of the last floating point instruction that was executed. This register is used for exception handling purposes.

The MC68881 supports four new data types: single precision, double precision, extended precision and packed-decimal string real, in addition to the three integer data types supported by all M68000 processors (byte, word and long word). Figure 6.12 shows the memory formats for the real data types.

The MC68881 supports five classes of instruction operations: data movement, dyadic operations, monadic operations, program

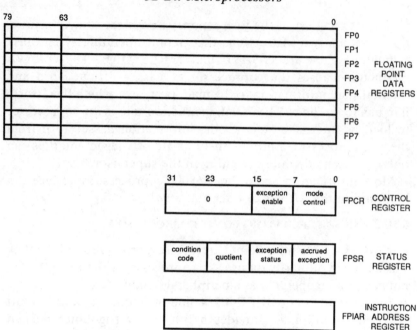

Fig. 6.11   MC68881 programming model.

control and system control. The data movement instructions on the MC68881 work in essentially the same way as the data movement instructions on the MC68020. They are used to move operands into, between and out of MC68881 registers. Dyadic operations require two operands and perform arithmetic functions such as add, subtract, multiply and divide. Monadic instructions provide arithmetic functions that require only one operand, such as sine, square root, negate, etc. Program control instructions affect the program flow based on conditions in the status register. These instructions include branch on condition, decrement and branch on condition, no operation, set on condition, and test operand. The system control operations are used to communicate with the operating system. The system control instructions are save state, restore state, and trap on condition.

More information on the MC68881 can be found in the *MC68881 User's Manual.*

### 6.10.3   MC68851 PAGED MEMORY MANAGEMENT UNIT

The MC68851 Paged Memory Management Unit (PMMU) is also manufactured in Motorola's HCMOS process. It was designed to support a demand paged virtual memory system. It operates as a

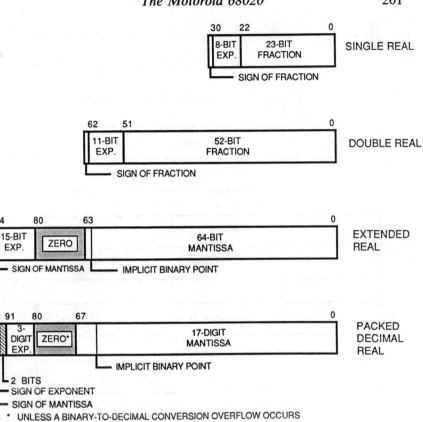

**Fig. 6.12** Memory formats for real data types.

coprocessor with the MC68020 but can be used with other processors. The remaining paragraphs of this section will discuss the coprocessor aspects of the PMMU, while the memory management capabilities will be discussed in Section 6.11.

Figure 6.13 shows the programmer's model for the MC68851. The CPU root pointer (CRP), DMA root pointer (DRP), supervisor root pointer (SRP), translation control (TC), cache status (CS), status (STATUS), current access level (CAL), validate access level (VAL), stack change control (SCC), and the access control (AC) registers control the translation and protection features of the PMMU. The other sixteen registers, breakpoint acknowledge data (BAD7–BAD0) and breakpoint acknowledge control (BAC7–BAC0), control the breakpoint functions available with the MC68020 BKPT instructions.

The CRP register is a 64-bit register that contains the pointer to the root of the translation table tree for the current user task.

## 32-Bit Microprocessors

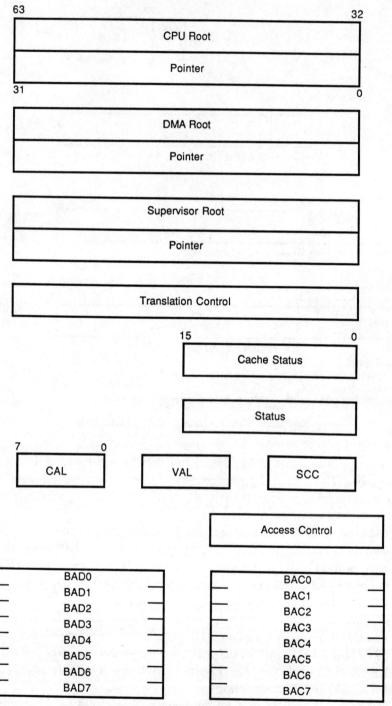

**Fig. 6.13**   MC68851 programming model.

The DRP is a 64-bit register that contains the root pointer to the translation table that is used when an alternate logical bus master is translating through the PMMU. The SRP is a 64-bit register whose contents point to the root of the translation table to be used for translating supervisor accesses. The TC register is a 32-bit register that contains bits that configure the translation mechanism of the PMMU. The CS register is a 16-bit read-only register that contains bits useful for maintaining a logical data cache. The STATUS register is a 16-bit register that contains bits for indicating bus error, supervisor violation, access level violation, invalid address, etc. The CAL and VAL registers are both 8 bits wide; however, only the upper three bits are implemented. The CAL register contains the access level of the currently executing routine and the VAL contains the access level of the caller of the current routine. The SCC register is an 8-bit register that determines if a stack change should occur during an MC68020 CALLM instruction. The AC register is 16 bits wide and controls access information for the PMMU (i.e. whether access levels are enabled, how many upper address bits contain access level information, etc.). The BAD and BAC registers are all 16 bits wide. The BAD registers hold op codes to be provided to the processor during a breakpoint acknowledge cycle and the BAC registers contain the enable and count functions for the breakpoint acknowledge instruction.

The MC68851 supports three classes of instructions: loading and storing of PMMU registers (PMOVE), testing access rights and conditionals (PVALID, PTEST, PLOAD, PFLUSH, PBcc, PDBcc, Scc, and PTRAPcc), and control functions (PSAVE and PRESTORE). All PMMU instructions are privileged except for the PVALID instruction.

More information on the MC68851 can be found in the *MC68851 User's Manual.*

### 6.11 Memory management

#### 6.11.1 MEMORY MANAGEMENT TECHNIQUES

Memory management basically has three functions: translate addresses, provide protection for the operating system from user access, and provide write protection for some user read-only pages. Without a memory management unit (MMU), an operating system would have the responsibility of handling address translation and access protection in software. Obviously, this would require an enormous amount of code. With an MMU in the system, an operating system need only set up the translation descriptors. The MMU then handles the tasks of translation and protection in hardware.

An MMU divides the system address bus, creating logical addresses and physical addresses. The logical side is the side with the main processor on it and the physical bus is used to access main memory. The MMU has two choices when it comes to translating logical addresses to physical addresses. In the first technique, the MMU adds a defined offset to the logical address to produce the physical address. In the second method, called the substitution technique, the MMU searches the translation tables to find the physical address mapping. Typically, the substitution method is preferred because physical addresses may be generated much more quickly than with the adder method.

Memory management can be implemented in one of two ways. The first implementation is called *segmented*. In this type of system, a segment descriptor contains three variables: the logical address, the length of the window or task, and the offset. The length defines a contiguous block of memory (known as a *page*) and the offset is used to generate the physical address. The second type of implementation is called *paged*. In a paged memory management system, two variables are defined, the logical address and the physical address. The length of the windows or pages are fixed. Each system has its own advantages and disadvantages.

The MC68851 discussed in the following section is a paged memory management unit.

### 6.11.2　MC68851

As stated in the previous section, the MC68851 PMMU supports a demand paged virtual memory environment. It supports multiple logical and/or physical bus masters, as well as logical and/or physical data caches. The primary functions of the PMMU are to provide logical-to-physical address translation, to monitor and enforce the protection/privilege mechanism set up by the operating system, and to support the MC68020 breakpoint operation. These three topics will be discussed further in the following paragraphs.

The task of translating logical to physical addresses occupies most of the PMMU's time, and thus has been optimised in terms of speed and minimum processor intervention. The MC68851 starts an address translation by searching for the descriptor that describes the translation for the incoming logical address in the on-chip address translation cache (ATC). The ATC is a very fast fully associative, 64-entry cache that stores recently used descriptors. If the descriptor is not resident in the ATC, the PMMU aborts the bus cycle and becomes bus master in order to 'walk' the translation tables in physical memory. A translation table is a hierarchical data structure that contains the page descriptors controlling the logical-to-physical address translations. The root pointer registers discussed in the previous section point to the top of these translation tables. When the PMMU finds the correct page descriptor, it loads it into the ATC and allows the logical bus master to retry the aborted cycle, which should now be correctly translated.

The MC68851 protection mechanism provides a cycle-by-cycle examination and enforcement of the access rights of the currently executing process. The PMMU supports eight levels of privilege in a hierarchical arrangement, which are encoded in the three most significant bits of the incoming logical address (LA31-LA29). The PMMU compares these bits with the value in the CAL (current access level) register. If the priority level of the incoming address is lower than the value in the CAL register, then the bus cycle is requesting a higher privilege than it is allowed. The PMMU will terminate this access as a fault. In addition, the PMMU supports the MC68020 module call and return instructions (CALLM/ RTM). Included is a mechanism to change privilege levels during module operation.

The MC68851 supports breakpoints for the MC68020 and other processors with its breakpoint acknowledge capability. When the MC68020 encounters a breakpoint instruction, it executes a breakpoint acknowledge cycle in CPU space. It reads a word from an address that is determined by the number of the breakpoint (specified in the instruction). The PMMU decodes this address and either places a replacement op code on the data bus or asserts bus error to indicate illegal instruction exception. The BAD (breakpoint acknowledge data) registers contain the replacement op codes.

For more information on the memory management capabilities of the MC68851, refer to the *MC68851 User's Manual*.

### 6.12 Development system support

The following paragraphs describe the development system support available for the MC68020.

### 6.12.1 BENCHMARK 20

The Benchmark 20 system provides to the first-time user of the MC68020 a tool for evaluating the processor and beginning code development and debug. It also allows the user to execute benchmarks on the MC68020 via its timer utilities.

The Benchmark 20, which is VERSAmodule based, supports Motorola resident assemblers on the EXORmacs and the VME/10 systems. It consists of two VERSAmodule boards (which are also available separately): the VM04 and the VM13-1. The VM04 consists of the MC68020, the MC68881, and the MMB (an MC68461 with an address translation cache). It also has both a VERSAbus and RAMbus interface, a programmable timer module, two serial I/O ports, and two ROM sockets. RAMbus is a 32-bit asynchronous multiplexed address/data extension bus designed for use with VERSAbus. A subsystem based on RAMbus can transfer data without waiting for or degrading the performance of the primary system bus. The VM13-1 is a 1024 kbyte dynamic RAM module with parity checking. Like the VM04, it supports both VERSAbus and RAMbus. It contains byte parity generation and error checking circuitry and is dual-ported.

The software package available with the Benchmark 20 is called 020bug. 020bug is an EPROM-resident system debug monitor that supports assembly and disassembly of both MC68020 and MC68881 instructions. In additon, it contains timer utilities for timing program execution.

### 6.12.2 HDS 400 EMULATOR

The HDS 400 Microprocessor Development Station provides real time emulation of the MC68020, as well as the other members of the M68000 processor family. It is compatible with the Real Time Bus State Analyser and can be supported by either EXORmacs, VME/10 or VAX hosts. It supports all of the features of the MC68020, including breakpoints, on-chip cache, and dynamic bus sizing. In addition, the user has unrestricted access to the full 4 gigabyte address space.

### 6.12.3 OTHER DEVELOPMENT TOOLS

In addition to the VM04/VM13 boards mentioned above, Motorola also offers VMEbus compatible MC68020 boards. The VME130 is a 12.5 MHz MC68020 board that contains sockets for the

MC68881 and the MC68851. It also contains sockets for 16 kbytes of ROM/EPROM. Also featured are two multi-protocol serial I/O ports, an MVMX32bus private memory bus interface, and a programmable timer module. The VME204 is a 1 Mbyte dynamic memory module designed to be used with the VME130. It is dual-ported, has an MVMX32bus interface, and provides byte parity and error checking.

### 6.12.4 SYSTEM 1131

The System 1131 supports the MC68020/MC68881/MC68851 combination using the VMEboard configuration. The system includes the MVME131 board, which contains the MC68020, the MC68881, and the MC68851, 1 Mbyte floppy, and a 15 Mbyte hard disk, all mounted in a rackmount VME chassis. A complete debug monitor is included in on-board ROM. UNIX System V/68 can be obtained for the board at a low cost.

### 6.13  Software support

Currently, there is a wide range of software support for the MC68020. The following paragraphs describe the cross assemblers and cross compilers available for the MC68020. Also described is UNIX and other third party software support.

*Cross assemblers.* Cross assemblers for the MC68020 are available for both the EXORmacs and VME/10 development stations. These cross assemblers support both VERSAdos and SYSTEM V/68 operating systems.

*Cross compilers.* Two versions of a cross C-compiler are available from Motorola. The first version runs with the SYSTEM V/68 operating system on either the EXORmacs or VME/10 development stations. The second version runs on the VAX/780 with UNIX™ SYSTEM V (release 1 and 2) operating system. This package includes both a C-compiler and a SYSTEM V/68 assembler. A FORTRAN 77 compiler is also available with the UNIX™ SYSTEM V(release 2).

*UNIX™ support.* UNIX™ support for the MC68020 is available from Motorola and other third party software houses. UNIX V™ (AT&T release 2 and 2+) is offered by Motorola to support both the VM04 and the VME130. These software packages also include FORTRAN 77. Additional UNIX™ support for the MC68020 is being offered by UNISOFT, again for both the VM04 and the VME130.

*Third party support.* The M68000 family of microprocessors has a large and diverse supply of third party software. The applications range from business and industry to operating systems and compilers. Motorola publishes a software catalogue that contains complete listings of software vendors and their products.

### 6.14 Performance

The designers of the MC68020 had one ultimate goal in mind: high performance. The fact that this goal was accomplished is

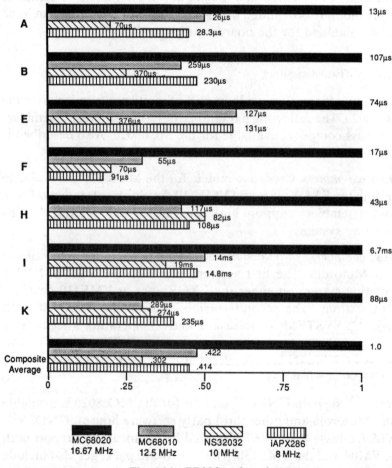

Fig. 6.14    EDN benchmarks.

evident by looking at a few numbers. First, the enhancements made to the MC68020 over the 8 MHz MC68000 will be noted. The MC68020 was designed to run at 16 MHz, giving a 2 times improvement over the MC68000. It has a 32-bit data bus, whereas the MC68000 has a 16-bit data bus, giving a 1.3 times improvement. Note that this is not a 2 times improvement because not all 32 bits of the bus are always used. An instruction cache was added to give a 1.25 times improvement. This takes into account faster bus cycle execution time, improved bus bandwidth, etc. Finally, new instructions, addressing modes, and a 32-bit ALU (arithmetic logic unit) were added to give a 1.25 times improvement. The result of all of these improvements is a processor that has 4.06 higher performance than the 8 MHz MC68000.

Figure 6.14 shows the execution time of the MC68020 compared to other processors for several EDN benchmarks.

In addition to performance, the designers of the MC68020 had other goals in mind. Most important, the MC68020 had to be compatible with the other members of the M68000 family. Thus, existing user software need not be rewritten in order to run on the MC68020. They also felt the need to add significant instruction set enhancements to the processor. This makes the MC68020 useful for a wide range of applications, such as robotics, graphics, and engineering workstations. Evidence of this can be found in the number and range of systems based on the MC68020 already introduced by various international companies.

## References

*MC68020 32-bit Microprocessor User's Manual*, (2 Ed.), Prentice-Hall, Inc., Englewood Cliffs, NJ, 1985.

*MC68881 Floating Point Coprocessor User's Manual*, Prentice-Hall, Inc., Englewood Cliffs, NJ, 1985.

*MC68851 Paged Memory Management Unit*, Motorola, Inc.

*Motorola Microprocessor Software Catalog*, (4 Ed.), Motorola, Inc., 1985.

'The Motorola MC68020', MacGregor, Doug, Mothersole, Dave and Moyer, Bill. IEEE, Aug. 1984.

# CHAPTER 7
# The Zilog Z80000 CPU*

BRADLY K. FAWCETT
*Zilog Inc., USA*

## 7.1 Introduction

Continuing Zilog's tradition in the design of state-of-the-art microprocessor components, the Z80000 32-bit microprocessor brings the performance of super minicomputers and mainframe computers into the realm of microprocessor based systems. Upward compatible with Z8000 family hardware and software, the Z80000 CPU features a high throughput, 32-bit architecture that directly supports operating systems and high level languages. Its flexible hardware interface provides for connection in a wide variety of system configurations.

The Z80000 CPU has full 32-bit address and data paths, and can directly address up to 4 gigabytes of virtual memory. Throughput is enhanced by an internal 6-stage instruction pipeline, on-chip cache memory, support for burst-mode memory transactions, on-chip demand paged memory management, a coprocessor interface, high clock speeds, and a rich instruction set.

Many Z80000 applications will involve the use of multi-tasking operating systems and high level languages. Architectural features that support the implementation of such systems include separate system and normal operating modes, on-chip memory management, sophisticated interrupt and trap handling, a large general purpose register file, and a large, powerful instruction set. Nine operand addressing modes are used within instructions to access numerous data types, including bits, bit fields, signed and unsigned integers, logical values, strings and BCD digits. The instruction set is highly regular in combining operations, addressing modes and data types. High level language compilation is supported by

---

* Z-Bus, Z8000, and Z80000 are trademarks of Zilog, Inc. UNIX is a trademark of AT&T Technologies, Inc. VAX is a trademark of Digital Equipment Corp.

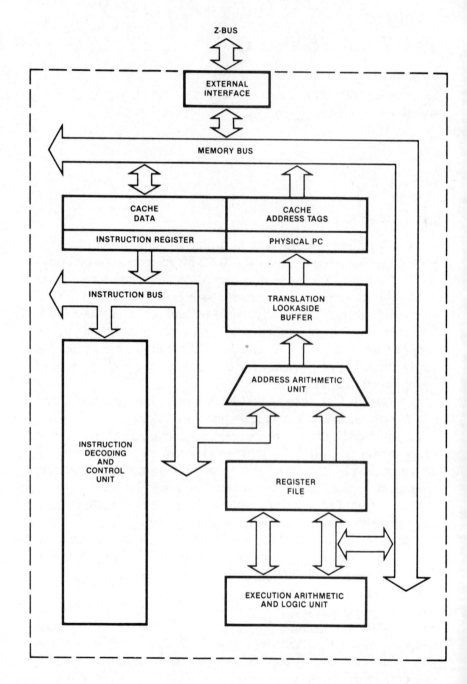

**Fig. 7.1**   Z80000 CPU functional block diagram.

instructions for procedure linkage, array index calculation, data type conversion and bounds checking; other instructions provide operating system functions such as system calls, semaphore testing and memory management.

The Z80000 CPU's external bus provides for easy connection to a wide variety of system environments spanning an extensive range of cost/performance requirements. The system designer can, by program control, configure the bus clock rate, data path width, and access time for bus transactions. Optionally, burst-mode memory transactions can be used to increase memory bandwidth further. Four types of multiprocessing configurations are directly supported: coprocessors, slave processors, tightly coupled multiple CPUs, and loosely coupled multiple CPUs. The bus structure is compatible with the entire Z-bus family of processors, coprocessors and peripherals.

Figure 7.1 shows a functional block diagram of the Z80000 CPU internal organisation. The external interface unit controls external bus transactions; the external Z-bus interface consists of a time multiplexed address/data bus and its associated status and control signals. An on-chip cache memory retains a copy of the most recently accessed instruction and data memory locations. The address arithmetic unit performs all effective address calculations and transmits them to the translation lookaside buffer (TLB), which translates the logical addresses to physical addresses. The register file contains sixteen general purpose 32-bit registers and several special purpose control registers. The execution arithmetic and logic unit (ALU) calculates the results of instruction execution; this unit has two paths to the register file, allowing two operands to be read simultaneously. The instruction decode and control unit decodes instructions and controls the operation of the other functional units. All of the functional units and data paths are 32 bits wide. The operation of the CPU is highly pipelined, with the functional units operating in parallel.

The design of the Z80000 CPU is based on a special 2 μm NMOS fabrication process featuring intrinsic transistors, high value polysilicon transistors, and multiple levels of interconnection. With this process, CPU clock speeds of up to 25 MHz are possible.

## 7.2 Address spaces

The Z80000 CPU can manipulate bit, byte (8 bit), word (16 bit), long word (32 bit), and quad word (64 bit) data. Data operands can be located within any of several logical address spaces, including four memory address spaces, an I/O address space, and the CPU register file.

For memory and I/O references, the Z80000 CPU translates the logical addresses specified in the program into physical addresses that are output on the address/data bus and presented to the actual memory or I/O device. Logical addresses (i.e. the addresses manipulated by the program) are in one of four logical memory address spaces or the logical I/O address space. Physical addresses are in the physical memory space or physical I/O space (Fig. 7.2).

The four logical memory address spaces are the system instruction space, system data space, normal instruction space and normal data space. The on-chip memory management unit can independently control each of the logical memory spaces. When in system mode, memory references access one of the system address spaces; in normal mode, memory references access one of the normal address spaces. The instruction space is used for instruction fetches, immediate mode operand fetches, and data accesses using the relative address or relative index addressing modes; the data address space is used for data references using any other addressing mode.

Logical memory addresses are always 32 bits in length. Any of three different memory address representation modes can be used: compact, segmented, or linear (Fig. 7.3).

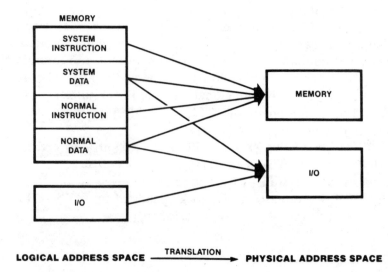

Fig. 7.2   Address spaces.

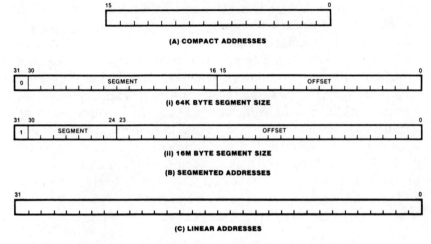

**Fig. 7.3** Memory address representations.

In compact mode, 16-bit memory addresses are manipulated by the program. Effective address calculations using compact addresses involve all 16 bits. Compact mode can be used for applications that require less than 64 kbytes of code and access less than 64 kbytes of data. Compact mode is more efficient and consumes less program space than segmented or linear mode, since memory addresses in the program are one word instead of two words in length. While in compact mode, the high order 16 bits of each 32-bit logical memory address are the high order 16 bits of the program counter.

In segmented mode, the logical memory address spaces are divided into distinct memory segments. The lower half of each address space is divided into 32 768 segments of up to 64 kbytes each and the upper half is divided into 128 segments of up to 16 Mbytes each. Each segment is a contiguous string of bytes at consecutive offsets. Each memory address is partitioned into a distinct segment number and offset address (Fig. 7.3). Effective address calculations involve only the offset portion of the address; the segment number is unaffected. Segmentation is a common memory organisation technique used in mini and mainframe computers; many applications benefit from the logical structure of segmentation by allocating individual program modules, stacks or data structures to separate segments.

In linear mode, effective address calculations involve all 32 bits of the address; the address space of 4 gigabytes is uniform and unstructured. Thus, the entire address space is a contiguous string

of bytes at consecutive addresses. Some applications benefit from
the flexibility of linear addressing, where objects can be assigned
to any arbitrary memory location.

Memory in Z80000 systems is byte-addressable – i.e. each byte
of memory has its own address. When storing word or long word
data in memory, the data is stored in consecutive memory locations,
starting with the most significant byte (Fig. 7.4). Words and long
words in memory are addressed using the lowest address of any
byte in the data element (i.e. the address of the most significant
byte). Word and long word data in memory can start at any address;
however, performance is improved when words begin at an even
address and long words begin at an address that is a multiple of
four. Instruction words must begin at even addresses.

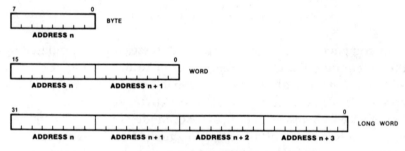

**Fig. 7.4**   Data storage in memory.

Logical I/O addresses are 32 bits in length, but only the low
order 16 bits are manipulated by the program; the CPU forces the
high order 16 bits of I/O addresses to all zeros. I/O ports can be
byte, word or long word ports.

Physical addresses are in the physical memory space or physical
I/O space. The two physical address spaces are distinguished by
different status signals on the bus and different transaction timing.
Physical addresses are 32 bits in length. An address in the logical
I/O address space maps to the identical address in the physical
I/O address space. The on-chip memory management device maps
logical memory addresses to the physical memory space or physical
I/O space (for memory-mapped I/O devices).

Storing data in CPU registers results in shorter instructions and
faster execution than with instructions that access the memory or
I/O address spaces. The Z80000 CPU is a register oriented processor containing sixteen 32-bit general purpose registers, a 32-bit
program counter (PC), a 16-bit flag and control word (FCW), and
nine other special purpose control registers.

The general purpose register file contains sixteen 32-bit registers, for a total of 64 bytes of storage (Fig. 7.5). Register data formats ranging from bytes to quad words are created by dividing and grouping the long word registers. For example, long word register RR0 is subdivided into word registers R0 and R1, word register R0 is subdivided into byte registers RH0 and RL0, and so on. Two long word registers are paired to form a quad word register; e.g. registers RR0 and RR2 together form quad word register RQ0. Thus, the Z80000 programmer can separately address 16 byte registers, 16 word registers, 16 long word registers and 8 quad word registers. The result is a register file that provides maximum flexibility for handling mixed data types. The programmer can specify the appropriate register size for each data element without sacrificing additional register space.

| Quad | Long | Col 1 | Col 2 | Col 3 | Col 4 | Word |
|---|---|---|---|---|---|---|
| RQ0 | RR0 | 7 RH0 0 | 7 RL0 0 | 7 RH1 0 | 7 RL1 0 | R0, R1 |
| | RR2 | 7 RH2 0 | 7 RL2 0 | 7 RH3 0 | 7 RL3 0 | R2, R3 |
| RQ4 | RR4 | 7 RH4 0 | 7 RL4 0 | 7 RH5 0 | 7 RL5 0 | R4, R5 |
| | RR6 | 7 RH6 0 | 7 RL6 0 | 7 RH7 0 | 7 RL7 0 | R6, R7 |
| RQ8 | RR8 | 15 R8 0 | | 15 R9 0 | | |
| | RR10 | 15 R10 0 | | 15 R11 0 | | |
| RQ12 | RR12 | 15 R12 0 | | 15 R13 0 | | |
| | RR14 | 15 R14 0 | | 15 R15 0 | | |
| RQ16 | RR16 | 31 0 | | | | |
| | RR18 | 31 0 | | | | |
| RQ20 | RR20 | 31 0 | | | | |
| | RR22 | 31 0 | | | | |
| RQ24 | RR24 | 31 0 | | | | |
| | RR26 | 31 0 | | | | |
| RQ28 | RR28 | 31 0 | | | | |
| | RR30 | 31 0 | | | | |

Fig. 7.5  General purpose register file.

These registers are general purpose in nature and can be used to hold data or addresses. Byte registers can be used as accumulators for 8-bit operations. Word registers can be used as accumulators for 16-bit operations, as index registers, or as memory pointers (in compact mode). Long word registers can be used as accumulators for 32-bit operations, as index registers or as memory pointers (in segmented and linear mode). Quad word registers can be used as accumulators for the 64-bit result of a Multiply, Divide or Extend Sign instruction. Since all the registers are general purpose, the particular use to which a register is put can vary during the course of a program, giving the programmer a great deal of flexibility. This architecture avoids the programming bottlenecks of an implied or dedicated register architecture, in which register contents must be saved and restored whenever the need for registers of a particular type exceeds the number of registers of that type in the processor.

Two of the general purpose registers are dedicated for the stack pointer and frame pointer used by the Call, Enter, Exit and Return instructions. The registers used depend on the current memory address representation mode. In compact mode, R15 is the stack pointer and R14 is the frame pointer, while in segmented or linear mode RR14 is the stack pointer and RR12 is the frame pointer. There are separate stack pointers for the system and normal modes of operation.

In addition to the general purpose register file, the Z80000 CPU also contains two program status registers and nine special purpose control registers. The program status registers are the program counter (PC), which indicates the address of the next instruction to be executed, and the flag and control word (FCW), which holds both the control bits that determine the CPU operating modes and the status flags from the last ALU operation. The special purpose registers are used for memory management, system configuration and other CPU control functions.

The 16-bit flag and control word holds control and status information. The lower byte of this register contains six flags (carry, zero, sign, parity/overflow, decimal-adjust, and half-carry) and the integer overflow mask. The flags reflect the result of the last operation, and are modified and used by many instructions. Through program control the integer overflow enable bit is used to enable and disable the integer overflow trap. The upper byte of the FCW holds eight control bits. Two bits select the current memory address representation mode (compact, segmented or linear). The extended processor architecture mode bit is used to inform the CPU if coprocessors are present in the system. Separate enable bits are provided for the vectored and non-vectored interrupt inputs. Trace and trace pending bits are used for single-stepping during a debugging process. The system/normal bit determines the current CPU operating mode.

The CPU's ability to operate in separate system and normal modes facilitates the implementation of protected operating systems. The operating mode dictates which instructions can be executed and which stack pointers are used. All instructions can be executed while in system mode; in normal mode, instructions that directly affect the hardware, such as I/O instructions, cannot be executed. (The instructions that cannot be executed in normal mode are called *privileged instructions*.) Operating system software would run in the system mode, controlling the system's resources and managing the execution of the applications programs, which would run in normal mode. The memory management mechanism allows system mode programs to access memory areas protected from normal mode use. Thus, the operating system and hardware itself are automatically protected from normal mode operations. Further protection is provided with separate stack pointers for the system and normal modes. Normal mode applications programs can use traps to request services from the operating system.

The Z80000 CPU's nine special control registers are described briefly below. Each is 32 bits in length and, since they control the configuration of the system, can be accessed only during system mode operations.

*Program status area pointer* (PSAP). Holds the starting physical memory address of the program status area. The program status area is the memory table that holds the values loaded into the program status registers during interrupt and trap processing.

*Normal stack pointer* (NSP). The stack pointer used while in normal mode (i.e. the normal mode RR14 or R15). This register allows the normal mode stack pointer to be accessed while in system mode.

*System instruction translation table descriptor* (SITTD). Contains the physical memory address of the translation table for system mode instruction fetches and other memory management control information.

*System data translation table descriptor* (SDTTD). Contains the physical memory address of the translation table for system mode data fetches and other memory management control information.

*Normal instruction translation table descriptor* (NITTD). Contains the physical memory address of the translation table for normal mode instruction fetches and other memory management control information.

*Normal data translation table descriptor* (NDTTD). Contains the physical memory address of the translation table for normal mode data fetches and other memory management control information.

*Overflow stack pointer* (OSP). Holds the physical address of the stack overflow area which is used when an address translation error occurs during interrupt or trap processing.

*Hardware interface control register* (HICR). Controls the configuration of the external bus interface, including bus speed, data path width and automatic wait states.

*System configuration control long word* (SCCL). Contains controls for the memory management unit, cache mechanism and exception processing logic.

## 7.3  Memory management

The Z80000 CPU contains an on-chip memory management mechanism that provides logical-to-physical address translation and memory access protection. By mapping logical memory addresses to physical addresses, a programming task can be located anywhere within physical memory. Thus, multiple programming tasks that use the same logical addresses can be mapped to different areas of physical memory. Conversely, sharing of memory can be implemented by mapping different logical addresses to the same physical address. The memory management device also limits the types of accesses that can be made to a physical memory area, providing a protection mechanism to ensure the security of sensitive code or data, such as operating system code. The Z80000 CPU's memory management supports demand paged virtual memory environments, wherein the range of logical addresses used exceeds the amount of available physical memory.

The memory management logic can be independently enabled or disabled for the system and normal mode memory address spaces via programming of the system configuration control long word register. When disabled, the physical address is identical to the logical address and all accesses are permitted.

The translation scheme of the memory management logic divides the logical address space into pages and the physical address space into frames; both pages and frames are always 1 kbyte in length. The translation process involves mapping a page, identified by the upper 22 bits of the logical address, to a specific frame, identified by the upper 22 bits of the starting physical address for that frame. The 10 least significant address bits, which indicate a specific location within the page or frame, are identical in the logical and physical address. The CPU includes a translate lookaside buffer (TLB) that stores the translation information for the 16 most recently referenced frames in a fully associative memory buffer. For each memory reference, the logical address is compared to the address tags in the TLB. If a match is found, the TLB entry is used to produce the physical address for that reference (Fig. 7.6). When the information for that page is not in the TLB, the CPU automatically references translation tables in memory, loading the new information into the TLB and replacing the TLB's least recently used entry. Thus, the TLB acts as a buffer that is automatically loaded with the most recently used translation information.

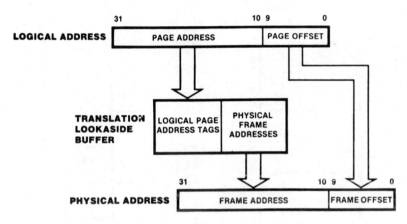

**Fig. 7.6** Address translation using the TLB.

The address translation and protection scheme employs three levels of tables. The logical address is partitioned into an 8-bit level 1 field, an 8-bit level 2 field, a 6-bit page number field, and a 10-bit page offset field (Fig. 7.7). When loading the TLB with translation information, the CPU automatically fetches entries from up to three levels of tables, with the fields in the logical address used as indexes into the corresponding tables. The transaction table descriptor registers in the CPU reference the starting address of the level 1 tables for that address space. The level 1 table entry contains the starting address for the level 2 table; the level 2 table entry contains the starting address for the page table; the page table entry holds the starting physical address for that frame, which is loaded into the TLB. There are several optional features that allow the number of levels and the size of the tables to be reduced. For example, when the address space is not fully used, levels of tables can be selectively skipped. Level 1 tables can

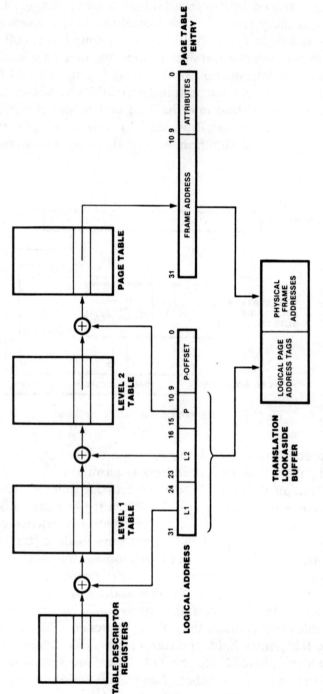

**Fig. 7.7** Loading of the TLB from tables in memory.

be skipped when an address space of 16 Mbytes is used; both level 1 and level 2 tables can be skipped for compact addresses.

Along with the pointer to the next level table, each entry in the translation table contains access protection information. Three types of accesses can be independently controlled: execute, read, and write. Separate protections can be assigned for system and normal mode accesses. The protections can be specified at any translation table level.

During a memory access, if the CPU's memory management logic detects an access protection violation or an invalid table entry, the instruction being executed is suspended and an address translation trap is executed. The CPU automatically saves the state of registers and memory so that the instruction can be restarted after eliminating the violating condition, in a manner compatible with virtual memory requirements.

## 7.4 Operand addressing modes

Z80000 instructions can manipulate data operands located in registers, memory or peripheral ports. Nine operand addressing modes are available for specifying the address of an operand within an instruction. Most operations can use any addressing mode, although some instructions support only a subset of the nine modes.

When accessing operands in memory, the CPU may be required to perform an effective address calculation of the operand's address. Effective address calculations involve adding an index value and/or a displacement value to a base address. The base address is located in the instruction, in a general purpose register, or in the PC; the index value is located in a general purpose word or long word register; the displacement is located in the instruction.

In compact mode, addresses are 16 bits long, and effective address calculations use 16-bit arithmetic. Carry and overflow from the most significant bit position are ignored. Thus, addresses wraparound with address 0 following address 65 535.

In segmented mode, only the offset portion of the base address is involved in the effective address calculation. The segment size and segment number of the effective address are always the same as the base address. Effective address calculations use 16-bit arithmetic for the 64 kbyte segments and 24-bit arithmetic for the 16 Mbyte segments. Carry and overflow from the most significant bit position are ignored. Thus, addresses wraparound within a segment.

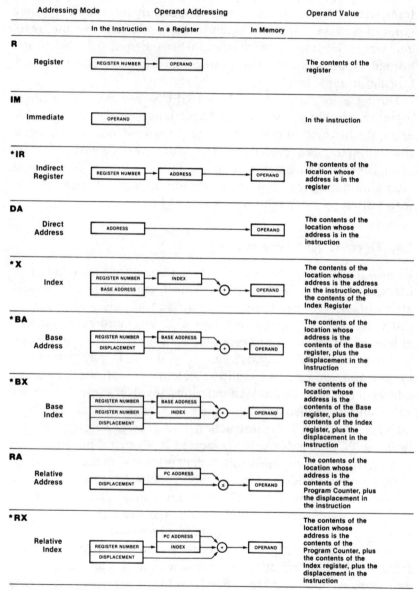

| Addressing Mode | Operand Addressing | | | Operand Value |
|---|---|---|---|---|
| | In the Instruction | In a Register | In Memory | |
| **R**<br><br>Register | REGISTER NUMBER → OPERAND | | | The contents of the register |
| **IM**<br><br>Immediate | OPERAND | | | In the instruction |
| **\*IR**<br><br>Indirect Register | REGISTER NUMBER → ADDRESS → OPERAND | | | The contents of the location whose address is in the register |
| **DA**<br><br>Direct Address | ADDRESS → OPERAND | | | The contents of the location whose address is in the instruction |
| **\*X**<br><br>Index | REGISTER NUMBER → INDEX<br>BASE ADDRESS → (+) → OPERAND | | | The contents of the location whose address is the address in the instruction, plus the contents of the Index Register |
| **\*BA**<br><br>Base Address | REGISTER NUMBER → BASE ADDRESS<br>DISPLACEMENT → (+) → OPERAND | | | The contents of the location whose address is the contents of the Base register, plus the displacement in the instruction |
| **\*BX**<br><br>Base Index | REGISTER NUMBER → BASE ADDRESS<br>REGISTER NUMBER → INDEX → (+) → OPERAND<br>DISPLACEMENT | | | The contents of the location whose address is the contents of the Base register, plus the contents of the Index register, plus the displacement in the instruction |
| **RA**<br><br>Relative Address | PC ADDRESS<br>DISPLACEMENT → (±) → OPERAND | | | The contents of the location whose address is the contents of the Program Counter, plus the displacement in the instruction |
| **\*RX**<br><br>Relative Index | PC ADDRESS<br>REGISTER NUMBER → INDEX → (+) → OPERAND<br>DISPLACEMENT | | | The contents of the location whose address is the contents of the Program Counter, plus the contents of the Index register, plus the displacement in the instruction |

\*R0 and RR0 cannot be used for Indirect, Base, or Index registers

**Fig. 7.8** Addressing modes.

In linear mode, effective address calculations use 32-bit arithmetic. Carry and overflow from the most significant bit position are ignored. Thus, addresses wraparound with address 0 following address $2^{32} - 1$.

The Z80000 CPU's addressing modes are illustrated in Fig. 7.8. For the register addressing mode, the operand is located in the specified general purpose register. For the immediate mode, the operand is located in the instruction itself. For the indirect register mode, the operand's data memory or I/O port address is contained in the specified general purpose register. For the direct address mode, the operand's data memory or I/O port address is specified within the instruction. For the index addressing mode, the operand's data memory address is calculated by adding the base address given in the instruction to the index value in the specified general purpose register. For the base address mode, the operand's data memory address is calculated by adding the displacement in the instruction to the base address contained in the specified general purpose register. For the base index mode, the operand's data memory address is calculated by adding the displacement given in the instruction to both the base address and index values located in the specified general purpose registers. For the relative mode, the operand's address is calculated by adding the displacement in the instruction to the program counter's contents; the operand is located in the instruction memory address space. For the relative index addressing mode, the operand is located at the address calculated by adding the displacement given in the instruction, the index value in the specified general purpose register, and the program counter's contents; the operand is located in the instruction memory address space.

## 7.5 Instruction set

The Z80000 CPU features a rich and powerful instruction set that supports operations on nine data types: bit, bit field, signed integer, unsigned integer, logical value, address, packed BCD integer, stack and string. Integers and logical values can be byte, word or long word operands. In addition, floating point operations are supported by a coprocessor. The regular combination of operations, addressing modes and data types results in an instruction set that is well suited to the compilation of high level languages such as C, Ada and Pascal.

The instruction set can be divided into eleven functional groups of instructions:

1. Load and exchange.
2. Arithmetic.
3. Logical.
4. Program control.
5. Bit manipulation.
6. Bit field.
7. Rotate and shift.
8. Block transfer and string manipulation.
9. Input/output.
10. CPU control.
11. Extended instructions.

Most instructions have byte, word and long word forms; a 'B' suffix on the instruction mnemonic indicates the byte form, and an 'L' suffix on the mnemonic indicates the long word form.

The Load and Exchange instructions (Table 7.1) move data between registers and memory. Load and Load Relative instructions provide basic moves, with special compactly encoded instructions for loading small constant values (LDK), loading a zero value (CLR), or exchanging two values (EX). Convert instructions allow a byte, word or long word value to be moved to a destination with a different size. Load Multiple instructions provide block transfers between the general purpose registers and memory for efficient saving and restoring of register values. Up to 16 long word registers can be loaded to or from consecutive memory locations with a single instruction. Stack operations are supported by the

**Table 7.1** Load and exchange instructions

| Mnemonic(s) | Operand(s) | Instruction name |
|---|---|---|
| CLR, CLRB, CLRL | dst | Clear |
| CVT | dst, src | Convert |
| CVTU | dst, src | Convert Unsigned |
| EX, EXB, EXL | dst, src | Exchange |
| LD, LDB, LDL | dst, src | Load |
| LDA | dst, src | Load Address |
| LDAR | dst, src | Load Address Relative |
| LDK, LDKL | dst, src | Load Constant |
| LDM, LDML | dst, src, num | Load Multiple |
| LDR, LDRB, LDRL | dst, src | Load Relative |
| POP, POPL | dst, src | Pop |
| PUSH, PUSHL | dst, src | Push |

Pop and Push instructions. The Load Address instructions calculate the effective address of the operand and load that address into the destination register.

The arithmetic group (Table 7.2) supports both signed and unsigned integer addition, subtraction, multiplication and division. Binary coded decimal arithmetic is also supported with the Decimal Adjust instruction. Instructions to perform twos complement negation (NEG), compare two operands (CP), and compare an operand with zero (TESTA) are also provided. The Increment and Decrement instructions add or subtract a constant between 1 and 16 from their destination; interlocked forms are available for fetching and reloading semaphores in memory. The Check instructions compare an operand against upper and lower bounds, generating a trap when the source is out of bounds. The Index instruction is used to compute an index into an array and compare the result to the upper and lower boundaries of the array; again, a trap is generated by an out-of-bounds condition.

**Table 7.2**  Arithmetic instructions

| Mnemonic(s) | Operand(s) | Instruction name |
|---|---|---|
| ADC, ADCB, ADCL | dst, src | Add with Carry |
| ADD, ADDB, ADDL | dst, src | Add |
| CHK, CHKB, CHKL | dst, src | Check |
| CP, CPB, CPL | dst, src | Compare |
| DAB | dst | Decimal Adjust |
| DEC, DECB, DECL | dst, src | Decrement |
| DECI, DECIB | dst, src | Decrement Interlocked |
| DIV, DIVL | dst, src | Divide |
| DIVU, DIVUL | dst, src | Divide Unsigned |
| EXTS, EXTSB, EXTSL | dst | Extend Sign |
| INC, INCB, INCL | dst, src | Increment |
| INCI, INCIB | dst, src | Increment Interlocked |
| INDEX, INDEXL | dst, sub, src | Index |
| MULT, MULTL | dst, src | Multiply |
| MULTU, MULTUL | dst, src | Multiply Unsigned |
| NEG, NEGB, NEGL | dst | Negate |
| SBC, SBCB, SBCL | dst, src | Subtract with Carry |
| SUB, SUBB, SUBL | dst, src | Subtract |
| TESTA, TESTAB, TESTAL | dst | Test Arithmetic |

The logical instructions (Table 7.3) perform logical operations on all the bits within the operands. The Test instruction performs a logical Or of the destination and zero, setting the flags appropriately.

**Table 7.3**  Logical Instructions

| Mnemonic(s) | Operand(s) | Instruction name |
|---|---|---|
| AND, ANDB, ANDL | dst, src | And |
| COM, COMB, COML | dst | Complement |
| OR, ORB, ORL | dst, src | Or |
| TEST, TESTB, TESTL | dst | Test |
| XOR, XORB, XORL | dst, src | Exclusive Or |

The program control instructions (Table 7.4) provide for controlling the program execution sequence for jumps, loops, procedure calls and exceptions. Conditional Jump instructions perform program branches based on the state of the ALU flags. Procedure invocations are supported by the Call, Enter, Exit and Return instructions. The Enter instruction is executed at the beginning of a procedure to establish the stack frame for that procedure call, including saving registers, establishing a frame pointer and allocating space for local variables; the Exit instruction releases the stack frame at the end of the procedure. These instructions provide all the essential functions for linking procedures in high level languages such as C and Pascal. The Decrement and Jump if Not Zero instructions are used to control loops by decrementing a loop counter, testing the counter, and jumping based on the outcome of the test. The Breakpoint, System Call and Conditional Trap instructions all generate trap conditions. Breakpoint traps are used for debugging, System Calls are used by normal mode routines to request service from an operating system, and Condi-

**Table 7.4**  Program control instructions

| Mnemonic(s) | Operand(s) | Instruction name |
|---|---|---|
| BRKPT | | Breakpoint |
| CALL | dst | Call |
| CALR | dst | Call Relative |
| DJNZ, DBJNZ, DLJNZ | r, dst | Decrement and Jump if Not Zero |
| ENTER | mask, siz | Enter |
| EXIT | | Exit |
| JP | cc, dst | Jump |
| JR | cc, dst | Jump Relative |
| RET | cc | Return |
| SC | src | System Call |
| TRAP | cc, src | Conditional Trap |

tional Traps allow the programmer to define trapping conditions based on the state of the flags.

The bit manipulation instructions (Table 7.5) allow the programmer to test, set or reset any bit in any byte, word or long word register or data memory location with a single instruction. The Test Condition Code instruction sets the least significant bit of its destination if the flags satisfy the specified condition code; this is often used when evaluating Boolean expressions. The Test and Set instruction is used to access the semaphores that control resource sharing in a multi-tasking or multiprocessing system.

The bit field instructions (Table 7.6) are used to insert and extract bit fields within long word operands. A bit field consists of between 1 and 32 contiguous bits. The Extract Field instructions extract a bit field from the destination and load it into a long word register. The Insert Field instruction inserts a bit field from a register into the destination. The starting position and size of the bit field are given as operands in these instructions.

Bytes, words and long words within general purpose registers can be shifted and rotated with the instructions listed in Table 7.7. Register contents can be rotated 1 or 2 bits to the left or right with a single rotate instruction. Digit rotate instructions act on 4-bit digits within byte registers, and are useful for manipulating BCD data. Shift instructions shift the contents of the destination register left or right by the number of bits specified by the source operand. Both logical and arithmetic shifts are provided. Arithmetic right shifts preserve the sign bit of the destination.

**Table 7.5** Bit manipulation instructions

| Mnemonic(s) | Operand(s) | Instruction name |
|---|---|---|
| BIT, BITB, BITL | dst, src | Bit Test |
| RES, RESB, RESL | dst, src | Reset Bit |
| SET, SETB, SETL | dst, src | Set Bit |
| TSET, TSETB, TSETL | dst | Test and Set |
| TCC, TCCB, TCCL | cc, dst | Test Condition Code |

**Table 7.6** Bit field instructions

| Mnemonic(s) | Operand(s) | Instruction name |
|---|---|---|
| EXTR | dst, src, pos, siz | Extract Field |
| EXTRU | dst, src, pos, siz | Extract Field Unsigned |
| INSRT | dst, src, pos, siz | Insert Field |

**Table 7.7** Rotate and shift instructions

| Mnemonic(s) | Operand(s) | Instruction name |
|---|---|---|
| RL, RLB, RLL | dst, src | Rotate Left |
| RLC, RLCB, RLCL | dst, src | Rotate Left through Carry |
| RLDB | dst, src | Rotate Left Digit |
| RR, RRB, RRL | dst, src | Rotate Right |
| RRC, RRCB, RRCL | dst, src | Rotate Right through Carry |
| RRDB | dst, src | Rotate Right Digit |
| SDA, SDAB, SDAL | dst, src | Shift Dynamic Arithmetic |
| SDL, SDLB, SDLL | dst, src | Shift Dynamic Logical |
| SLA, SLAB, SLAL | dst, src | Shift Left Arithmetic |
| SLL, SLLB, SLLL | dst, src | Shift Left Logical |
| SRA, SRAB, SRAL | dst, src | Shift Right Arithmetic |
| SRL, SRLB, SRLL | dst, src | Shift Right Logical |

The block transfer and string manipulation instructions (Table 7.8) act on entire strings of data in contiguous memory locations. Strings of up to 65 536 bytes, words or long words can be manipulated by a single instruction. A block of memory can be moved to another memory area, strings of data in memory can be searched for a given value or values, two strings can be compared, and data

**Table 7.8** Block transfer and string manipulation instructions

| Mnemonic(s) | Operand(s) | Instruction name |
|---|---|---|
| CPD, CPDB, CPDL | dst, src, r, cc | Compare and Decrement |
| CPDR, CPDRB, CPDRL | dst, src, r, cc | Compare, Decrement and Repeat |
| CPI, CPIB, CPIL | dst, src, r, cc | Compare and Increment |
| CPIR, CPIRB, CPIRL | dst, src, r, cc | Compare, Increment and Repeat |
| CPSD, CPSDB, CPSDL | dst, src, r, cc | Compare String and Decrement |
| CPSDR, CPSDRB, CPSDRL | dst, src, r, cc | Compare String, Decrement and Repeat |
| CPSI, CPSIB, CPSIL | dst, src, r, cc | Compare String and Increment |
| CPSIR, CPSIRB, CPSIRL | dst, src, r, cc | Compare String, Increment and Repeat |
| LDD, LDDB, LDDL | dst, src, r | Load and Decrement |
| LDDR, LDDRB, LDDRL | dst, src, r | Load, Decrement and Repeat |
| LDI, LDIB, LDIL | dst, src, r | Load and Increment |
| LDIR, LDIRB, LDIRL | dst, src, r | Load, Increment and Repeat |
| TRDB | dst, src, r | Translate and Decrement |
| TRDRB | dst, src, r | Translate, Decrement and Repeat |
| TRIB | dst, src, r | Translate and Increment |
| TRIRB | dst, src, r | Translate, Increment and Repeat |
| TRTDB | src1, src2, r | Translate, Test, and Decrement |
| TRTDRB | src1, src2, r | Translate, Test, Decrement and Repeat |
| TRTIB | src1, src2, r | Translate, Test, and Increment |
| TRTIRB | src1, src2, r | Translate, Test, Increment and Repeat |

strings can be translated from one 8-bit code to another. The indirect register addressing mode is used to access the elements of a memory string. All operations can proceed through the string in either direction; the pointer register is automatically incremented or decremented after each iteration of the operation. A count register, the third operand in these instructions, is decremented after each iteration of the operation. Repetitive forms automatically repeat the operation until the count register is zero. The repetitive forms of these instructions are interruptible after each iteration.

The input/output instructions (Table 7.9) transfer data between an I/O port and a register or memory. The Input and Output instructions transfer a single byte, word or long word of data between an I/O device and a register. The remaining instructions are block moves that allow the transfer of entire blocks of data between a peripheral port and a string of contiguous memory locations. As with the other block move instructions, memory strings can be accessed in either direction and the repetitive forms are interruptible after each iteration. All I/O instructions are privileged instructions.

**Table 7.9**  Input/output instructions

| Mnemonic(s) | Operand(s) | Instruction name |
|---|---|---|
| IN, INB, INL | dst, src | Input |
| IND, INDB, INDL | dst, src, r | Input and Decrement |
| INDR, INDRB, INDRL | dst, src, r | Input, Decrement, and Repeat |
| INI, INIB, INIL | dst, src, r | Input and Increment |
| INIR, INIRB, INIRL | dst, src, r | Input, Increment, and Repeat |
| OTDR, OTDRB, OTDRL | dst, src, r | Output, Decrement, and Repeat |
| OTIR, OTIRB, OTIRL | dst, src, r | Output, Increment, and Repeat |
| OUT, OUTB, OUTL | dst, src | Output |
| OUTD, OUTDB, OUTDL | dst, src, r | Output and Decrement |
| OUTI, OUTIB, OUTIL | dst, src, r | Output and Increment |

The CPU control instructions (Table 7.10) are privileged instructions, with the exception of the No Operation and flag manipulation (COMFLG, RESFLG, SETFLG) instructions. The Enable Interrupt and Disable Interrupt instruction allow for software control of the vectored and non-vectored interrupt inputs. The Halt instruction suspends further instruction execution in the CPU until the next interrupt, allowing instruction execution to be synchronised with an external event. The Interrupt Return instruction

**Table 7.10** CPU control instructions

| Mnemonic(s) | Operand(s) | Instruction name |
|---|---|---|
| COMFLG | flag | Complement Flag |
| DI | int | Disable Interrupt |
| EI | int | Enable Interrupt |
| HALT | | Halt |
| IRET | | Interrupt Return |
| LDCTL, LDCTLB, LDCTLL | dst, src | Load Control Register |
| LDND, LDNDB, LDNDL | dst, src | Load Normal Data |
| LDNI, LDNIB, LDNIL | dst, src | Load Normal Instruction |
| LDPND, LDPNI, LDPSD, LDPSI | dst, src | Load Physical Address |
| LDPS | src | Load Program Status |
| NOP | | No Operation |
| PCACHE | | Purge Cache |
| PTLB | | Purge TLB |
| PTLBEND, PTLBENI, PTLBESD, PTLBESI | | Purge TLB Entry |
| PTLBEN | | Purge TLB Normal |
| RESFLG | flag | Reset Flag |
| SETFLG | flag | Set Flag |

is used to return from an interrupt or trap service routine. The Load Control instruction transfers data between a special purpose CPU register and a general purpose register. Load Normal Data and Load Normal instruction are used to access the normal mode memory address spaces from within a system mode routine. The Load Physical Address instructions load the physical address of the source operand to the destination register, setting the flags to indicate access protections. The Purge Cache instruction invalidates the on-chip cache's contents. Several instructions invalidate TLB entries: Purge TLB invalidates all TLB contents, Purge TLB Normal purges only normal mode TLB entries, and the Purge TLB Entry instructions can invalidate only the entries associated with a particular memory address space. Purging cache and TLB entries is often necessary when changing the memory map during task switching in multi-tasking systems.

The basic instruction set can be extended through the use of coprocessors called *extended processing units* (EPUs). Certain opcodes are reserved for use by EPUs. The instructions associated with EPUs are called *extended instructions*.

## 7.6  Instruction execution and exceptions

Instruction execution in the Z80000 CPU is highly pipelined to maximise instruction throughput. Figure 7.9 shows the 6-stage

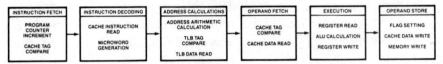

| INSTRUCTION FETCH | INSTRUCTION DECODING | ADDRESS CALCULATIONS | OPERAND FETCH | EXECUTION | OPERAND STORE |
|---|---|---|---|---|---|
| PROGRAM COUNTER INCREMENT<br><br>CACHE TAG COMPARE | CACHE INSTRUCTION READ<br><br>MICROWORD GENERATION | ADDRESS ARITHMETIC CALCULATION<br><br>TLB TAG COMPARE<br><br>TLB DATA READ | CACHE TAG COMPARE<br><br>CACHE DATA READ | REGISTER READ<br><br>ALU CALCULATION<br><br>REGISTER WRITE | FLAG SETTING<br><br>CACHE DATA WRITE<br><br>MEMORY WRITE |

**Fig. 7.9** Instruction pipeline.

synchronous pipeline used to execute instructions. The various pipeline stages can be working simultaneously on separate instructions or on separate portions of a single complex instruction. The pipeline and on-chip cache allow simple instructions, such as register-to-register loads, to execute at a rate of one instruction per processor cycle (two clock cycles). Thus, peak performance of the CPU is 12.5 million instructions per second (MIPS) with a 25 MHz clock. Actual performance is typically about one-third to one-half of this peak due to the execution of multiple-cycle instructions, contention among pipeline stages for use of the bus interface, and main memory accesses for cache and TLB misses.

Four types of exceptions can alter the normal flow of program execution in a Z80000 CPU: resets, bus errors, interrupts and traps. Resets occur when the $\overline{\text{RESET}}$ line is activated. Bus errors occur when external hardware indicates an error condition during a bus transaction. Interrupts are asynchronous events detected at one of the CPU's three interrupt inputs. Traps are synchronous events detected internally during instruction execution.

The CPU responds to a reset by fetching values for the program status registers (FCW and PC) from physical memory locations 2 and 4. These values determine the starting address and operating modes for the initialisation routine. Certain CPU control registers are initialised to establish a default bus configuration, all cache and TLB entries are invalidated, and the cache and memory management logic are disabled.

Response to the other exceptions involves saving the current program status values and an identifier word on the stack; some exceptions cause additional status information to be saved. New program status values are then fetched from a table in memory called the program status area. These new program status values determine the starting address and operating modes of the service routine for that exception. The starting address of the program status area must be stored in the CPU's program status area pointer register. Each type of exception has its own unique entry within the program status area from which the program status of that service routine can be read. The Interrupt Return instruction is used to terminate the service routine and transfer control back to the programming task that was executing at the time of the exception.

A bus error exception causes the currently executing instruction to terminate immediately. The state of the bus status signals and the physical address being accessed when the error occurred are automatically saved on the stack along with the program status information when processing this exception.

Three separate Z80000 CPU inputs are used to detect three interrupt types: non-maskable, vectored and non-vectored. The vectored and non-vectored interrupts can be enabled and disabled by program control, but the non-maskable interrupt is always enabled. Non-maskable and non-vectored interrupts have a single service routine; vectored interrupts can have many potential service routines. When an interrupt is detected, the CPU generates an interrupt acknowledge cycle to fetch an identifier word from the interrupting device. For vectored interrupts, the low order byte of the identifier is the vector used to select one of up to 256 possible service routines. The identifier is automatically stored on the system stack with the program status information during interrupt processing.

The Z80000 CPU recognises ten different types of trap conditions: extended instruction traps, privileged instruction traps, system call traps, address translation traps, breakpoint traps, integer arithmetic traps, conditional traps, unimplemented instruction traps, odd PC traps and trace traps. The CPU's trap mechanisms simplify program debugging and improve software reliability through run-time detection of error conditions.

An enable bit for the extended processor architecture is contained within the flag and control word register. This bit is used to inform the CPU of the presence of coprocessors in the system. If an extended instruction is encountered by the CPU and the extended processor architecture is disabled, an extended instruction trap is performed. This trap allows software to simulate execution of the extended instruction when coprocessors are not present.

The privileged instruction trap occurs when a program attempts to execute a privileged instruction while in the normal mode.

The system call trap occurs when a System Call instruction is executed. This trap allows normal mode programs to make requests to the operating system. An 8-bit request code that is specified as an immediate operand in the instruction is passed to the service routine on the stack as part of this trap's identifier word.

If the memory management logic detects an invalid table entry or access violation during a memory access, the address translation trap occurs. The current instruction is immediately terminated in a manner consistent with virtual memory implementations.

The breakpoint trap occurs when a Breakpoint instruction is executed. The Breakpoint instruction can be used by a software debugger to replace an instruction where a breakpoint is to be set.

The integer arithmetic trap occurs when an integer overflow, bounds check or index error is detected during execution of integer arithmetic instructions. Overflows during arithmetic instructions cause this trap only if integer overflow traps are enabled in the flag and control word. A bounds check error is detected when a Check instruction is executed and the destination operand is out of bounds. An index error occurs when an Index instruction is executed and the subscript is out of bounds.

The conditional trap occurs when a Trap instruction is executed and the specified condition is true. This trap allows the programmer to define trapping conditions that detect user-defined run-time errors.

If a program attempts to execute an instruction code that does not correspond to one of the defined Z80000 instructions, an unimplemented instruction trap is executed.

The odd PC trap occurs before execution of an instruction if the program counter contains an odd value. Since instructions are always aligned on word boundaries in memory, an odd value in the program counter indicates an error has occurred.

The trace trap occurs before execution of each instruction if trace traps are enabled in the flag and control word. The trace trap provides for single-stepping of programs in a debugging environment.

During exception processing, the program status values, identifier word, and other status information is saved on the system stack. If the memory management logic detects an access violation during this status saving process, the system stack pointer is restored to the value it held before the exception occurred, and the overflow stack is used to save the status information for the exception. The physical address of the overflow stack is determined by the contents of the CPU's overflow stack pointer register. New program status is then fetched from locations in the program status area dedicated to processing this type of system stack error.

## 7.7 Multiprocessing

The Z80000 CPU architecture provides support for four different types of multiprocessor configurations: slave processors, tightly coupled multiple CPUs, loosely coupled multiple CPUs, and co-processors (Fig. 7.10).

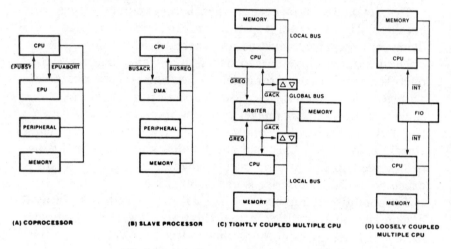

**Fig. 7.10** Multiprocessor configurations.

Slave processors, such as DMA controllers, perform dedicated functions asynchronous to CPU operation. The CPU and slave processors share a local bus. The CPU is the default bus master; slave processors must request the use of the bus from the CPU. The Z80000 CPU has a bus request input that slave processors can use to request the bus, and a bus acknowledge output used to inform slave processors when the CPU has relinquished the bus in response to a request.

Tightly coupled multiprocessing systems are systems where multiple CPUs execute independent instruction streams from their own (local) memory and communicate through some shared (global) memory. Each CPU is the default bus master of its local bus, but the global bus master is chosen by an external arbiter. Control bits in the CPU's hardware interface control register allow the programmer to enable this multiprocessing mode for the Z80000 CPU and choose the range of addresses dedicated to the local and global buses. A global request ($\overline{\text{GREQ}}$) output and global acknowledge ($\overline{\text{GACK}}$) input are provided to implement this multi-processing configuration. While in control of its local bus, a CPU can attempt to initiate transactions on the global bus. For each memory or I/O transaction, the CPU checks to see if the global bus is required. Before performing a transaction on the global bus, the CPU must request the bus by asserting $\overline{\text{GREQ}}$ and wait for an active $\overline{\text{GACK}}$ in response. Once $\overline{\text{GACK}}$ is asserted, the CPU can perform the transaction.

Loosely coupled CPUs communicate through a multiple-port memory or peripheral device, such as the Z8038 FIFO Input/Output Unit. The Z80000 CPU's I/O and interrupt facilities support loosely coupled multiprocessing through peripherals. The CPU provides external status information about interlocked memory references that can be used to control multi-port memories.

The Z80000 CPU's architecture supports the use of coprocessors called extended processing units (EPUs). EPUs perform specialised functions in parallel with the CPU. EPUs connect directly to the Z-Bus and perform operations on data resident in their internal registers. Up to four EPUs can be connected to a single CPU. The Z8070 Floating-Point Arithmetic Processor is one example of an EPU.

Four types of extended instructions are used to control EPUs:

1. Data transfers between an EPU and memory.
2. Data transfers between an EPU and the CPU.
3. Status flag transfers between an EPU and the CPU.
4. Internal EPU operations.

Each EPU continuously monitors the instruction stream, capturing and executing instructions intended for it. The CPU and EPU cooperate in the execution of extended instructions. When the CPU receives an extended instruction (and the extended processor architecture is enabled) the CPU broadcasts the instruction to the EPUs in the system. If the instruction involves a data transfer (as for the first three types of extended instructions listed above), the CPU is responsible for generating the appropriate bus transactions, including effective address calculations. The EPUs monitor the bus activity, capturing or supplying data at the appropriate times, as if they were part of the CPU. Up to 16 words can be transferred to or from an EPU as a result of a single instruction.

While an EPU is executing an internal operation extended instruction, the CPU can fetch and execute subsequent instructions. Thus, EPUs and the CPU can be operating in parallel. The $\overline{\text{EPUBUSY}}$ signal is used to synchronise CPU and EPU activity in the case of overlapping extended instructions. If another extended instruction for an EPU is encountered while that EPU is still

busy processing an earlier extended instruction, the EPU asserts
the EPUBUSY signal until it is ready to accept the new instruction.
While the CPU's EPUBUSY input is active, the CPU cannot
initiate any new bus transactions. If the CPU detects an address
translation trap while executing an extended instruction, the CPU's
EPUABORT output is asserted, informing the selected EPU to
abort execution of that instruction.

If EPUs are not present in the system, EPU activity can be
simulated in software using the extended instruction trap.

## 7.8 Cache memory

The Z80000 CPU contains 256 bytes of high speed memory that
can be configured as an associative cache or as dedicated fixed
physical memory locations. When configured as a cache, this
memory can be a cache for instruction fetches, data references, or
both, as determined by the contents of the CPU's system configuration control long word register. Individual pages can be
configured as cacheable or non-cacheable in the memory management logic. When configured as a cache, the set of memory locations mapped into the cache at a given time is determined by the
action of the executing program, and the memory locations that
were most recently accessed are stored in the cache. Memory reads
from locations already stored in the cache do not generate external
bus transactions and, therefore, are faster than accesses to external
memory. Thus, use of the cache results in faster program execution.

The cache's organisation is illustrated in Fig. 7.11. Cache
memory is arranged as 16 rows of eight words each, with a 28-bit
address tag and eight validity bits associated with each row. Each
row of the cache contains storage for eight contiguous words of
memory, where the tag address indicates the physical addresses

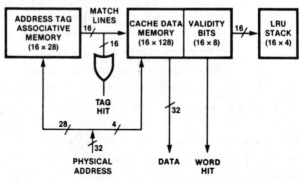

**Fig. 7.11**   Cache organisation.

stored in that row. For each memory access, the tags are checked to see if that location is currently mapped into the cache. A valid bit associated with each word in the row indicates if that word holds a valid copy of the data at the associated physical memory location. The cache is fully associative, so that any memory location can be assigned to any row.

Lines in the cache are replaced using a least recently used (LRU) algorithm. If a cacheable read transaction accesses a physical memory location not currently mapped into the cache, the row in the cache that was least recently accessed is selected to hold the newly read data.

When the cache is enabled, each memory access is a 'cache hit' or a 'cache miss'. For read operations, a cache hit means that valid data for that memory reference is in the cache and no external transaction is required. A cache miss on a read means that the accessed data is not valid in the cache, in which case an external bus transaction is generated, and the cache contents are updated to include the newly read data. This may involve replacing a row in the cache using the LRU algorithm. For write operations, a cache hit means that the accessed location is in a row of the cache. An external bus transaction is generated, and the data is written to both external memory and the cache. A cache miss on a write results in an external bus transaction and has no effect on the cache. Data is always written to external memory regardless of the state of the cache, ensuring that external memory always holds valid data.

If burst-mode memories are employed in the system, the CPU will use a burst-mode transaction to prefetch a block of memory into the cache for a cache miss on an instruction fetch. Burst-mode transactions are also used to store and fetch data operands when more than one transfer is necessary, as with unaligned operands, string instructions and Load Multiple instructions.

A control bit in the system configuration control long word register can be used to disable the cache replacement algorithm, putting the on-chip memory into a fixed address mode. Thus, selected locations can be locked into the cache for fast, on-chip access.

## 7.9   External interface

To complete a computer system, the Z80000 CPU needs to interface to other devices, including memories, peripherals, DMA control-lers, coprocessors and other CPUs. Zilog has established the Z-Bus as a convention to describe the signals involved in interfacing components of a microprocessor system. The Z80000 is compatible with the Z-Bus family of processors, support chips and peripheral devices (Table 7.11). The multi-function Z-Bus peripherals are extensively programmable, so each can be precisely tailored for a given application.

**Table 7.11**   Current Z-Bus family components

| | |
|---|---|
| *Z-Bus CPUs:* | |
| Z80000 | 32-bit CPU |
| Z8001/2/3/4 | 16-bit CPUs |
| Z8 | Single-chip 8-bit microcomputer family |
| *Z-Bus processor support devices:* | |
| Z8070 | Floating-point arithmetic processing unit |
| Z8016 | Dual-channel DMA controller |
| Z8581 | Clock generator and controller |
| *Z-Bus peripherals:* | |
| Z8030 | Dual-channel, multi-protocol serial communications controller |
| Z8031 | Dual-channel, asynchronous serial communications controller |
| Z8036 | Counter/timer and parallel I/O unit |
| Z8038 | FIFO input/output interface unit |
| Z8060 | FIFO buffer unit |
| Z8065 | Burst error processor |
| Z8068 | Data ciphering processor |
| Z8052 | CRT controller |
| Z8090, Z8094 | Universal peripheral controller |

The Z80000 CPU's external interface has 59 signal lines and 4 power supply connections (Fig. 7.12). A summary of the pin functions is given below:

AD0–AD31, Address/Data (bidirectional, active high, 3-state). Time-multiplexed address and data bus lines that carry memory or I/O port addresses and data during bus transactions.

$\overline{AS}$, Address Strobe (output, active low, 3-state). A bus timing signal whose rising edge marks the beginning of a bus transaction and indicates that the address and bus status signals are valid.

$\overline{BRST}$, Burst (output, active low, 3-state). Status signal indicating that the CPU is performing a burst-mode memory access.

$\overline{BRSTA}$, Burst Acknowledge (input, active low). Signal indicating that the responding memory device can support burst-mode transfers.

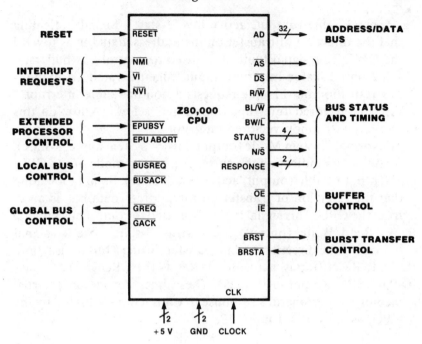

**Fig. 7.12** Pin functions.

$\overline{\text{BUSREQ}}$, Bus request (input, active low). Signal indicating that a bus requestor has obtained or is trying to obtain control of the local bus.

$\overline{\text{BUSACK}}$, Bus Acknowledge (output, active low). Signal indicating that the CPU has relinquished control of the local bus in response to a bus request.

$\text{BL}/\overline{\text{W}}$, $\text{BW}/\overline{\text{L}}$ (outputs, 3-state). Status signals indicating the size of the current transaction's data (byte, word or long word).

CLK, Clock (input). Clock input used to generate all CPU timing.

$\overline{\text{DS}}$, Data Strobe (output, active low, 3-state). Signal used to time all data transfers.

$\overline{\text{EPUBSY}}$, EPU Busy (input, active low). Signal indicating when an EPU is busy, used to synchronise CPU and EPU activity.

$\overline{\text{EPUABORT}}$, EPU Abort (output, active low). Signal indicating that the CPU is aborting an extended instruction due to an address translation trap.

$\overline{\text{GACK}}$, Global Acknowledge (input, active low). Signal indicating that the CPU has been granted control of a global bus.

$\overline{\text{GREQ}}$, Global Request (output, active low, 3-state). Signal indicating that the CPU has obtained or is trying to obtain control of a global bus.

$\overline{\text{IE}}$, Input Enable (output, active low, 3-state). Signal indicating that the direction of transfer on the address/data bus is toward the CPU. This signal typically is used to control bus buffers.

$\overline{\text{NMI}}$, Non-maskable Interrupt (input, edge-activated). A high-to-low transition on this line requests a non-maskable interrupt.

$\overline{\text{NVI}}$, Non-vectored Interrupt (input, active low). A low on this line requests a non-vectored interrupt.

$N/\overline{S}$, Normal/System Mode (output, low = system mode, 3-state). Status signal indicating the current operating mode of the CPU.

$\overline{\text{OE}}$, Output Enable (output, active low, 3-state). Signal indicating that the direction of transfer on the address/data bus is away from the CPU. This signal typically is used to control bus buffers.

$R/\overline{W}$, Read/Write (output, low = write, 3-state). Status signal indicating the direction of data transfer during a bus transaction.

$\overline{\text{RESET}}$, Reset (input, active low). Resets the CPU.

RSP0–RSP1, Response (inputs). These lines encode an external memory or peripheral's response to transactions initiated by the CPU, as shown in Table 7.12.

Table 7.12    Encoding of response inputs

| RSP0 | RSP1 | Response |
|------|------|----------|
| 1 | 1 | Ready |
| 0 | 1 | Bus error |
| 1 | 0 | Bus retry |
| 0 | 0 | Wait |

ST0–ST3, Status (outputs, active high, 3-state). These lines encode the type of transaction occurring on the bus, as shown in Table 7.13.

$\overline{\text{VI}}$, Vectored Interrupt (input, active low). A low on this line requests a vectored interrupt.

The Z80000 CPU performs transactions on its external interface to transfer data during instruction fetches, data operand reads and writes, exception processing and memory management operations. The CPU also performs internal operation and halt transactions, which do not involve a data transfer.

The CPU's hardware interface control register (HICR) specifies the characteristics of the bus interface, including bus speed, memory data path width, and the number of automatic wait states.

**Table 7.13**    Encoding of ST3-ST0 status lines

| ST3-ST0 | Definition |
|---------|------------|
| 0000 | Internal operation |
| 0001 | CPU-EPU data transfer |
| 0010 | I/O transaction |
| 0011 | Halt |
| 0100 | CPU-EPU instruction transfer |
| 0101 | Non-maskable interrupt acknowledge |
| 0110 | Non-vectored interrupt acknowledge |
| 0111 | Vectored interrupt acknowledge |
| 1000 | Cacheable CPU-memory data transfer |
| 1001 | Non-cacheable CPU-memory data transfer |
| 1010 | Cacheable EPU-memory data transfer |
| 1011 | Non-cacheable EPU-memory data transfer |
| 1100 | Cacheable instruction fetch |
| 1101 | Non-cacheable instruction fetch |
| 1110 | Reserved |
| 1111 | Interlocked CPU-memory data transfer |

For purposes of specifying the bus configuration, physical memory is divided into two sections, $M_0$ and $M_1$, selected by bit 30 of the physical address. Similarly, the physical I/O space is divided into two sections, $I/O_0$ and $I/O_1$. For example, a system might have slow, 16-bit wide EPROM in $M_0$, and fast 32-bit wide RAM in $M_1$. The HICR contents specify the following bus interface parameters:

$M_0$ wait count – the number of automatic wait states (0 to 7) inserted during accesses to $M_0$.

$M_0$ data path width – the data path width (16 or 32 bits) for accesses to $M_0$.

$M_1$ wait count – the number of automatic wait states (0 to 7) inserted during accesses to $M_1$.

$M_1$ data path width – the data path width (16 or 32 bits) for accesses to $M_1$.

$I/O_0$ wait count – the number of automatic wait states (0 to 7) inserted during access to $I/O_0$.

$I/O_1$ wait count – the number of automatic wait states (0 to 7) inserted during access to $I/O_1$.

Interrupt acknowledge wait count – the number of automatic wait states (0 to 7) inserted into interrupt acknowledge transactions.

Bus clock speed – frequency of bus clock ($\frac{1}{2}$ or $\frac{1}{4}$ CPU clock frequency).

EPU overlap mode – degree of overlap of CPU and EPU operations.(Execution overlap can be disabled for debugging purposes.)

Minimum address strobe – when enabled, ensures an address
strobe is generated at least once every 16 bus clock cycles. (This
is useful for refreshing pseudo-static RAMs.)

Global enable and local address – enables global/local bus mode
and determines the range of addresses on the global and local
busses.

Bus transactions begin when the address strobe $(\overline{AS})$ is asserted
and then negated. If an address is required, the address is valid
on the rising edge of $\overline{AS}$. The bus status lines are also valid on
the positive edge of $\overline{AS}$. ST0 through ST3 indicate the type of
transaction occurring, $R/\overline{W}$ indicates the direction of transfer,
$BW/\overline{L}$ and $BL/\overline{W}$ indicate the size of the data being transferred,
and $N/\overline{S}$ indicates the current CPU operating mode. The data
strobe $(\overline{DS})$ signal is used to time the data transfer. For writes, an
active $\overline{DS}$ indicates that the CPU has placed valid data on the
address/data bus. For reads, the CPU 3-states the address/data
bus before asserting $\overline{DS}$, so the addressed device can drive the
data onto the bus.

During each data transaction, the responding device returns a
code to the CPU on the response inputs indicating ready, wait,
bus error, or bus retry. The response lines are sampled by the CPU
prior to sampling the data during a read cycle or negating $\overline{DS}$
during a write cycle. The ready response indicates the successful
completion of the transaction. The wait response indicates that
the responding device needs more time to complete the transaction;
another bus cycle, called a wait state, is then added to the transaction before sampling the response again. There is no limit to the
number of wait states that can be added to a single transaction in
this manner. Wait states can also be added to a transaction via
programming of the HICR. Programmed wait states are inserted
in the transaction before sampling the response lines. The bus
error response triggers the bus error exception, which is processed
in a manner similar to an interrupt or trap. The bus retry response
causes the CPU to try to perform that transaction again.

Memory read transactions, by default, span two bus clock periods. The address and status are emitted during the first clock
period, and the response lines and data are sampled during the
second clock period. Two-cycle reads are intended for use with

very fast memories, such as an external cache. More moderate memory speeds require the use of a wait state during the read operation. Memory write and I/O read and write transactions, by default, take three bus clock cycles.

To increase memory transaction bandwidth, burst-mode transactions can be used. Burst-mode memory transactions use multiple assertions of data strobe after a single address strobe to transfer data at consecutive memory addresses. The CPU uses burst-mode transactions to prefetch a block for a cache miss on an instruction fetch, or to read or write data operands for instructions with multiple transfers. At the beginning of a burst-mode transaction, the CPU asserts the $\overline{BRST}$ output. The acknowledging $\overline{BRSTA}$ signal is sampled along with response lines to indicate if memory will support a burst-mode transaction before the CPU proceeds with the burst-mode access.

### 7.10 Development systems and languages

Since the Z80000 CPU is upward compatible with the 16-bit Z8000 microprocessor, the development tools already available for the Z8000 family can be easily applied to Z80000-based designs. New tools optimised for the Z80000 are also available.

Zilog's System 8000 family of high performance microcomputers provide an ideal software development environment. The System 8000's hardware combines the Z8000 CPU with a high performance Winchester disk and intelligent disk and tape controllers. Family members range from 8-user systems with 512 kbytes of main memory and a 23 Mbyte Winchester disk to 40-user systems with 4 Mbytes of main memory and a 168 Mbyte Winchester disk. Zilog's enhanced UNIX operating system is specifically designed for software development and testing. Numerous development tools including debuggers, libraries, compilers and assemblers allow code development for a number of different target processors. Standard RS-232 serial links on the System 8000 microcomputer provide for the uploading and downloading of programs to hardware emulation systems. The System 8000 features a 32-bit backplane for easy upgrade to a full 32-bit system based on the Z80000. Furthermore, Zilog is supplying support to original equipment manufacturers wishing to port Unix System V to the Z80000 CPU.

Languages currently available for the Z8000 (and therefore for the Z80000) include Ada, C, Pascal, FORTRAN, COBOL, and

BASIC. Versions of these compilers optimised for the Z80000 are available or forthcoming. The Z80000 cross-assembler supports macros and conditional assembly, and is available for System 8000, VAX or IBM-PC compatible hosts.

Besides the development systems, emulators and development software available from Zilog, numerous support products are available from third-party vendors.

### 7.11 Summary

In summary, the Z80000 CPU meets and surpasses the requirements of medium and high end microprocessor systems. Its abundant architectural features allow its use in applications previously delegated only to super minicomputers or mainframe computers, such as office automation, engineering workstations, graphics processing, digital signal processing, robotics, expert systems and speech recognition and synthesis. The Z80000 architecture makes a wide range of configuration options available to the designer, allowing for integration into applications ranging from dedicated controllers to large multiprocessing systems. Its highly pipelined design, on-chip cache and memory management, coprocessor interface, high clock speed and large instruction set all contribute to the achievement of previously unattainable throughput rates. Software program development is easily accomplished with the CPU's sophisticated architecture. While Zilog continues to develop further support for the Z80000 CPU, the well established Z8000 family of peripherals, processors and support devices and the System 8000 family development systems and development software are fully compatible with the Z80000 32-bit microprocessor, the latest in Zilog's line of high performance state-of-the-art VLSI components.

# Index